plurall

CB137491

Esta obra está no **Plurall**.
Baixe o app no seu celular
ou acesse **http://plurall.net**
e descubra uma nova
forma de estudar!

GCG2CR8SJ

Atenção! Somente serão liberados conteúdos
e serviços relacionados a esta obra.

Ajuda: @plurallnet

SOMOS EDUCAÇÃO

TIME TO SHARE Jornadas

Workbook 8

Organizadora:
Editora Saraiva
Obra coletiva organizada e produzida pela Editora Saraiva

Editor responsável:
Vicente Martínez
Licenciado em Tradução/Interpretação pela Universidad Pontificia de Comillas (Madrid)
Editor de conteúdos didáticos

Coordenadora:
Gisele Aga
Licenciada em Letras pela FMU – Faculdades Metropolitanas Unidas
Professora de Inglês na rede particular de ensino e em cursos de idiomas
Coordenadora pedagógica em cursos de idiomas
Editora de conteúdos didáticos

Editora Saraiva

PRESENTATION

Caro estudante,

Este caderno foi elaborado com a finalidade de ajudá-lo a organizar seu conhecimento. Ao resolver as atividades propostas, você terá a oportunidade de buscar informações, utilizar a própria experiência e conhecimento prévio sobre os assuntos tratados, desenvolver habilidades, elaborar opiniões sobre assuntos da atualidade, refletir sobre atitudes e comportamentos e ampliar a sua visão do mundo.

As atividades estão distribuídas em oito unidades, correspondendo às unidades do livro para que possa retomar e ampliar os tópicos estudados. A cada unidade, você encontrará as seguintes seções: *Review the journey*, *Another look* e *Reading the world*.

- Em *Review the journey*, você irá aplicar os conceitos gramaticais apresentados na unidade.
- A seção *Another look* propõe uma leitura complementar (verbal ou não verbal) ligada a algum tema ou gênero trabalhado na unidade do livro. As atividades visam trabalhar aspectos que não foram abordados no livro ou que são tratados sob outro aspecto. Além disso, nas últimas atividades você será incentivado a refletir e se posicionar em relação ao assunto tratado na seção.
- Em *Reading the world*, você lerá textos com temáticas instigantes, como aspectos culturais de diversos países, novas tecnologias, entre outras. Ao final das atividades, você poderá contar com uma produção (oral ou escrita).

Esperamos que sua jornada por este caderno seja bastante produtiva e o auxilie a desenvolver a autonomia nos estudos.

Os editores

CONTENTS

1 Speaking English helps us..., 4
- Review the journey, 4
- Another look, 6
- Reading the world, 8

2 What were you doing there?, 10
- Review the journey, 10
- Another look, 12
- Reading the world, 14

3 What are you going to recycle?, 16
- Review the journey, 16
- Another look, 18
- Reading the world, 22

4 What do you know about her?, 24
- Review the journey, 24
- Another look, 26
- Reading the world, 30

5 Which painting do you prefer?, 32
- Review the journey, 32
- Another look, 34
- Reading the world, 38

6 What's this story about?, 40
- Review the journey, 40
- Another look, 42
- Reading the world, 46

7 A world of possibilities, 48
- Review the journey, 48
- Another look, 50
- Reading the world, 54

8 Families, 56
- Review the journey, 56
- Another look, 58
- Reading the world, 62

Connecting ideas, 64

UNIT 1

Speaking English helps us...

Review the journey

1. Underline the verbs in the simple past.

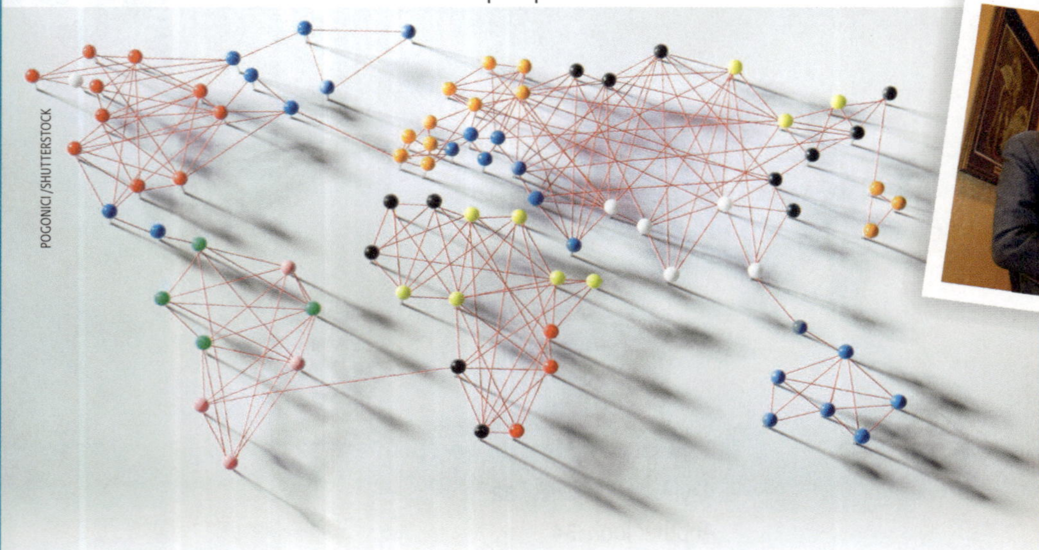

POGONICI /SHUTTERSTOCK

PETER POWER/TORONTO STAR/GETTY IMAGES

borrowed: peguei emprestado
frenchman: francês
coined: criou
posted: enviado
mother tongue: língua materna
Anglophone: anglófonas, que falam inglês
christened: batizou

THE RISE OF GLOBAL ENGLISH

Robert McCrum

'Globish' is not my word. In the best traditions of the English language, I borrowed it from a frenchman who first coined it in 1995. Jean-Paul Nerriere was a senior executive with IBM. Posted to Japan in the 1990s, he made one simple, but brilliant, observation. In his work for IBM, Nerriere noticed in meetings that non-native English speakers in the Far East were communicating far more successfully with their Korean and Japanese clients than competing British or American executives, for whom English was the mother tongue. Standard English might be all very well for Anglophone societies, but out there in the developing world, this non-native 'decaffeinated English', declared Nerriere, was becoming the new global phenomenon. In a moment of inspiration, he christened it 'Globish'.

Extracted from: <http://blog.oxforddictionaries.com/2015/05/the-rise-of-global-english/>. Accessed on: Mar. 24, 2016.

2. Write the infinitive form of the verbs you underlined in activity 1.

____

____

____

3. Guess where these famous people were born and their native language. Use the words from the boxes.

Egypt	England
Germany	The Netherlands
Poland	Brazil

English	Dutch
Brazilian Portuguese	Egyptian
German	Polish

a. William Shakespeare: ____________________ / ____________________

b. Cleopatra: ____________________ / ____________________

c. Santos Dumont: ____________________ / ____________________

d. Albert Einstein: ____________________ / ____________________

e. Rembrandt: ____________________ / ____________________

f. Marie Curie: ____________________ / ____________________

4. Correct the sentences below. There is one example.

BIS

a. John Green wrote *Harry Potter and the Philosopher's Stone*. (*The Fault in Our Stars*)

John Green didn't write *Harry Potter and the Philosopher's Stone*. He wrote *The Fault in Our Stars*.

b. Alexander Graham Bell invented the airplane. (the telephone)

____

c. Tim Burton and Mike Johnson directed *Shrek the Third*. (*Corpse Bride*)

____

d. Rihanna recorded "The Climb." ("Diamonds")

____

Another look

1. Look at the text in activity 3. Then check the elements you can identify in it.

a. ☐ numbers
b. ☐ maps
c. ☐ pictures
d. ☐ texts
e. ☐ quotations
f. ☐ colors
g. ☐ charts
h. ☐ hypertext
i. ☐ stanzas

2. Which text genre is it?

a. ☐ a magazine article
b. ☐ an infographic

3. Look at the title. What is the text about? Read the text and confirm your answer.

___

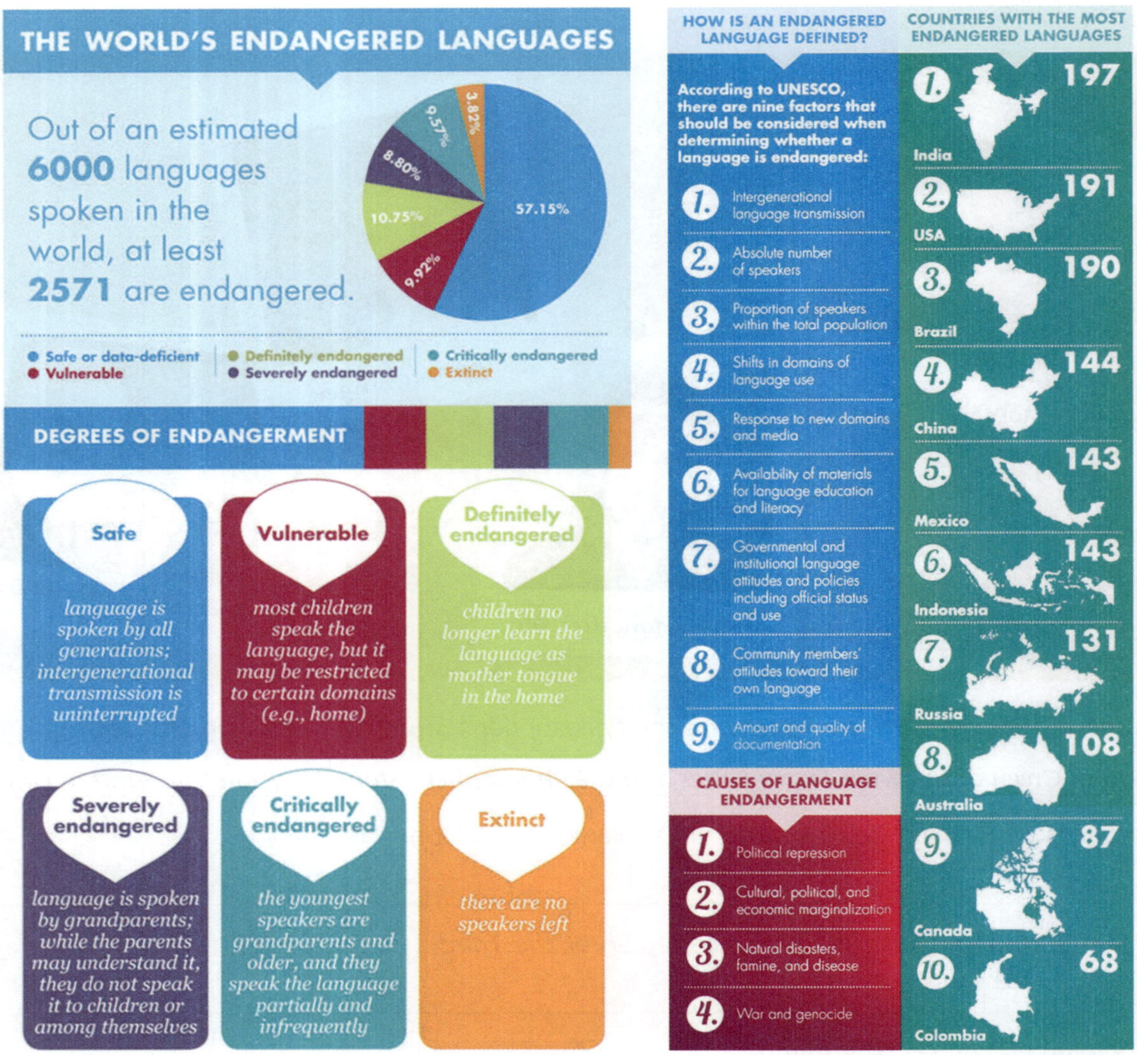

OXFORD DICTIONARIES/OXFORD UNIVERSITY PRESS

Adapted from: <http://blog.oxforddictionaries.com/2016/02/endangered-languages/>. Accessed on: Mar. 24, 2016.

4. Complete the sentences with items from the box.

2,571	3.82%	57.15%	Brazil
critically endangered	India	six degrees	vulnerable

a. At least ____________________ of 6,000 languages spoken in the world are endangered.

b. ____________________ of the languages are safe or data-deficient, and ____________________ are extinct.

c. There are ____________________ of endangerment: safe, ____________________, definitely endangered, severely endangered, ____________________, and extinct.

d. The top 5 countries with the most endangered languages are ____________________, USA, ____________________, China, and Mexico.

5. Write the name of the countries in the correct place according to the map.

Italy	31	Austria	5
______________	26	Hungary	5
Germany	18	Latvia	5
Ukraine	14	Slovakia	5
Romania	11	______________	5
______________	11	Albania	4
Greece	10	Czech Republic	4
Belgium	8	Lithuania	4
Croatia	8	Belarus	3
Poland	8	Denmark	3
Sweden	8	Estonia	3
Switzerland	8	Luxembourg	3
Finland	7	Slovenia	3
Macedonia	7	Bosnia and Herzegovina	2
Bulgaria	6	Moldova	2
______________	6	Ireland	1
Norway	6	Montenegro	1
Serbia	6	______________	1

OXFORD DICTIONARIES/OXFORD UNIVERSITY PRESS

www.oxforddictionaries.com OXFORD UNIVERSITY PRESS

Adapted from: <http://blog.oxforddictionaries.com/2016/02/endangered-languages/>. Accessed on: Mar. 24, 2016.

Reading the world

1. Read the text.

HOP-ON AND TAKE A RIDE!

GREG BALFOUR EVANS/ALAMY/FOTOARENA

City Sightseeing London is a special city tour that visits the main tourist attractions in London, England.

The hop-on hop-off bus will take you to all the sights you want to see in a city. The bus stops at each location just for a few minutes. The service counts with double decked vehicles, equipped with sound system, bilingual translation, bilingual tourist guides and drivers.

One of the most famous hop-on hop-off buses in the world are the lines that drive you through the streets of London. But there are similar services in many other locations such as Paris, New York, Edinburgh, Rome... You can also find this service in Brazilian cities such as Curitiba, Salvador, and São Paulo. Let's take a closer look at some of these tourism lines:

MAURICIO SIMONETTI/PULSAR IMAGENS

Linha Turismo (Tourism Line) is a special city tour that visits the main tourist attractions in Curitiba, Paraná. It is possible to visit parks, squares and the rest of the city's tourist attractions.

FERNANDO VIVAS/AG. A TARDE/FOLHA IMAGEM

Salvador Bus was the first service to adopt the regular sightseeing model in Brazil, in 2008. With a wristband ticket, the tourist will be able to visit the main tourist attractions in Salvador, Bahia.

RICARDO BASTOS / FOTOARENA

Circular Turismo Sightseeing SP is a city tour that visits the main tourist attractions in São Paulo. The buses are equipped with sound system, Wi-Fi, and travel information in three languages: Portuguese, English and Spanish.

sightseeing: visita rápida a pontos turísticos
hop-on hop-off bus: ônibus circular que faz paradas para embarque e desembarque de turistas
double decked: com dois andares
wristband ticket: pulseira que dá acesso a *shows*, passeios, parques etc.

Adapted from: <www.city-sightseeing.com/tours/united-kingdom/london.htm?set-lang=en>; <www.curitiba.pr.gov.br/idioma/ingles/linhaturismo>; <www.salvadorbus.com.br/en/buy-your-ticket/cart/>; <www.cidadedesaopaulo.com/sp/br/linha-circular-turismo>. Accessed on: May 20, 2016.

2. Can you find any words in English in the pictures from Brazilian bus tour services? Write them down below.

___

___

3. Why are there words and expressions in English in Brazilian tourist services?

___

___

4. Which expressions would you use on a hop-on hop-off tour?

a. ☐ Excuse me!
b. ☐ One ticket, please!
c. ☐ Where exactly am I?
d. ☐ Where is...?
e. ☐ Thank you!
f. ☐ How much is the ticket?
g. ☐ Does this bus go to...?
h. ☐ Is it open on Sundays?
i. ☐ Can you show me on the map?
j. ☐ Where can I find...?
k. ☐ How long to get to...?
l. ☐ Is this seat taken?

5. Can you think of another places in Brazil where you usually find words in English? Name the places and write what common words or expressions you usually see.

___

___

___

1. Would you like to take a city tour? Where? What attractions would you like to see in this place? Why?

___

___

___

___

___

___

___

UNIT 2

What were you doing there?

Review the journey

1. Complete the texts. Use the past continuous.

a.

Last month I was on holiday in Ireland with my mum and dad. One day, we ______________________ (drive) through a small village. It was time for lunch, so we stopped at a restaurant.

b.

I dreamt I was at a restaurant, but there was something strange about the "customers". They were animals: dolphins, sea lions, sharks, stingrays – and they ______________________ (wear) human clothes. They ______________________ (eat), ______________________ (drink) and ______________________ (chat). A crocodile ______________________ (play) the violin. It was a very strange dream!

2. Match the pictures with their caption.

a.

b.

c.

d.

☐ In the spring seeds take root, vegetation begins to grow, and flowers blossom.

☐ In the summer temperatures may increase to their hottest of the year.

☐ In the autumn/fall temperatures cool again and tree leaves fall down.

☐ Winter often brings a chill. Some areas may experience snow.

3. Write an affirmative statement about what people were doing. Use the cues.

a.

IVASHSTUDIO/SHUTTERSTOCK

BORYANA MANZUROVA/SHUTTERSTOCK

Laura / ride a bike / Paris / Seth / take a nap

b.

AKHENATON IMAGES/SHUTTERSTOCK

THINKSTOCK/GETTY IMAGES

Paul / travel / Hawaii / Sandra / work

c.

LIVIA CORONA/GETTY IMAGES

BYCHYKHIN OLEXANDR/SHUTTERSTOCK

Susan / take pictures / in Mexico / Claire / take a balloon ride

Another look

1. Look at the leaflet in activity 2. What is it about?

a. ☐ A museum. **b.** ☐ A train station. **c.** ☐ A toy store.

2. Use the words from the box to complete the text about leaflets.

free	information	key	museum	opening times	pictures	show

Most leaflets are ____________ and are made to attract customers. Many contain beautiful ____________. They spread specific ____________. They often summarize the ____________ information. You may keep them and ____________ them to other people.

This one is about a ____________. It presents ____________ and admission prices.

BRIGHTON TOY MODEL MUSEUM/MATHEW KELLER INC.

3. Read the leaflet and answer the questions.

NIAMH BALDOCK/ALAMY/FOTOARENA

JULIE EDWARDS/ALAMY/FOTOARENA

a. Where's the museum? Write the complete address.

____

b. What is the telephone number of the museum?

____

c. How much would it cost for you to visit the museum?

____

d. What is the website of the museum?

____

e. Is it possible to organize special events at the museum?

____

f. When is the museum closed?

____

4. Where in the museum can you enter without paying the admission fee? What can you do there?

____

____

1. What museums have you already visited? Which one was your favorite? Why?

____

____

2. Would you visit Brighton Toy and Model Museum? Why?

____

____

Reading the world

1. Read the text. Underline the transparent words.

What's Your Travel Personality? What's Your Travel Style?

If you're considering an extended multi-destination or around-the-world journey chances are you've got a pretty advanced sense of adventure and a strong personality to boot. We've pinpointed a series of traveling personalities to help establish an identity that will create an overarching theme for your trip, a way to help divide up the world into those places you should see and those that aren't as worthy of your time.

ZOOM TEAM/SHUTTERSTOCK

ADVENTUROUS – You don't need to be a part of a tour to have an adventure, but if you're not sure what adventure travel means or if you just want an idea of what kind of companies do operate tours, that's a great place to start. Recommended destinations: New Zealand, Brazil rainforest, Bolivia, Nepal/Tibet, Tanzania, India.

THINKSTOCK/GETTY IMAGES

ROMANTIC – Travel can be an amazing way to connect with your partner, or even meet someone new! Romantic places can help you get a sense of what's out there. The notion of taking off to far-flung places is a romantic idea in itself. Recommended stops: Santorini, Venice, Paris, Buenos Aires, Goa, Bali, Phuket, Fiji, Tahiti.

ANTONELLO LANZELLOTTO AGF FOTO RM/ DIOMEDIA

INTELLECTUAL – Days filled with museums, archeological sites, groundbreaking architecture and traditional experiences. If these things are your style, the world awaits. There are destinations all over the world that will cater to the student inside you. Recommended regions: Europe, India, Japan, Machu Picchu, Istanbul, Cairo.

EKATERINA POKROVSKY/SHUTTERSTOCK

FIRST TIME TRAVELER – Will this be your first time traveling internationally? A little nervous about flying overseas? Concerned that you don't know what you don't know? There are places much less of a cultural shock to ease you into the world at large. Recommended stops: London, Paris, Rome, Costa Rica, Australia, New Zealand.

The truth is that most travelers have some elements of all of the things we mentioned above in their ideal travel experience. It's important to think about this aspect of your trip, not just what cities you want to visit or on what airlines you'll be flying.

pinpointed: apontamos; marcamos no mapa
stops: pontos de parada

Adapted from: <www.airtreks.com/ready/where-do-you-want-to-go/what-is-your-traveling-personality/>. Accessed on: Apr. 4, 2016.

2. How would you describe yourself? Choose the best alternative.

a. ☐ Adventurous.

b. ☐ Romantic.

c. ☐ Intellectual.

d. ☐ First time traveler.

3. Why do you identify yourself with this travel personality?

____

____

____

4. Can you think of other travel personalities that are not in the text? Name and describe at least one.

____

____

____

5. Mix two or even all the traveler types and create a new one. Use your imagination.

____

____

____

6. Read about the first time traveler again. Why do you think the countries mentioned are considered less of a cultural shock?

____

____

____

1. Which stops recommended for your travel personality would you choose? Why?

____

____

2. Which stops recommended for another travel personality would you choose? Why?

____

____

UNIT 3

What are you going to recycle?

Review the journey

1. Complete the conversation with verbs from the box in the present continuous.

answer buy have leave write

FILIPE FRAZAO /SHUTTERSTOCK

Maysa: Did you buy recycled paper?

SEBRA/SHUTTERSTOCK

Lilian: No. I ______________ recycled paper tomorrow morning.

FILIPE FRAZAO /SHUTTERSTOCK

Maysa: And Sandra? Did she answer the quiz already?

SEBRA/SHUTTERSTOCK

Lilian: No. Sandra ______________ the quiz this evening.

FILIPE FRAZAO /SHUTTERSTOCK

Maysa: And your parents? Are they fine?

SEBRA/SHUTTERSTOCK

Lilian: Yes, my parents are great. They ______________ to Japan tonight.

FILIPE FRAZAO /SHUTTERSTOCK

Maysa: Daniele ______________ only trash-free lunch this weekend. Is it true?

Lilian: Yes, it's true.

Maysa: Will you write the essay about sustainability today?

SEBRA/SHUTTERSTOCK

Lilian: No, I ______________ the essay next Friday.

2. Underline the correct option.

a. **Do you/Are you going to** plant a tree tomorrow?

b. She **is going to separate/is separate** the trash tonight.

c. Dad **is take/is going to take** a shower in 10 minutes.

d. I **am going to/go** unplug all the cables after using the computer tonight.

e. Where **are you go/are you going** this afternoon?

3. What is going to happen? Use the correct verbs from the box.

have	jump	rain	sneeze

a.

DARRYL LENIUK/GETTY IMAGES

Brad ______________________________.

b.

JOANA LOPES/SHUTTERSTOCK

Emily _______________________ a baby.

c.

THINKSTOCK/GETTY IMAGES

It ______________________________.

d.

PEGGY BLUME/SHUTTERSTOCK

Wagner _________________________.

Another look

TEXT 1

1. Look at the text in activity 2 and write **T** (true) or **F** (false).

a. ☐ This is a brief test of knowledge.

b. ☐ There are questions and four possible answers for each of them.

c. ☐ It isn't found on the internet, magazines, etc.

d. ☐ This is a recipe.

2. Read and take the quiz.

WAYS TO GO GREEN!

1. Which is the best alternative to a plastic water bottle?

a. ☐ Plastic water bottles are the best choice.

b. ☐ Metal water bottle.

c. ☐ Paper cup.

d. ☐ Plastic cup.

2. What should you do with your computer when you're not using it?

a. ☐ Put it in sleep mode.

b. ☐ Leave it on.

c. ☐ Turn it off and unplug it.

d. ☐ Turn it off but leave the wall switch on.

3. What is the name for the alternative to gasoline that can be made from corn?

a. ☐ Corn gasoline.

b. ☐ Ethanol.

c. ☐ Methane.

d. ☐ You can't make fuel from corn.

4. Which of the following is a renewable energy source?

a. ☐ Coal.

b. ☐ Oil.

c. ☐ Gasoline.

d. ☐ Wind.

1b, 2c, 3b, 4d.

Adapted from: <www.funtrivia.com/html5/index.cfm?qid=311452>. Accessed on: Apr. 29, 2016.

3. Circle the correct answers.

A quiz is a short **test/composition/text**. It is a set of **answers/questions/sentences** about a particular subject. People sometimes **read/answer/copy** it as a game or competition.

4. Usually a quiz scores the correct and the incorrect answers. Correct the quiz you took on page 18 and add 2 (two) points to each correct answer. How many points did you score?

____

5. Some quizzes bring the feedback for all answer you give. Read the feedback and check the items.

Correct – add 2 points

Metal water bottle

Plastic water bottles are not the best choice for a few reasons. They are made from petroleum, which is a finite resource and can run out. Metal water bottles are the best choice because you can refill them without worrying about chemicals from a plastic bottle leaching into your water. They do not create waste because you don't have to throw them away.

Adapted from: <www.funtrivia.com/html5/index.cfm?qid=311452>. Accessed on: May 23, 2016.

a. ☐ The feedback explains correct answers.

b. ☐ The feedback shows another question.

c. ☐ If you are wrong, it presents explanations.

d. ☐ It shows points you score.

1. Have you ever taken a quiz about being green before? How many points did you score?

____

____

2. If you had to create a quiz, what would it be about? Why?

____

____

TEXT 2

1. Do you think people today are more concerned about the planet than they were 10 years ago? Why?

____

2. What do you do to help save natural resources?

____

3. Read the following text. Why is it called *Earth is amazing!*?

____

____

Earth is amazing!

Our world is a beautiful place and it has sustained everything living on it for millions of years. Although our presence has done much damage to it, we still have a chance to change it.

The wonderful thing that's happening today is that people are becoming more aware of the needs of our environment and are showing signs of willingness to make a change. When we talk of environment, it involves everything around us, not just the weather. It includes all the animals, plants and the human beings living in this planet.

Here are some amazing environmental facts that you need to know about.

- 27,000 trees are cut down each day so we can have toilet paper.
- Aluminum can be recycled continuously, as in forever. Recycling 1 aluminum can save enough energy to run our TVs for at least 3 hours. 80 trillion aluminum cans are used by humans every year.
- American companies alone use enough paper to encircle the Earth 3x! (It's a good thing that businesses are moving towards going paperless.)
- We can save 75,000 trees if we recycled the paper used on the daily run of the New York Times alone.
- When you throw plastic bags and other plastic materials in the ocean, it kills as many as 1 million sea creatures annually.
- A glass bottle made in our time will take more than 4,000 years to decompose.
- Only 1% of our planet's water supply can be used. 97% is ocean water and 2% is frozen solid in the Arctic, for now.
- Our planet gains inhabitants numbering to 77 million people a year.
- An estimated 50,000 species inhabiting our tropical forests become extinct annually. That's an average of 137 species a day.
- Rainforests are cut down at a rate of 100 acres per minute.
- The world's oldest trees are more than 4,600 years old.
- Landfills are composed of 35% packaging materials.

BIRGIT BRANDLHUBER/SHUTTERSTOCK

Aluminum swarfs.

Extracted from: <www.theworldcounts.com/stories/amazing_environmental_facts>. Accessed on: Jun. 23, 2016.

4. Read the text again and write **T** (true) or **F** (false).

a. [ ] If people used reusable packaging, we would decrease the amount of trash in a significant way.

b. [ ] It is possible to recycle aluminum over and over again.

c. [ ] We consume almost all the water available in the planet.

d. [ ] Recycling paper is an alternative to producing more and more paper all the time.

e. [ ] Plastic bags do not harm the environment at all.

5. Why is it important to go digital, according to the data presented in this article?

____

____

____

____

6. Research another curious fact about our planet. Write it down and share it with your classmates.

____

____

____

____

____

1. Read your answer in activity 2 again. After reading the text, is there anything else you can do to help save natural resources?

____

____

____

2. What is the most interesting fact about our planet you have learned in this unit?

____

____

____

Reading the world

1. Read the following web article and answer the questions that follow.

BIS

www.criticalcactus.com/beautiful-recycled-homes/

4 Awesome Homes Built With Recycled Material

Did you think sustainable building is boring? Think again. Or wait, let us help you rethink with these 4 amazing houses that are built with trash.

MARIAKRAYNOVA/SHUTTERSTOCK

This house built with 25,000 recycled bottles cemented together is situated in Calico, California, United States of America.

ZORAN MILICH/GETTY IMAGES

This (not so) tiny home is built with reclaimed shipping containers and some additional material to create the part that unites the partially opened up containers to one stunning home.

PAUL WESTON / ALAMY/FOTOARENA

There are also many houses built from trash. To know more about them, watch Dan Phillips's entertaining and pretty funny TED Talk presentation, available at: www.ted.com/talks/dan_phillips_creative_houses_from_reclaimed_stuff

JAY GOEBEL / ALAMY/FOTOARENA

This structure was built using beer and soda cans, wooden windows, hubcaps, screen doors, bicycle reflectors and more.

Based on: <www.criticalcactus.com/beautiful-recycled-homes/>. Accessed on: Apr. 2, 2016.

TED Talk: *TED* é o acrônimo de *Technology*, *Education* e *Design*; *talk* é seminário ou colóquio

a. Do you think building houses with recycled materials is a way of protecting the environment and saving natural resources? Explain.

____

____

____

____

b. People who build houses with trash are seen as wise persons and pioneers. What do you think about that?

____

____

____

c. Would you use trash to build a house for you and your family? Which material would you use?

____

____

2. Use your imagination! Draw a sketch of your sustainable building.

UNIT 4 What do you know about her?

Review the journey

1. Do you know what a student council or government is? Describe it with your own words. Then read the text below and check if your answer is correct.

> **Student council** is a group of students elected by peers to participate in designated areas of school government. [...] Generally, councils participate in the planning of school events such as prom and spirit rallies; they also assist administration with events for the local community such as blood drives or donation collections. The student council works with the district's school board, school administration, parent organizations, student body, and local community to decide on and approve projects and initiatives for the school, students, and community. [...]

Extracted from: <http://study.com/academy/lesson/what-is-student-council-definition-purpose-positions.html>. Accessed on: Jun. 24, 2016.

2. Imagine you are running for president of the student council. Combine verbs and expressions and make a list of what you intend to do.

debate	develop	end
enjoy	fight	improve

antibullying campaign	detention rules	fun times
gender equality	student participation	unhealthy meals

3. Study the chart and think about your school's rules and requirements. Check the correct column.

	Required	Not required	Prohibited
be late for class			✓
wear a uniform			
eat in the classroom			
do homework			
carry a student ID			

CAIAIMAGE/ROBERT DALY/GETTY MAGES

4. Now write full sentences to describe the rules and requirements at your school.

- Use the information in the chart of activity 3.
- Use **must** and **must not** to describe rules and requirements.
- Use **don't have to** to describe what is not a rule or requirement.

Students must not be late for class .

____

____

____

____

____

5. Complete the sentences with **may** or **must**.

a. There are some new rules that the student government _______________ approve. Nothing is for certain yet.

b. I think that comment _______________ have offended some people in the student meeting. It is not a kind of comment we are used to hear in these meetings. I think you should ask people if they are OK with it, and apologize if they are not.

c. She _______________ take the test tomorrow. There is no other option!

d. The situation in the student committee _______________ change. It is unacceptable that it just stays the same.

e. We _______________ be informed about our city politics, or else, it will be impossible for us to demand our rights and comply with our obligations.

Another look

1. Which elements can you identify in the text in activity 4?

a. ☐ personal data

b. ☐ an interview

c. ☐ a picture

d. ☐ a story

e. ☐ activity description

f. ☐ actions that made the person special or famous

g. ☐ titles and subtitles

h. ☐ a strip with drawings

2. What text genre is it?

a. ☐ a fast fact

b. ☐ news

c. ☐ an interview

d. ☐ a biographical fact sheet

3. What is the text about?

____

4. Read the text below.

MICHELLE LAVAUGHN ROBINSON OBAMA

Born: January 17, 1964 in Chicago, Illinois, U.S.
Nationality: American
Job: first lady of US

Michelle Obama attended Princeton University, graduating in 1985, and went on to earn a degree from Harvard Law School in 1988 – she would later become a lawyer, Chicago city administrator, community-outreach worker. Following her graduation from Harvard, she worked at a Chicago law firm, where she met her husband, future U.S. President Barack Obama. The couple married on October 3, 1992. As first lady of U.S., she has focused her attention on current social issues, such as poverty, healthy living and education.

Supporting the U.S. President Barack Obama

In 2007, Michelle scaled back her own professional work to attend to family and campaign obligations during Barack's run for the Democratic presidential nomination. Barack Obama eventually won the nomination and was elected the 44th President of the United States. He was sworn in on January 20, 2009.

When her husband sought reelection in 2012, facing a challenging race against Republican presidential nominee Mitt Romney, Michelle Obama diligently campaigned on his behalf. She traveled the country, giving talks and making public appearances.

Issues and Causes

As the first lady of the United States, Michelle Obama has focused her attention on issues such as the support of military families, helping working women balance career and family and encouraging national service. During the first year of the Obama presidency, Michelle and her husband volunteered at homeless shelters and soup kitchens in the Washington D.C. area. Michelle also has made appearances at public schools, stressing the importance of education and volunteer work.

Michelle Obama remains committed to her health-and-wellness causes. In 2012, she announced a new fitness program for kids, as part of her *Let's Move!* initiative. Along with the U.S. Olympic team and other sports organizations, she has worked to get young people to try out a new sport or activity.

Some facts you didn't know about Michelle Obama

- She was assigned Barack's mentor when he came to her Chicago firm for a summer job.
- At Princeton, Michelle majored in sociology. She got her law degree from Harvard.
- She worked for Chicago's Mayor Daley in the city's office of planning and development.
- As vice president of community and external affairs at the University of Chicago Medical Centre, Michelle supervised a five hundred per cent increase of volunteerism in the hospital.
- She was on the board of six major organisations, including the prestigious Chicago Council on Global Affairs, the University of Chicago Laboratory Schools and Tree House Foods; and Vice President, Community and External Affairs at the University of Chicago Hospitals.

WORLD HISTORY ARCHIVE/ALAMY/FOTOARENA

Based on: <www.biography.com/people/michelle-obama-307592>; <www.telegraph.co.uk/news/worldnews/michelle-obama/4317226/50-things-you-didnt-know-about-Michelle-Obama.html>. Accessed on: Apr. 2, 2016.

5. Check what is correct about Michelle Obama.

a. ☐ She is the 44th president of the United States.

b. ☐ She is American.

c. ☐ As a first lady, Michelle Obama is not an active person. She doesn't participate in the political life.

d. ☐ Michelle created the *Let's Move!* initiative.

6. When Barack Obama sought reelection in 2012, what did Michelle do?

____

____

7. Write **T** (true) or **F** (false).

a. ☐ Michelle Obama hasn't made any efforts to improve students' well-being.

b. ☐ She is not committed with causes such as volunteering, health and nutrition.

c. ☐ Michelle Obama has a major in sociology and a law degree.

d. ☐ *Let's Move!* initiative is part of Michelle's work to promote physical activity among kids.

e. ☐ Michelle Obama is not concerned about physical activity, as she cares most about her husband's campaigns.

8. Read about *Let's Move!*. Answer the questions.

BIS

www.letsmove.gov/learn-facts/epidemic-childhood-obesity

LET'S MOVE!

JOE RAEDLE/GETTY IMAGES

Let's Move! is a comprehensive initiative, launched by the First Lady, dedicated to solving the challenge of childhood obesity within a generation, so that children born today will grow up healthier and able to pursue their dreams. Combining comprehensive strategies with common sense, *Let's Move!* is about putting children on the path to a healthy future during their earliest months and years. Giving parents helpful information and fostering environments that support healthy choices. Providing healthier foods in our schools. Ensuring that every family has access to healthy, affordable food. And, helping kids become more physically active.

Everyone has a role to play in reducing childhood obesity, including parents, elected officials from all levels of government, schools, health care professionals, faith-based and community-based organizations, and private sector companies. Your involvement is key to ensuring a healthy future for our children.

Extracted from: <www.letsmove.gov/learn-facts/epidemic-childhood-obesity>. Accessed on: Jun. 7, 2016.

a. What is *Let's Move!* goal?

____

b. Who must help achieve this goal, according to the text?

____

9. Which activities are part of the *Let's Move!* campaign? Check the correct alternatives.

a. ☐

GM VISUALS/BLEND IMAGES/GETTY IMAGES

b. ☐

MONKEY BUSINESS IMAGES/SHUTTERSTOCK

c. ☐

ALISTAIR BERG/GETTY IMAGES

d. ☐

STEVE DEBENPORT/GETTY IMAGES

10. Match the following captions to the pictures in activity 9.

a. ☐ Children choosing unhealthy food at the school's cafeteria.

b. ☐ Children practicing sports.

c. ☐ Teaching people about healthy nutrition.

d. ☐ Access to healthy food.

1. Do you think it is necessary to be the first lady of a country to help people in need?

____

____

____

2. Do you help people? How? If not, would you like to? Make a list of the things you do or would like to do.

____

____

____

3. Do you consider yourself to be physically active? What could you do to improve your physical activity routine?

____

____

____

Reading the world

1. Read the text below to meet Cassandra Clare, author of *The Mortal Instruments* book series.

MY BIO

DAVID LIVINGSTON/GETTY IMAGES

MARGARET K. MCELDERRY BOOKS

Cassandra Clare was born to American parents in Teheran, Iran and spent much of her childhood travelling the world with her family, including one trek through the Himalayas as a toddler where she spent a month living in her father's backpack. She lived in France, England and Switzerland before she was ten years old.

Since her family moved around so much she found familiarity in books and went everywhere with a book under her arm. She spent her high school years in Los Angeles where she used to write stories to amuse her classmates, including an epic novel called *The Beautiful Cassandra* based on a Jane Austen short story of the same name (and which later inspired her current pen name).

After college, Cassie lived in Los Angeles and New York where she worked at various entertainment magazines and even some rather suspect tabloids where she reported on Brad and Angelina's world travels and Britney Spears' wardrobe malfunctions. She started working on her YA novel, *City of Bones* in 2004, inspired by the urban landscape of Manhattan, her favorite city. She turned to writing fantasy fiction full time in 2006 and hopes never to have to write about Paris Hilton again.

Cassie's first professional writing sale was a short story called *The Girl's Guide to Defeating the Dark Lord* in a Baen anthology of humor fantasy. Cassie hates working at home alone because she always gets distracted by TV reality shows and the tricks of her two cats, so she usually sets out to write in local coffee shops and restaurants. She likes to work in the company of her friends, who see that she sticks to her deadlines.

The Mortal Instruments is a series of six young adult fantasy novels written by her: *City of Bones* (2007), *City of Ashes* (2008), *City of Glass* (2009), *City of Fallen Angels* (2011), *City of Lost Souls* (2012), and *City of Heavenly Fire* (2014).

Why teen books, Cassandra?

Why not teen books? More seriously, when I started out writing *City of Bones*, I didn't think of it as young adult, just as a fantasy novel. The characters simply happened to be teenagers. At some point I was approached by a publisher who was interested in the book, but they wanted me to "age up the characters" and make them adults. I toyed with the idea for a while, but I knew it wouldn't work. I wanted to tell a story about characters at that crucial life stage just between adolescence and adulthood, where your choices determine the kind of person you're going to be rather than reflecting who you already are.

Based on: <www.cassandraclare.com/about/>; <www.cassandraclare.com/faq/why-teen-books/>. Accessed on: May 31, 2016.

2. Why did Cassandra Clare start to write stories?

____

____

3. Which Cassandra's story is based on a Jane Austen's short story?

____

____

4. When did she start to write *City of Bones*?

____

5. Why did Cassandra choose to write stories for teenagers?

____

____

____

____

6. Would you like to write for teenagers too? What kind of story would you like to create?

____

____

____

7. Read the following review of *The Mortal Instruments* series. What is the series really about according to the review?

> "Clare's atmospheric setting is spot-on, informed equally by neo-gothic horror films and the modern fantasy leanings of Neil Gaiman. Werewolves, vampires, angels and fairies all fit in this ambitious milieu. At the core, though, this is a compelling story about family secrets and coming-of-age identity crises. Fans of the smart/chic horror typified by *Buffy the Vampire Slayer* will instantly fall for this new series."
>
> – Publishers Weekly

Extracted from: <www.cassandraclare.com/my-writing/novels/the-mortal-instruments/>. Accessed on: Jun. 22, 2016.

____

____

____

8. Do you know any other books or movies that have a similar core story?

____

____

____

UNIT 5

Which painting do you prefer?

Review the journey

1. Observe the paintings and their captions. Then make comparisons.

a. Portinari's painting / Velázquez's painting / small

MOMA, NY/PROJETO PORTINARI

PORTINARI, Candido. *Hill*. 1933. Oil on canvas. 144 cm × 145.7 cm. Museum of Modern Art, New York, USA.

REPRODUÇÃO/MUSEU DO PRADO, MADRI, ESPANHA

VELÁZQUEZ, Diego. *The maids of honour*. 1656. Oil on canvas. 3.18 m × 2.76 m. Museo Nacional del Prado, Madrid, Spain.

____

b. Van Gogh's painting / Monet's painting / old

REPRODUÇÃO/COURTAULD INSTITUTE GALLERIES, LONDON

VAN GOGH, Vincent. *Self-portrait with bandaged ear*. 1889. Oil on canvas. 60.5 cm × 50 cm. Courtauld Institute Galleries, London, England.

THE BRIDGEMAN LIBRARY/KEYSTONE BRASIL

MONET, Claude. *Women in the garden*. 1866. Oil on canvas. 255 cm × 205 cm. Musée d'Orsay, Paris, France.

____

c. Pissaro's painting / Segall's painting / colorful

MUSEU LASAR SEGALL, SÃO PAULO

SEGALL, Lasar. *Paisagem brasileira.* 1925. Oil on canvas. 64 cm × 54 cm. Museu Lasar Segall, São Paulo, Brazil.

THE BRIDGEMAN LIBRARY/KEYSTONE BRASIL

PISSARRO, Camile. *White frost.* 1873. Oil on canvas. 65 cm × 93 cm. Musée d'Orsay, Paris, France.

____

2. Describe the pictures in activity 1. Use the adjectives from the box.

beautiful colorful dramatic famous hazy large pale
realistic shadowy simple small ugly unknown unusual

a. ____

____

____

____

b. ____

____

____

____

c. ____

____

____

____

Another look

TEXT 1

1. How do you usually buy a book? What do you look first when choosing one?

____

____

2. Look at the pictures. What do you expect to find in this book?

____

3. Use the words and expressions from the box to identify the elements from the front and back covers below.

> authors' names   ISBN number/barcode
> publisher's name   title

____

____

____

____

4. The painting on the book cover in activity 3 is called *Dream Caused by the Flight of a Bee around a Pomegranate a Second before Waking up*, by Salvador Dalí. Look at the painting below. How would you describe it? Try to describe all the elements that you see.

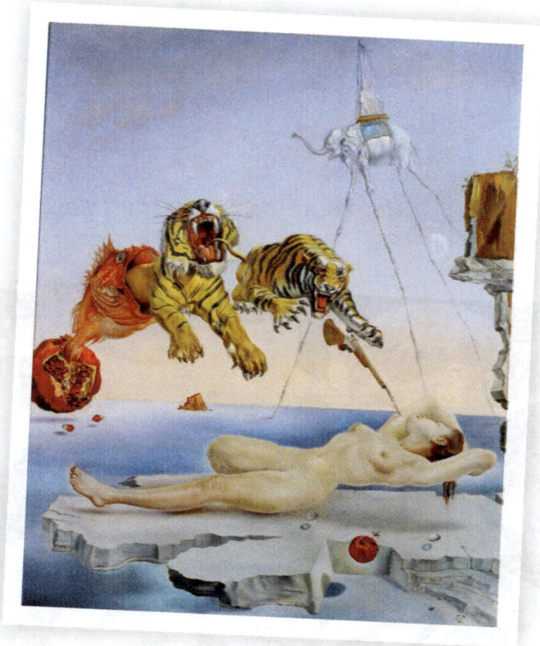

ERICH LESSING/ALBUM/FOTOARENA

____

____

____

____

5. In pairs, compare your answers to activity 4. Did you describe the picture in a similar way? List the differences between your answers below. Then discuss them.

____

____

____

____

1. How do you feel about the painting? Do you like it or not? Justify your answer.

____

____

____

TEXT 2

1. When you look at a picture or a painting, what do you normally observe?

a. ☐ colors
b. ☐ details
c. ☐ landscape
d. ☐ light
e. ☐ location
f. ☐ originality

2. Look at the paintings and read the texts. Then underline the transparent words.

REPRODUÇÃO/MUSEU NACIONAL CENTRO DE ARTE REINA SOFÍA, MADRI

PICASSO, Pablo. *Guernica*. 1937. Oil on canvas. 349.3 cm × 776.6 cm. Museo Reina Sofía, Madrid, Spain.

Guernica is considered for the most important artwork of the twentieth century, as it is an appeal about the bombing of civilians in the town of Guernica by the Germans. It is an oil canvas painting with size 349.3 cm × 776.6 cm. The artwork is exposed in the Reina Sofía Museum in Madrid since 1992.

Adapted from: <http://artcocktail.mallforarts.com/2012/06/brief-description-of-the-ten-most-famous-paintings-in-the-world/>. Accessed on: Apr. 30, 2016.

It is an oil canvas painting with size 92 cm × 73 cm. It was painted in 1888; now it is exposed in the Neue Pinakothek museum in Munich. Its bright colors are warm and bring delight to the visitors. Some of the sunflowers are almost wither; others are fully blooming and others have started to wither. There were seven versions of the painting *Sunflowers*, but now there are only six because one was destroyed during World War II in Japan.

Adapted from: <http://artcocktail.mallforarts.com/2012/06/brief-description-of-the-ten-most-famous-paintings-in-the-world/>. Accessed on: Apr. 30, 2016.

wither: murchos, secos
blooming: florescidos

REPRODUÇÃO/NEUE PINAKOTHEK, MUNICH, GERMANY

VAN GOGH, Vincent. *Sunflowers*. 1888. Oil on canvas. 92 cm × 73 cm. Neue Pinakothek, Munich, Germany.

3. Read the texts from activity 2 again and answer the questions.

a. Who painted *Guernica*?

____

b. When did he paint it?

____

c. Who painted *Sunflowers*?

____

d. When did he paint it?

____

4. Match questions and answers.

a. Who bombed the town of Guernica?

b. How large is *Guernica*?

c. Where is Van Gogh's *Sunflowers* exposed?

d. Where was one of its versions destroyed?

☐ In Japan.

☐ The Germans.

☐ In Munich, Germany.

☐ 349.3 cm × 776.6 cm.

5. Find in the paintings' description words that have the same meaning as:

a. non-combatants: ______________________________

b. piece of cloth specially prepared for painting: ______________________________

c. lively; vibrant: ______________________________

d. enjoyment; happiness: ______________________________

1. Have you ever been to a museum or to an art exhibit?

____

2. Read the quote and answer the questions below.

> Seeing artistically does not happen automatically. We must constantly develop our powers of observation.
>
> *Eugene Delacroix*

Extracted from: <www.azquotes.com/quote/1048058>. Accessed on: May 2, 2016.

a. Are you a good observer?

____

____

b. Do you agree with the quote? Explain.

____

____

Reading the world

1. Read both texts and answer the questions.

TEXT 1

How could someone steal a painting from a museum?

When Leonardo da Vinci's *Mona Lisa* disappeared from the Louvre museum in Paris in 1911, the world was shocked. The theft went undetected for days. Museum staff saw the empty space on the wall and assumed the painting had been moved to the Louvre's restoration center for upkeep. But by the second day, the Louvre called the police.

The theft of the *Mona Lisa* by museum worker Vincenzo Perugia was brilliant in its simplicity. He hid in a room. When everyone had gone home, he left his hiding place, took the *Mona Lisa* off the wall, stuck the priceless work under his shirt and walked out into the night.

VELISHCHUK YEVHEN/SHUTTERSTOCK

theft: roubo
undetected: não detectado; insuspeito
upkeep: manutenção

Extracted from: <http://people.howstuffworks.com/steal-painting-from-museum.htm>. Accessed on: May 2, 2016.

TEXT 2

Stolen Picasso recovered undamaged in Brazil

Police in Brazil have recovered two paintings worth a total of £28m, three weeks after they were stolen from one of South America's most prestigious galleries.

Escorted by a helicopter and more than a dozen police vehicles, the works by Pablo Picasso and the Brazilian artist Candido Portinari were returned yesterday to the Sao Paulo Museum of Art (Masp). Picasso's *Portrait of Suzanne Bloch* and Portinari's *The Coffee Worker*, which were stolen by masked men on December 20, were found on Tuesday at a house in Greater Sao Paulo. Two arrests were made, but police are still hunting for the mastermind behind the theft.

THIAGO LEITE/SHUTTERSTOCK

Extracted from: <www.theguardian.com/world/2008/jan/10/artsfunding.artnews>. Accessed on: May 2, 2016.

2. Number the sentences accordingly. In which text...

a. ☐ is the value of two paintings mentioned?

b. ☐ is the name of the robber mentioned?

c. ☐ do they say how the robber stole the painting?

d. ☐ do they say when the robber left the museum?

e. ☐ do we know the number of robbers arrested?

f. ☐ do we know when the paintings were returned?

3. Have you ever heard of museum or church robberies? Which objects do robbers often steal?

____

____

____

4. What do robbers steal works of art for?

____

____

____

5. Try to guess. Underline the correct answers. Then look on the internet, books, or talk to your teacher for the correct answer.

a. The most stolen artist in the world is **Da Vinci/Picasso**.

b. Someone who produces copies or imitations is named a **forger/forgerer**.

c. It **is/isn't** a crime to copy an artwork.

d. It isn't a crime to sell a copy, if you say it's the **fake/original** artwork.

6. Look at the following painting. Do you know the painter who made it? Search about her story and write how it relates to activity 5.

____

____

____

____

____

____

____

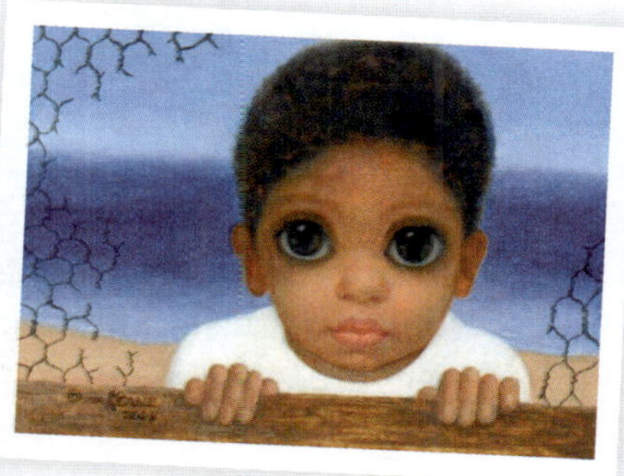

KEANE EYES GALLERY, SAN FRANCISCO, CA

KEANE, Margaret. *A day at the beach*. 2004. Fine art giclee print on canvas. 20.3 cm × 30.5 cm. Keyne Eyes Gallery, San Francisco, USA.

UNIT 6

What's this story about?

Review the journey

1. Underline the correct answer.

THE BRIDGEMAN LIBRARY/KEYSTONE BRASIL

a. Once upon a time, in a land beyond the high mountains and over the sea, **there was/there were** three billy goats who lived on a rocky hillside. **There were/There was** a big billy goat, a middlesized billy goat, and a little billy goat, and they were all called Gruff.

Jonathan Langley. *The Three Billy Goats Gruff*. London: HarperCollins, 2011.

b. Many years ago, **there were/there was** an emperor, who was so excessively fond of new clothes, that he spent all his money on the finest suits. He did not trouble himself in the least about his soldiers; nor did he care to go to the theatre or out hunting, except when **there was/there were** a chance to show off his new clothes.

Hans Christian Andersen. *The Emperor's New Clothes*. Extracted from: <www.storynory.com/2008/06/23/the-emperors-new-clothes/>. Accessed on: Mar. 3, 2016.

c. Once upon a time **there was/there were** a great king of China. This king had everything he wanted. He had rare treasures, a beautiful palace, fine horses, the bravest warriors and a people who loved him. But one thing the king lacked. He didn't have a wife.

The Tale of The Sad Queen. Extracted from: <http://fairytalesoftheworld.com/quick-reads/the-tale-of-the-sad-queen/>. Accessed on: Mar. 3, 2016.

d. **There was/There were** three little pigs. One pig built a house of straw while the second pig built his house with sticks. They built their houses very quickly and then sang and danced all day because they were lazy. The third little pig worked hard all day and built his house with bricks.

The Three Little Pigs. Extracted from: <http://shortstoriesshort.com/story/the-three-little-pigs/>. Accessed on: Mar. 3, 2016.

2. Complete the dialogues using the superlative form of the adjectives in bold.

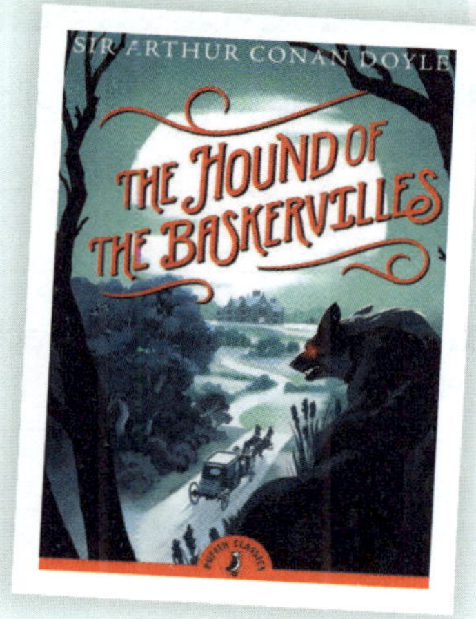

PENGUIN BOOKS

a. A: *The Hound of the Baskervilles*, by Arthur Conan Doyle, is a **great** mystery book.

B: Yes, in my opinion, it is one of ____________________ mystery books ever written.

PENGUIN BOOKS

b. A: Carlos Drummond de Andrade was an **influential** Brazilian poet. The book *Multitudinous Heart* reunited some of his **powerful** poems.

B: In my opinion, Carlos Drummond de Andrade was ____________________ Brazilian poet and *Multitudinous Heart* reunited his ____________________ poems.

MACMILLAN PUBLISHERS LIMITED

c. A: Jane Austen's *Pride and Prejudice* is a **popular** romance novel.

B: Yes, Jane Austen's *Pride and Prejudice* is one of ____________________ romance novels of all times.

PENGUIN BOOKS

d. A: Jules Verne is a very **well-known** science fiction author. He wrote *Around the World in 80 Days*.

B: Yes, Jules Verne is one of ____________________ science fiction authors who ever lived. I love *Around the World in 80 Days*.

Another look

1. Read the title of the following story. Do you know this story? If you do, what happens in the end?

____

____

2. Read the story and check if your answer in activity 1 is correct. If not, write what is different.

____

____

LITTLE RED RIDING-HOOD

There was once upon a time a little village girl, the prettiest ever seen or known, of whom her mother was dotingly fond. Her grandmother was even fonder of her still, and had a little red hood made for the child, which suited her so well, that wherever she went, she was known by the name of Little Red Riding-Hood.

One day, her mother having baked some cakes, said to her, "Go and see how your grandmother is getting on, for I have been told she is ill; take her a cake and this little jar of butter." Whereupon Little Red Riding-Hood started off without delay towards the village in which her grandmother lived. On her way she had to pass through a wood, and there she met that sly old fellow, Mr Wolf, who felt that he should very much like to eat her up on the spot, but was afraid to do so, as there were woodcutters at hand in the forest. He asked her which way she was going, and the poor child, not knowing how dangerous it is to stop and listen to a wolf, answered, "I am going to see my grandmother, and am taking a cake and a little jar of butter, which my mother has sent her."

"Does she live far from here?" asked the Wolf.

"Oh, yes!" replied Little Red Riding-Hood, "on the further side of the mill that you see down there; hers is the first house in the village."

"Well, I was thinking of going to visit her myself," rejoined the Wolf, "so I will take this path, and you take the other, and we will see which of us gets there first."

The Wolf then began running off as fast as he could along the shorter way, which he had chosen, while the little girl went by the longer way, and amused herself with stopping to gather nuts, or run after butterflies, and with making little nosegays of all the flowers she could find.

It did not take the Wolf long to reach the grandmother's house; he knocked: tap, tap.

"Who is there?"

"It is your grand-daughter, Little Red Riding-Hood," answered the Wolf, imitating the child's voice. "I have brought a cake and a little jar of butter, which my mother has sent you." The good grandmother, who was ill in bed, called out, "Pull the bobbin, and the latch will go up." The Wolf pulled the bobbin, and the door opened. He leaped on to the poor old woman, and ate her up in less than no time, for he had been three days without food. He then shut the door again, and laid himself down in the grandmother's bed, to wait for Little Red Riding-Hood. Presently she came and knocked at the door: tap, tap.

bobbin: tramela
latch: trinco

"Who is there?" Little Red Riding-Hood was frightened at first, on hearing the Wolf's gruff voice, but thinking that her grandmother had a cold, she answered,—

"It is your grand-daughter, Little Red Riding-Hood. I have brought a cake and a little jar of butter, which my mother has sent you."

The Wolf called out, this time in rather a softer voice, "Pull the bobbin, and the latch will go up." Little Red Riding-Hood pulled the bobbin, and the door opened.

When the Wolf saw her come in, he hid himself under the bedclothes, and said to her, "Put the cake and the little jar of butter in the cupboard, and come into bed with me."

Little Red Riding-Hood undressed, and went to the bedside, and was very much astonished to see how different her grandmother looked to what she did when she was up and dressed.

"Grandmother," she exclaimed, "what long arms you have!"

"All the better to embrace you with, my little girl."

"Grandmother, what long legs you have!"

"All the better to run with, child."

"Grandmother, what long ears you have!"

"All the better to hear with, child."

"Grandmother, what large eyes you have!"

"All the better to see with, child."

"Grandmother, what large teeth you have!"

"All the better to eat you with!" and saying these words, the wicked Wolf sprang out upon Little Red Riding-Hood, and ate her up.

'Grandma, what great ears you have!'
Little Red Riding-Hood

Extracted from: <www.gutenberg.org/files/33511/33511-h/33511-h.htm>. Accessed on: Jun. 7, 2016.

3. This version of *Little Red Riding-Hood* was taken from the book *Tales of Passed Times*, by Charles Perrault, which was published in London, in 1900. Who are the characters in the text?

____

____

____

4. Which character is usually part of the story, but not in this version?

____

5. What does the character you mentioned in activity 4 usually do in the story?

____

____

____

6. Charles Perrault wrote many stories and most of them had morals. What do you think the moral of the story you read is?

____

____

____

7. Read the moral of the story below and write **T** (true) or **F** (false).

MORAL

Now, children, take warning, and chiefly, I pray,
You maidens so gentle and fair,
When you come across all kinds of folk, have a care
Not to listen to what they may say;
For it can't be thought strange if you do,
Should the Wolf choose to eat up a few.
The Wolf, I say here, for you'll find
Wolves are many, and vary in kind;
There are some, easy-mannered and tame,
Without malice, or temper, the same,
Most obliging and sweet in their way,
Like to follow their tender young prey,
And will track them right into their homes—lack-a-day!
Who among us has not learnt by this time to know,
The most dangerous of wolves is the soft, smooth-tongued foe!

maidens: senhoritas
tame: dócil
smooth-tongued: de fala mansa
foe: inimigo

Extracted from: <www.gutenberg.org/files/33511/33511-h/33511-h.htm>. Accessed on: Jun. 7, 2016.

a. ☐ The moral is directed mostly to girls.
b. ☐ It is about learning how to listen to older people's advice.
c. ☐ It says the most dangerous wolves are not necessarily scary.
d. ☐ Wolves can be understood as people in general, or men specifically, that assault women.
e. ☐ The moral is about wolves because there were many wolves where Charles Perrault lived.

8. Why do you think Perrault's stories had morals? Do you know any other stories that have morals?

____

____

____

9. Now, read the ending for *The Little Red Riding-Hood*, by Jacob and Whilhelm Grimm. What is different from Perrault's version of the story?

____

____

____

____

"Oh, grandmother, what a horribly big mouth you have!"

"All the better to eat you with!" And with that he jumped out of bed, jumped on top of poor Little Red Cap, and ate her up. As soon as the wolf had finished this tasty bite, he climbed back into bed, fell asleep, and began to snore very loudly.

A huntsman was just passing by. He thought it strange that the old woman was snoring so loudly, so he decided to take a look. He stepped inside, and in the bed there lay the wolf that he had been hunting for such a long time. "He has eaten the grandmother, but perhaps she still can be saved. I won't shoot him," thought the huntsman. So he took a pair of scissors and cut open his belly.

He had cut only a few strokes when he saw the red cap shining through. He cut a little more, and the girl jumped out and cried, "Oh, I was so frightened! It was so dark inside the wolf's body!"

And then the grandmother came out alive as well. Then Little Red Cap fetched some large heavy stones. They filled the wolf's body with them, and when he woke up and tried to run away, the stones were so heavy that he fell down dead.

The three of them were happy. The huntsman took the wolf's pelt. The grandmother ate the cake and drank the wine that Little Red Cap had brought. And Little Red Cap thought to herself, "As long as I live, I will never leave the path and run off into the woods by myself if mother tells me not to."

Extracted from: <www.pitt.edu/~dash/type0333.html#grimm>. Accessed on: Jun. 7, 2016.

10. Read the last sentence of the story again. Check the alternative that expresses the moral of the story, according to this sentence.

a. ☐ Never listen to a huntsman.

b. ☐ When a wolf appears, go the other way around.

c. ☐ Never walk alone in the woods.

d. ☐ Do not disobey your parents, or you might get into trouble.

1. What version of the story do you prefer? Why?

____

____

Reading the world

1. Do you read manga or watch anime? Do you know the difference between them?

____

____

____

2. Read the report below.

HOW DO JAPANESE PEOPLE VIEW ANIME AND MANGA VS. OTHER PEOPLE?

Curt Tigges, studied abroad in Japan for a semester

From my time in Japan, it seemed that most people were not terribly interested in watching anime. The majority of adults didn't watch it, and even among young people (college students) most of the ones I talked to were not very familiar with the ones that are most popular in the United States. Generally, anime is targeted towards teenager, geek, or otaku demographics, though a few are intended for wider appeal.

Many young men (through their 30s) read manga, however. It's very popular, and you will often see people on the subway reading it. Fewer women read it.

EIICHIRO ODA/SHONEN JUMP/VIZ MEDIA

Gee Daigo, Japanese

Honestly, there is a great synergy between the internet and anime/manga, but once you go offline, there is no sign of Manga or Anime in Japan.

I don't watch anime (or read comics or manga at all) and most professionals I know from Japan don't care much about anime either.

Manga, on the other hand, is widely accepted and considered to be reasonable entertainment you see everywhere. Adults read all different types of mangas available.

geek: pessoa fascinada por ciências, tecnologia (aparelhos, aplicativos, *games*) e cultura *pop* (quadrinhos, filmes etc.)

otaku: são os *geeks* japoneses, fascinados por tecnologia, mangás, *animes* e *games*

Adapted from: <www.quora.com/How-do-Japanese-people-view-anime-and-manga-vs-other-people-Americans-for-example/>. Accessed on: May 3, 2016.

3. Answer each request.

a. Copy three Japanese words: ______________________________

b. Write how long Curt studied in Japan: ______________________________

c. Find out who the target public for anime is: ______________________________

d. Mention a place where the Japanese frequently read manga: ______________________________

e. Write who does not care much about anime in Japan: ______________________________

f. Find out what is better known than anime: ______________________________

4. Was there any otaku in your school or neighborhood? Which manga or anime did she/he like?

____

____

____

5. Are there magazine stands that sell manga or comics in your neighborhood? Do you or your friends go there? What do you usually buy or read?

____

____

____

6. Can you draw manga? Try to create a character inspired by manga art style. Search the internet for examples and use your imagination!

UNIT 7

A world of possibilities

Review the journey

1. Read the text. Then complete the sentences with the relative pronouns from the box.

5 Fascinating Facts About The Paralympics

Until the Paralympics came along athletes with disabilities did sometimes compete in the Olympics. In fact, in 1904, American gymnast George Eyser won three gold medals in just one day, with an artificial leg.

The first attempt to organise a specific contest for those with disabilities came in 1948. Sixteen veterans took part in an archery competition.

The Games got an international dimension in 1952 when the Dutch joined. The tournament continued to grow and in 1960 what is now considered the first Paralympic Games was held in Rome, Italy, with 400 athletes from 23 countries taking part in eight sports.

From then on the Paralympic Games were held every four years and athletes with different disabilities were allowed to participate from the 1976 Games held in Toronto, Canada.

The Paralympic symbol is made up of three "agitos", coloured red, blue, and green, being the colours most widely included in national flags. The "para" in the title is because the Games run parallel to the Olympic Games.

Adapted from: <www.huffingtonpost.co.uk/2012/08/23/20-fascinating-facts-about-the-paralympics_n_7375398.html>. Accessed on: Apr. 2, 2016.

when	where	which	who	whose

a. The Dutch joined the Paralympics in 1952, __________ the games got an international dimension.

b. Red, blue, and green are the colours __________ the Paralympic symbol is made up.

c. George Eyser was an American gymnast __________ won three gold medals in one day. Eyser, __________ leg was artificial, competed in the 1904 Paralympics.

d. The first Paralympic Games was held in Rome, Italy, __________ 400 athletes from 23 countries took part in eight sports.

2. Complete the text using **should** or **shouldn't**.

U.S. athletes ______ consider skipping Rio if fear Zika

The United States Olympic Committee told U.S. sports federations that athletes and staff concerned for their health over the Zika virus ______ consider not going to the Rio 2016 Olympic Games in August. [...]

Federations were told that no one ______ go to Brazil "if they don't feel comfortable going. Bottom line," said Donald Anthony, president and board chairman of USA Fencing. Anthony, a former Olympian, said: "One of the things that they immediately said was, especially for women that may be pregnant or even thinking of getting pregnant, that whether you are scheduled to go to Rio or not, that you ______ go. And no one ______ go if they feel at all as though that that threat could impact them."

Will Connell, Director of Sport at the U.S. Equestrian Federation, said the USOC was leaving the decision up to individual athletes and staff members. "They said no one who has reasons to be concerned ______ feel obliged to go," Connell said. "If an athlete feels that way, of course they may decide not to go."

Adapted from: <www.reuters.com/article/us-health-zika-usa-olympics-exlusive-idUSKCN0VH0BJ>. Accessed on: Apr. 3, 2016.

3. Do the crossword.

a.

BOB DAEMMRICH/ALAMY/FOTOARENA

b.

LEFTERIS PITARAKIS/AP PHOTO/GLOW IMAGES

c.

DEAN MOUHTAROPOULOS/GETTY IMAGES

d.

DENNIS GROMBKOWSKI/GETTY IMAGES

e.

DAN KITWOOD/GETTY IMAGES

Another look

1. Read the headline below and answer the questions.

a. What's the topic of the text?

____

b. What's the athlete's name?

____

c. Which country did he represent?

____

2. Read the text.

THE INFLUENCE OF SPORT – AN INTERVIEW WITH AUSTRALIAN PARALYMPIC ATHLETE AHMED KELLY

If you followed the Paralympics in London, you may have heard of this rising Australian sports star. Ahmed Kelly was born in 1991 with significant disabilities to all 4 limbs as a result of chemical warfare in Iraq. He was subsequently chosen to represent Australia at the 2012 Paralympic Games in London.

What do you remember about the first 7 years of your life prior coming to Australia? Did you have any exposure to sport during this time?

No, none at all. I didn't have any exposure to sports at all. I loved running around as I had so much energy at the time. One of my favourite memories of Bagdad would be the times when I played with my brother Emmanuel. When I arrived in Australia, I had double below knee amputation surgery. This operation changed my childhood dramatically as it allowed me to use prosthetic legs and with these legs I am able to walk straighter, run, jump and all of them for a good length of time.

IAN MACNICOL/GETTY IMAGES

Was sport always an integral part of your life? Was there any person or persons who were key to your development or growth in sport?

I loved my sport, so you could say that it was an integral part of my life. I was physically active just about every day whether it was training or in my own time. As soon as I finished my school work I would be out practising or trying to get fit. From the early days, my friend Ervis persevered trying to teach me how to kick the footy and I must admit that the height of Spider Burton had me in awe when we first met. Spider was a great footy mentor and one most people including myself would look up to regularly. The footy and swimming coaches definitely played a key role in my sporting development and success.

Extracted from: <http://bluestoneedge.com/bluestone-edge-news-hub/news-and-views-feature-articles/the-influence-of-sport-an-interview-with-australian-paralympic-athlete-ahmed-kelly/>. Accessed on: May 4, 2016.

footy: abreviação para *Australian football* (futebol australiano)
awe: admiração; reconhecimento

3. Underline the correct answers.

a. The text has the format of **a quiz/an interview/a leaflet**.

b. There is **a reporter and a referee/a coach and a sportsperson/an interviewer and an interviewee** talking.

c. The main purpose of the interview is to **obtain information and opinions of the interviewee/sell newspapers/talk about the athlete's problems**.

d. Nowadays interviews **don't have to/have to/shouldn't** be face to face.

4. Read another piece of the interview. Insert the labels.

interviewee's answers   interviewer's questions

MICHAEL WILSON/AFL MEDIA/GETTY IMAGES

What age did you first start playing sport and how much opportunity was there to compete in Australia? Was there much encouragement to participate and or excel?

I was around 11 years old before I was able to have a decent crack at sports. I had a go at several sports such as soccer, basketball, T-Ball and Australian football but I thoroughly enjoyed getting involved in Australian football. I had many wonderful opportunities to compete in sports. My involvement in sport really started when I attended our local school, St. Patrick's Primary in Kilmore. It wasn't anything serious and more focused on having fun. Once I went on to Assumption and Carey it started to get serious so I concentrated on getting better at my specific sports which were footy and swimming.

5. Read the excerpt above again and answer.

a. Are the interviewer's or interviewee's names present in the text?

____

b. How did you differentiate questions and answers?

____

____

c. Did the interviewee answer all the interviewer's questions?

____

____

6. Write the name of the sports Ahmed has already practiced.

____

____

7. Insert the phrases into the correct blanks.

a few sports | in his life | Paralympic swimmer | prosthetic legs | to Australia

Ahmed Kelly is a ______________________ born in Iraq. He lived in Baghdad until he was seven and then was brought ______________________. He wears ______________________ because of chemical warfare injuries. He used to play ______________________ like soccer and basketball. Swimming was one of his favorites. He can walk, run and jump. His coaches played a very significant role ______________________.

8. Correct the wrong pieces of information according to the text.

a. Ahmed participated in the Olympics in Rio.

____

b. He was born in Australia.

____

c. He started practicing sports in Baghdad.

____

d. One of his favourite memories from his first 7 years prior going to Australia is when he played alone.

____

e. He didn't have much energy when he was a kid.

____

f. His friend Ervis taught him how to swim.

____

9. Which adjectives do you think best describe Ahmed Kelly? Choose them and then write a sentence about Ahmed using the adjectives you chose.

a. ☐ brave
b. ☐ hardworking
c. ☐ jealous
d. ☐ persistent
e. ☐ selfish
f. ☐ strong-willed

____

____

10. In your opinion, which characteristics should an athlete have? Do you think Paralympic and Olympic athletes should have the same characteristics or not? Why?

____

____

____

____

11. If you met people who wanted to become Paralympic athletes, what advice would you give them?

____

____

____

____

1. Do you know Daniel Dias? He's a Brazilian Paralympic athlete. Search for more information about him and write a short biographical fact sheet. You can search his official website: <www.danieldias.esp.br/> (accessed on: Jun. 7, 2016), or the International Paralympic Committee website as well: <www.paralympic.org/athletes/biographies> (accessed on: Jun. 7, 2016).

CLIVE ROSE/GETTY IMAGES

____

____

____

____

____

____

Reading the world

1. Do you know what it means to be visually impaired?

a. ☐ Not being able to hear properly.

b. ☐ Not being able to speak.

c. ☐ Having a decreased ability to see in a way that cannot be fixed by usual means.

d. ☐ Not being able to walk.

2. According to an IBGE census, in 2013, there were about 200 million people in Brazil, and 3.6% of them were visually impaired. How many visually impaired people are there in Brazil according to this data?

a. ☐ There are about seven hundred people.

b. ☐ There are about seven million people.

c. ☐ There are about seven thousand people.

d. ☐ There are about seven people.

3. Read the text.

BIS

http://ns.umich.edu/new/releases/22083-technology-changing-for-visually-impaired-people-in-developing-countries

Technology changing lives for visually impaired people in developing countries

BSIP/UIG/GETTY IMAGES

ANN ARBOR – He was planning to be a lawyer because he didn't think visually impaired people like him could do high-tech jobs in India. But after discovering special technology that allows him to use computers, he changed his mind and now wants to be a software engineer. "I became crazy about computers. Now I want to do something with computers only," said the man, one of 176 people surveyed in India, Peru and Jordan about how their lives were changed by technology that enables blind people to use computers and other devices.

The study shows that assistive technology – screen readers and other communication software – can boost the economic and social aspirations of visually impaired people, enabling them to pursue work they once thought was impossible. The technology also makes them less marginalized in low- and middle-income countries, where they are often stuck at home or limited to low-skilled jobs.

Many of the respondents said they didn't know that a blind person could use a computer until early adulthood. Several only found out about assistive technology when they were applying for jobs either directly or through resource centers.

Extracted from: <http://ns.umich.edu/new/releases/22083-technology-changing-lives-for-visually-impaired-people-in-developing-countries>. Accessed on: May 4, 2016.

boost: aumentar

4. Underline the correct word to complete the sentences.

   a. He can be a software engineer using special **technology/prosthetics**.

   b. In countries like India, Peru and Jordan technology **allows/concerns** visually impaired people to use different devices.

   c. In many countries, the visually impaired have **low-skilled/high-skilled** jobs.

   d. Ann Arbor is the author of the **article/study**.

5. Do you know what **assistive technology** is? Take a look at the pictures. What object doesn't seem to belong to the group?

a.

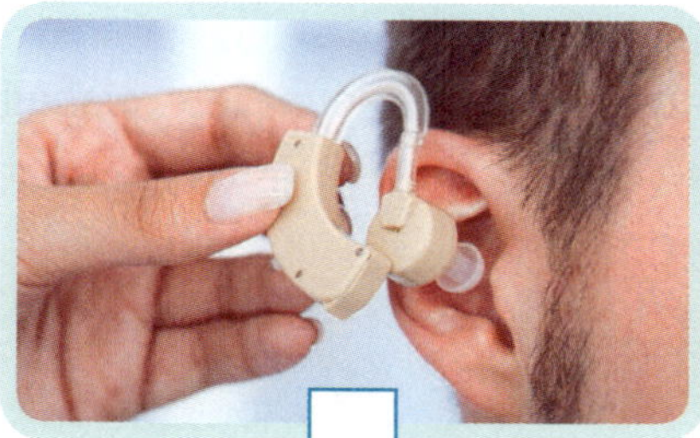

ANDREY_POPOV/SHUTTERSTOCK

c.

AH86/SHUTTERSTOCK

b.

THINKSTOCK/GETTY IMAGES

d.

ZLIKOVEC/SHUTTERSTOCK

6. The pictures that you didn't check show examples of assistive technology. Now, describe what it is.

___

___

1. Have you ever heard of people who read or record books for the blind?

___

___

___

2. Would you like to be a volunteer in one of these projects? Why?

___

___

___

UNIT

8 Families

Review the journey

1. Have you ever heard of foster families? Insert words from the box to complete the explanation.

The word ________ means to help someone (or something) ________ and develop. It also means to take ________ of someone's ________. Foster parents are people – other than a kid's parents who give a kid a ________ place to live and grow. Foster parents take kids into their homes and take care of them for as long as the kids need. Together, they become a foster family.

care
foster
grow
needs
safe

Adapted from: <http://kidshealth.org/en/kids/foster-families.html#>. Accessed on: May 5, 2016.

2. Now read the text and underline the verbs in the present perfect tense.

www.fosterforward.net/about--success-stories--how-foster-care-defined-a-family

How Foster Care Defined a Family

A TESTIMONIAL FROM MAYA COLANTUONO

Our biological children have grown into more compassionate, understanding and open-minded young people as a result of being foster siblings. Last year we attended an open house at our 11 year old daughter Sophie's school and her teacher directed us to a questionnaire hanging on the wall. One of the questions asked "What is the best thing your parents ever did for you?" Sophie's answer was "The best thing my parents ever did for me was to become a foster family".

DAVID SACKS/GETTY IMAGES

siblings: irmãs ou irmãos

The classmate next to Sophie answered the same question with "My parents took me to Disney World". Sophie has never been to Disney World but I don't think she feels she is missing anything!

[...]

Foster care has defined us in a way we were never defined before. We were The Colantuonos, a generally happy family with all of the regular triumphs and tribulations of a middle class suburban family. We did not, however, stand all together for anything that really mattered until we discovered foster care. Foster care has defined us in a way that religion, sports and community involvement did not. It has made our home and our family into something that matters outside of ourselves. It has taken us beyond just the daily meeting of our own needs and put everything into perspective. It isn't easy, but it's worth doing. I hope you will consider it. I hope you will jump right in and get too attached. Believe me, you will regret not having done it years ago!

Extracted from: <www.fosterforward.net/about--success-stories--how-foster-care-defined-a-family>. Accessed on: May 5, 2016.

3. The sentences in the present perfect describe actions that

a. ☐ happened at unspecified times in the past and have consequences in the present.

b. ☐ happened at specific times in the past and the reader knows when they happened.

c. ☐ are happening now, at the moment of the speech.

4. Check the sentences that are in the simple past.

a. ☐ Last year we were attending an open house at our 11 year old daughter Sophie's school.

b. ☐ The classmate next to Sophie answered the same question.

c. ☐ It isn't easy, but it's worth doing.

d. ☐ Foster care has defined us.

5. In sentence **a** above, if we remove the adverb of time **last year**, the sentence can be rewritten in the present perfect. Rewrite it:

____

____

6. Write **T** (true), **F** (false) or **NM** (not mentioned).

a. ☐ Maya has her own birth children.

b. ☐ Sophie doesn't approve being part of a foster family.

c. ☐ Sophie has been to New York City.

d. ☐ Sophie is the oldest child.

e. ☐ The Colantuonos love being foster parents.

f. ☐ Sophie's parents took her to Disney World.

Another look

1. How do you think you would feel if you had foster siblings? If you already do, what is that like for you?

____

____

2. Read the title of the text below. Whose point of view do you think will be presented?

____

3. Read the text. Then write **T** (true) or **F** (false).

www.fosteringperspectives.org/fp_v11n1/birthkid.htm

VIEWS OF FOSTER CARE AND ADOPTION IN NORTH CAROLINA

fostering perspectives

WWW.FOSTERINGPERSPECTIVES.ORG

Sponsored by the NC Division of Social Services and the Family and Children's Resource Program

Vol. 11, No. 1 • November 2006

What's It Like to be a Birth Child in a Foster Home?

1 The writing contest in the last issue of *Fostering Perspectives* was a departure in some ways. Instead of asking for responses from children and youth who are or have been in foster care, as we usually do, this time we put the focus on a group of kids that is unquestionably affected by the child welfare system but often overlooked — the birth children of foster parents. For this contest, we asked them to tell us what it was like to be a birth child in a foster home and what they had learned from this experience.

2 Their answers, which you'll find on these pages, are diverse and eye-opening, reassuring and surprising. The lessons these children say they have learned include:

- How to handle stress
- People don't always love you back (sometimes they don't know how yet)
- It's important to listen to everyone
- Kids need a home and a parent to love

3 I hope that as you read the words of these children you will think about your own experience and what you have learned from your own work in foster care.

— John McMahon, Editor

child welfare system: sistema de proteção e bem-estar da criança dos EUA

Eli, age 10

JGI/JAMIE GRILL/GETTY IMAGES

4 I live with my grandmother. Last year she asked me if I would like to help her keep foster kids in our home. I said I'd love to! We both enjoy having kids around.

5 The first kids to come stay with us were twins, a boy and a girl... When they went to live with another family I was sad and missed them.

6 Now we have a boy my age living with us. This has been harder for me. Sometimes we fight and sometimes we are friends. He's even in my class at school, so sometimes I get tired of seeing him so much. I'm glad he lives with us, even if we do fight. I don't always like sharing my room and toys, but I like having a brother.

7 My granny has thought up ways to help us get along better. She lets us both have quiet time when we need it. And we each get at least one day a week to spend with her by ourselves doing whatever we want to do. The hardest thing for me was learning to share my granny. This has helped a lot.

8 I hope we get lots of other kids to live with us. It is fun learning about them and making new friends.

Extracted from: <www.fosteringperspectives.org/fp_v11n1/birthkid.htm>. Accessed on: May 5, 2016.

a. ☐ *Fostering Perspectives* is most probably a periodical.

b. ☐ They have a writing contest for children and teens.

c. ☐ The publication doesn't think children and teens have something interesting to say about fostering.

d. ☐ This publication has an editor.

e. ☐ The text has the format of a letter.

f. ☐ This is an article and Eli's text is a testimonial.

g. ☐ The text is in topics.

h. ☐ There is the date the issue was published.

4. Which words best complete the paragraph? Underline them.

HIYA IMAGES/FANCY RF/GETTY IMAGES

Testimonial/Design pages serve as a platform to show how other people have **benefited/learned** from a product or service (or from an experience). Companies often include testimonial pages to **buy/advertise** their products.

5. Finish the sentences.

a. Birth children who have a foster home can learn how ________________________.

b. Eli is a ten-year-old kid who lives with ________________________.

c. The first children to come stay with Eli and his grandma ________________________.

d. Eli doesn't always like sharing ________________________.

e. He believes it is fun making ________________________.

6. Does the editor think the children's answers are predictable? Copy from the text the sentence that proves your answer.

7. Why has it been harder for Eli to have a boy his age living with him?

8. What did Eli's grandmother do to help him and the foster kid get along?

9. In which paragraph do we know

a. ☐ what the contest is about?

b. ☐ what the answers were like?

c. ☐ what happened when the twins moved out?

d. ☐ who is living with Eli and his grandmother now?

e. ☐ how many kids Eli would like to live with?

10. Check an answer to each question. Explain your reasons.

	YES	NO	WHY
a. Would you like your family to become a foster family?			______ ______ ______
b. Do you think that foster families should get some financial help from the government?			______ ______ ______
c. Do foster children usually feel comfortable with strangers?			______ ______ ______

1. Even if your family is not a foster family, is there any way to help orphanages or other institutions that take care of children whose family is not able to assume them?

____

____

____

2. Why do you think *Fostering Perspectives* wanted to hear and publish the biological children in foster families' point of view on the subject? Is it important to publish testimonials such as Eli's? Why?

____

____

____

Reading the world

1. Can a foreigner adopt a Brazilian child? Read the text and check your answer.

____

BIS

https://adopt.com/brazil

ADOPTION CONNECT TECHNOLOGIES INC./WWW.ADOPT.COM

Adopt

Family: What Every Child Deserves.

BRAZIL

Brazil is party to the Hague Convention on Protection of Children and Co-operation in Respect of Intercountry Adoption (Hague Adoption Convention). Therefore, all adoptions between Brazil and the United States must meet the requirements of the Convention and U.S. law implementing the Convention.

Brazilian law does not allow for a Brazilian child to travel to the United States to be adopted. Therefore, prospective adoptive parents must obtain a full and final adoption under Brazilian law before the child can immigrate to the United States. [...]

Who can adopt?

Adoption between the United States and Brazil is governed by the Hague Adoption Convention. Therefore to adopt from Brazil, you must first be found eligible to adopt by the U.S. Government. The U.S. Government agency responsible for making this determination is the Department of Homeland Security, U.S. Citizenship and Immigration Services (USCIS).

Adoption in Brazil can be a complicated process, sometimes involving long waits. Brazilian adoption law gives preference to Brazilian citizens and citizens of countries that have implemented the Hague Adoption Convention. Please be aware that without Brazilian citizenship, it is unlikely that a U.S. citizen will be able to adopt a healthy, single child under the age of 5 years. The following types of children are most commonly available to U.S. citizens without Brazilian citizenship:

- Single, healthy children, age 5+
- Sibling groups of any number and of all ages
- Special needs children of all ages

[...]

therefore: assim, consequentemente
eligible: qualificado; elegível

Extracted from: <https://adopt.com/brazil>. Accessed on: May 6, 2016.

2. In "…all adoptions between Brazil and the United States must meet the requirements of the Convention and U.S. law implementing the Convention", which convention is that?

____

____

____

3. Are prospective adoptive parents considered foster adoptive parents or potential adoptive parents?

____

4. Choose the statement that is **not true** according to the information given.

a. ☐ The USCIS is responsible for determining whether Americans can adopt a Brazilian child or not.

b. ☐ Adopting a kid in Brazil is easy.

c. ☐ The American person who wants to adopt a single child under the age of five should have Brazilian citizenship.

d. ☐ If you are American and want to adopt a brother and a sister in Brazil, you don't necessarily have to have Brazilian citizenship.

5. Do you believe that it should be easier for a foreigner to adopt a Brazilian child? Justify your answer.

____

____

6. Read the text below about the Hague Adoption Convention and answer: Why do you think this convention was created?

> The Hague Convention on the Protection of Children and Co-operation in Respect of Inter-Country Adoption (Hague Adoption Convention) is an international agreement to safeguard intercountry adoptions. Concluded on May 29, 1993 in The Hague, the Netherlands, the Convention establishes international standards of practices for intercountry adoptions.

Extracted from: <https://adopt.com/international/hague>. Accessed on: Jun. 23, 2016.

____

____

____

____

____

Connecting ideas

UNIT 1

- **http://exame.abril.com.br/carreira/noticias/10-curiosidades-surpreendentes-sobre-a-lingua-inglesa**
  10 curiosidades surpreendentes sobre a língua inglesa
- **www.youtube.com/watch?v=CjXn3lW5wQ4**
  English vs Globish
- **www.biography.com/people/william-shakespeare-9480323#mysterious-origins**
  William Shakespeare's biography

UNIT 2

- **www.history.com/topics/niagara-falls**
  Niagara Falls
- **www.brightontoymuseum.co.uk/**
  Brighton Toy and Model Museum
- **http://besttripchoices.com/travel-personalities/quiz/**
  Take the Travel Personality Quiz!
- **www.buzzfeed.com/jadayounghatchett/what-type-of-traveler-are-you?utm_term=.ttbg6RNkn#.on7LbeOPW**
  What's Your Travel Personality?

UNIT 3

- **http://webecoist.momtastic.com/2009/04/10/9-of-the-worlds-most-amazing-wind-farms/**
  9 of the World's Most Amazing Wind Farms
- **www.dummies.com/how-to/content/ten-ways-to-live-sustainably.html**
  Ten Ways to Live Sustainably
- **www.criticalcactus.com/beautiful-recycled-homes/**
  12 Awesome Homes Built With Recycled Material
- **www.garbagewarrior.com/press**
  Garbage Warrior movie website

UNIT 4

- **www.letsmove.gov/**
  Let's Move! campaign official website
- **www.youtube.com/watch?v=2oBeuSCfGeg**
  Michelle Obama introduces *Let's Move!*
- **www.theguardian.com/childrens-books-site/2015/nov/08/mortal-instruments-cassandra-clare-review**
  A review of *The Mortal Instruments* series by Cassandra Clare
- **www.bbc.co.uk/history/historic_figures/austen_jane.shtml**
  Jane Austen's biography
- **www.youtube.com/watch?v=LIYiThAyY8s**
  An online class about Jane Austen and her work

UNIT 5

- **www.youtube.com/watch?v=7KQWs5az2V4**
  Destiny, a short animation movie by Salvador Dalí and Walt Disney
- **www.youtube.com/watch?v=jc1Nfx4c5LQ**
  A recreation of Pablo Picasso's *Guernica* in 3D
- **www.youtube.com/watch?v=oBfMOmR4S9M**
  Monuments Men movie trailer

UNIT 6

- **www.youtube.com/watch?v=1dYv5u6v55Y**
  Pride and Prejudice movie trailer
- **www.youtube.com/watch?v=OU8Uig-1NEo**
  Around The World In 80 Days
- **www.japanesegallery.co.uk/default.php?Sel=manga&Submenu=4**
  History of Japanese Manga Comics

UNIT 7

- **www.youtube.com/watch?v=f9Vp5LM_lEs**
  Trailer do filme *Pauê – O passo de um vencedor*
- **www.paralympic.org/athletes/biographies**
  Biography of Paralympic athletes
- **www.youtube.com/watch?v=gtx47hO0lLs**
  Interview with Brazilian Paralympic athlete Daniel Dias
- **www.youtube.com/watch?v=oEQy__GGprk**
  Youtuber Julia Tolezano talks to Brazilian Paralympic athlete Daniel Dias

UNIT 8

- **www.hcch.net/en/instruments/conventions/full-text/?cid=69**
  Hague Adoption Convention full text
- **www.childwelfare.gov/topics/adoption/nam/spread-the-word/video/**
  An adoption story

Organizadora:

Editora Saraiva

Obra coletiva organizada e produzida pela Editora Saraiva

Editor responsável:

Vicente Martínez

Licenciado em Tradução/Interpretação pela
Universidad Pontificia de Comillas (Madrid)
Editor de conteúdos didáticos

Coordenadora:

Gisele Aga

Licenciada em Letras pela FMU - Faculdades Metropolitanas Unidas
Professora de Inglês na rede particular de ensino e em cursos de idiomas
Coordenadora pedagógica em cursos de idiomas
Editora de conteúdos didáticos

TIME TO SHARE

Jornadas 8

Editora Saraiva

DESENVOLVIMENTO DOS CONTEÚDOS:

Adriana Beatriz Saporito
Licenciada em Letras e graduada em Tradução/Interpretação (Inglês-Português) pela Faculdade Ibero-Americana de Letras e Ciências Humanas.
Professora de Português e de Inglês da rede particular de ensino.
Editora de conteúdos didáticos.
Autora de Inglês para os anos iniciais do Ensino Fundamental.

Ana Lúcia Militello
Licenciada em Letras pela Faculdade Ibero-Americana de Letras e Ciências Humanas com habilitação em Tradução/Interpretação.
Editora de conteúdos didáticos.

Carla Maurício Coelho da Silva Vianna
Licenciada em Letras pela UFRJ.
Professora de Inglês da rede particular de ensino.
Editora de conteúdos didáticos.
Autora de Inglês para os anos finais do Ensino Fundamental.

Daniella Bergamo
Graduada em Tradução/Interpretação e licenciada em Inglês e Português pela Faculdade Ibero-Americana de Letras e Ciências Humanas.
Pós-graduada em Educação — Currículo e Prática Educativa — pela PUC-RJ.
Professora de Inglês da rede particular de ensino e em cursos de idiomas.

Gisele Aga
Licenciada em Letras pela
FMU — Faculdades Metropolitanas Unidas.
Professora de Inglês da rede particular de ensino e em cursos de idioma.
Coordenadora pedagógica em cursos de idiomas.
Editora de conteúdos didáticos.

Lisiane Ott Schulz
Doutoranda em Letras pela Universidade de Caxias do Sul (UCS) em associação com a UniRitter.
Mestre em Educação pela Universidade de Caxias do Sul (UCS).
Bacharel em Letras — Tradução/Interpretação (Português-Inglês) — e licenciada em Letras — Inglês e Literatura — pela UFRGS.
Professora do curso de Letras — Português e Literatura Brasileira — pela UCS.
Professora de Inglês das redes pública e particular de ensino e em cursos de idiomas.

Luciana Santos Pinheiro
Especialista em Estudos Avançados da Língua Inglesa pela PUC-RS.
Mestre em Letras pela Universidade de Caxias do Sul (UCS).
Doutora em Linguística Aplicada pela UFRGS.
Autora e editora de conteúdos didáticos.
Professora universitária e da rede particular de ensino.

Time to Share – 8º ano (Ensino Fundamental)

Dados Internacionais de Catalogação na Publicação (CIP)
(Câmara Brasileira do Livro, SP, Brasil)

Jornadas Time to Share, 8º ano / organizadora Editora Saraiva; obra coletiva organizada e produzida pela Editora Saraiva; editor responsável Vicente Martínez; coordenadora Gisele Aga. – 1. ed. – São Paulo : Saraiva, 2016.

Suplementado pelo manual do professor.
Bibliografia.
ISBN 978-85-472-0840-0 (aluno)
ISBN 978-85-472-0841-7 (professor)

1. Inglês (Ensino fundamental) I. Martínez, Vicente. II. Aga, Gisele.

16-04732 CDD-372.652

Índice para catálogo sistemático :
1. Inglês : Ensino fundamental 372.652

Gerente editorial M. Esther Nejm
Editor responsável Vicente Martínez
Editores Alice Silvestre, Caroline Zanelli, Myrian Yamamoto, Renata Chimim, Renato Malkov, Vinicius Oliveira, Vivian Viccino
Coordenador de revisão Camila Christi Gazzani
Revisores Diego Carbone, Larissa Vazquez, Patrícia Cordeiro
Produtor editorial Roseli Said
Revisor linguístico Robert Caudle Garner
Coordenador de iconografia Cristina Akisino
Pesquisa iconográfica Fernando Cambetas, Beatriz Micsik, Juliana Prado, Mariana Valeiro
Licenciamento de textos Ricardo Corridoni, Erica F. Brambila
Gerente de artes Ricardo Borges
Coordenador de artes Narjara Lara
Design Casa Paulistana de Comunicação
Capa Sergio Candido com imagens de EQRoy / Shutterstock.com
Diagramação C2 Artes
Assistente Camilla Felix Cianelli
Ilustrações Leo Teixeira, Vicente Mendonça, Zubartez
Tratamento de imagens Emerson de Lima
Produtor gráfico Thais Mendes Petruci Galvão
078.452.001.001 **Impressão e acabamento** Intergraf Ind. Gráfica Eireli
Edição 1
Impressão 2

Editora Saraiva
SAC 0800-0117875
De 2ª a 6ª, das 8h às 18h
www.editorasaraiva.com.br/contato
Avenida das Nações Unidas, 7221 – 1º andar – Setor C – Pinheiros – CEP 05425-902

INTRODUCTION

In The Company Of Words

It is truly marvellous, wonderful and comforting

To know that I have eyes to read

Hands that can write

And an enormous love for words

I am lucky to be speaking a few extremely beautiful languages

For I love words [...]

Gcina Mhlophe

Extracted from: <www.gcinamhlophe.co.za/gcinamasiko-arts-and-heritage-trust/poetry.html>. Accessed on: Jun. 8, 2016.

Aprender a ler e escrever é dominar um código antes indecifrável. E decifrar o código é acessar um novo mundo de possibilidades e conhecimento. Acessar o passado, compreender o presente e pensar no futuro. Aprender outro idioma é expandir ainda mais nosso alcance de mundo, entrando em contato com novas culturas e saberes. Nesta coleção, você encontrará textos e áudios autênticos, expressões artísticas com diferentes linguagens (música, tirinhas, fotografia, pintura, grafite etc.). Você terá a possibilidade de refletir sobre temas polêmicos e atuais, de pensar sobre sua escola, sua comunidade e sobre seu próprio aprendizado, além de, é claro, atividades linguísticas. Esteja aberto ao conteúdo apresentado, veja, reveja, leia quantas vezes for necessário, pergunte aos amigos e professores quando tiver dúvidas, ouça as interpretações que cada um tem, use livros, revistas, a internet, compartilhe suas impressões, seja ativo no processo de aprendizagem à sua maneira. Descubra um novo mundo!

SHUTTERSTOCK

GET TO KNOW YOUR BOOK

The units are organized by sections. Get to know a little bit more about them.

OPENING PAGES

This section presents several artistic manifestations and questions to activate your previous knowledge about the theme you are going to explore throughout the unit.

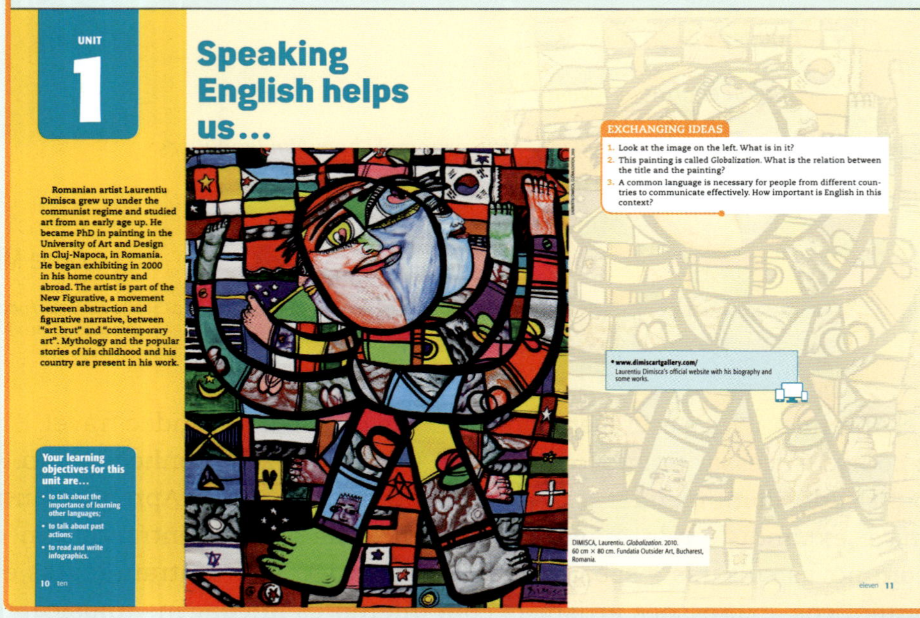

UNIT 1

Speaking English helps us...

Romanian artist Laurentiu Dimisca grew up under the communist regime and studied art from an early age up. He became PhD in painting in the University of Art and Design in Cluj-Napoca, in Romania. He began exhibiting in 2000 in his home country and abroad. The artist is part of the New Figurative, a movement between abstraction and figurative narrative, between "art brut" and "contemporary art". Mythology and the popular stories of his childhood and his country are present in his work.

Your learning objectives for this unit are...

- to talk about the importance of learning other languages;
- to talk about past actions;
- to read and write infographics.

EXCHANGING IDEAS

1. Look at the image on the left. What is in it?
2. This painting is called *Globalization*. What is the relation between the title and the painting?
3. A common language is necessary for people from different countries to communicate effectively. How important is English in this context?

• www.dimiscartgallery.com/ Laurentiu Dimisca's official website with his biography and some works.

DIMISCA, Laurentio. *Globalization*. 2010. 60 cm × 80 cm. Fundatia Outsider Art, Bucharest, Romania.

10 ten

eleven 11

READING COMPREHENSION

It brings authentic texts about relevant topics, in a variety of genres. The texts will help you get prepared for the real use of the language.

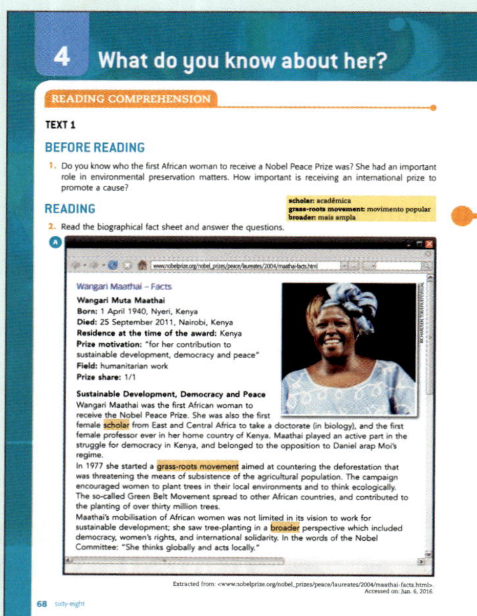

4 What do you know about her?

READING COMPREHENSION

TEXT 1

BEFORE READING

1. Do you know who the first African woman to receive a Nobel Peace Prize was? She had an important role in environmental preservation matters. How important is receiving an international prize to promote a cause?

READING

scholar: acadêmica
grass-roots movement: movimento popular
broader: mais ampla

2. Read the biographical fact sheet and answer the questions.

A

Wangari Maathai – Facts

Wangari Muta Maathai
Born: 1 April 1940, Nyeri, Kenya
Died: 25 September 2011, Nairobi, Kenya
Residence at the time of the award: Kenya
Prize motivation: "for her contribution to sustainable development, democracy and peace"
Field: humanitarian work
Prize share: 1/1

Sustainable Development, Democracy and Peace
Wangari Maathai was the first African woman to receive the Nobel Peace Prize. She was also the first female scholar from East and Central Africa to take a doctorate (in biology), and the first female professor ever in her home country of Kenya. Maathai played an active part in the struggle for democracy in Kenya, and belonged to the opposition to Daniel arap Moi's regime.
In 1977 she started a grass-roots movement aimed at countering the deforestation that was threatening the means of subsistence of the agricultural population. The campaign encouraged women to plant trees in their local environments and to think ecologically. The so-called Green Belt Movement spread to other African countries, and contributed to the planting of over thirty million trees.
Maathai's mobilisation of African women was not limited in its vision to work for sustainable development; she saw tree-planting in a broader perspective which included democracy, women's rights, and international solidarity. In the words of the Nobel Committee: "She thinks globally and acts locally."

Extracted from: <www.nobelprize.org/nobel_prizes/peace/laureates/2004/maathai-facts.html>. Accessed on: Jan. 6, 2016.

68 sixty-eight

FOCUS ON VOCABULARY

Vocabulary practice is contextualized, so it will be easier for you to understand it. You will also have the opportunity to expand the vocabulary related to the topic of the unit.

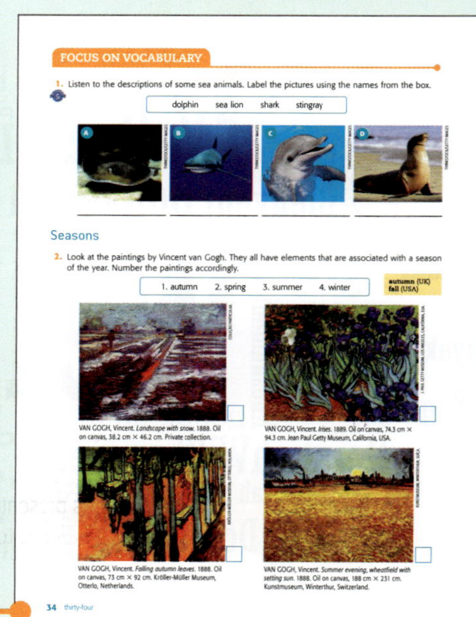

FOCUS ON VOCABULARY

1. Listen to the descriptions of some sea animals. Label the pictures using the names from the box.

dolphin sea lion shark stingray

Seasons

2. Look at the paintings by Vincent van Gogh. They all have elements that are associated with a season of the year. Number the paintings accordingly.

1. autumn 2. spring 3. summer 4. winter

autumn (UK) **fall** (USA)

VAN GOGH, Vincent. *Landscape with snow*. 1888. Oil on canvas, 38.2 cm × 46.2 cm. Private collection.

VAN GOGH, Vincent. *Irises*. 1889. Oil on canvas, 74.3 cm × 94.3 cm. Jean Paul Getty Museum, California, USA.

VAN GOGH, Vincent. *Falling autumn leaves*. 1888. Oil on canvas, 73 cm × 92 cm. Kröller-Müller Museum, Otterlo, Netherlands.

VAN GOGH, Vincent. *Summer evening, wheatfield with setting sun*. 1888. Oil on canvas, 188 cm × 231 cm. Kunstmuseum, Winterthur, Switzerland.

34 thirty-four

LANGUAGE IN USE

This section will help you reflect about language in context and practice it with different kinds of activities.

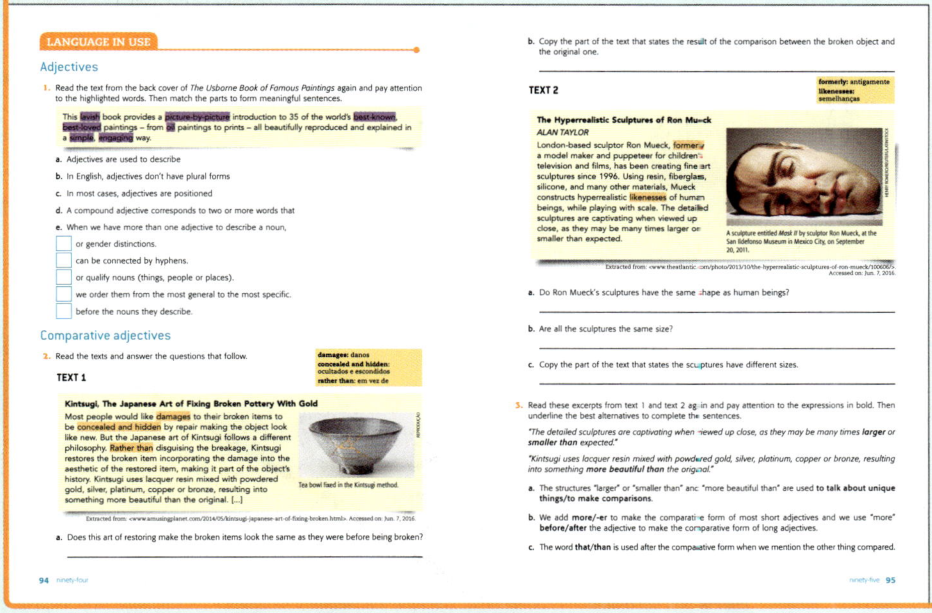

LANGUAGE IN USE

Adjectives

1. Read the text from the back cover of *The Usborne Book of Famous Paintings* again and pay attention to the highlighted words. Then match the parts to form meaningful sentences.

> This lavish book provides a picture-by-picture introduction to 35 of the world's best-known, best-loved paintings – from oil paintings to prints – all beautifully reproduced and explained in a simple, engaging way.

a. Adjectives are used to describe
b. In English, adjectives don't have plural forms
c. In most cases, adjectives are positioned
d. A compound adjective corresponds to two or more words that
e. When we have more than one adjective to describe a noun,

☐ or gender distinctions.
☐ can be connected by hyphens.
☐ or qualify nouns (things, people or places).
☐ we order them from the most general to the most specific.
☐ before the nouns they describe.

Comparative adjectives

2. Read the texts and answer the questions that follow.

damages: danos
concealed and hidden: ocultados e escondidos
rather than: em vez de

TEXT 1

Kintsugi, The Japanese Art of Fixing Broken Pottery With Gold

Most people would like damages to their broken items to be concealed and hidden by repair making the object look like new. But the Japanese art of Kintsugi follows a different philosophy. Rather than disguising the breakage, Kintsugi restores the broken item incorporating the damage into the aesthetic of the restored item, making it part of the object's history. Kintsugi uses lacquer resin mixed with powdered gold, silver, platinum, copper or bronze, resulting into something more beautiful than the original. [...]

Tea bowl fixed in the Kintsugi method.

Extracted from: <www.amusingplanet.com/2014/05/kintsugi-japanese-art-of-fixing-broken.html>. Accessed on: Jun. 7, 2016.

a. Does this art of restoring make the broken items look the same as they were before being broken?

______

94 ninety-four

b. Copy the part of the text that states the result of the comparison between the broken object and the original one.

______

formerly: antigamente
likenesses: semelhanças

TEXT 2

The Hyperrealistic Sculptures of Ron Mueck
ALAN TAYLOR

London-based sculptor Ron Mueck, formerly a model maker and puppeteer for children's television and films, has been creating fine art sculptures since 1996. Using resin, fiberglass, silicone, and many other materials, Mueck constructs hyperrealistic likenesses of human beings, while playing with scale. The detailed sculptures are captivating when viewed up close, as they may be many times larger or smaller than expected.

A sculpture entitled *Mask II* by sculptor Ron Mueck, at the San Ildefonso Museum in Mexico City, on September 20, 2011.

Extracted from: <www.theatlantic.com/photo/2013/10/the-hyperrealistic-sculptures-of-ron-mueck/100606/>. Accessed on: Jun. 7, 2016.

a. Do Ron Mueck's sculptures have the same shape as human beings?

______

b. Are all the sculptures the same size?

______

c. Copy the part of the text that states the sculptures have different sizes.

______

3. Read these excerpts from text 1 and text 2 again and pay attention to the expressions in bold. Then underline the best alternatives to complete the sentences.

"The detailed sculptures are captivating when viewed up close, as they may be many times ***larger*** *or* ***smaller than*** *expected."*

"Kintsugi uses lacquer resin mixed with powdered gold, silver, platinum, copper or bronze, resulting into something ***more beautiful than*** *the original."*

a. The structures "larger" or "smaller than" and "more beautiful than" are used **to talk about unique things/to make comparisons**.
b. We add **more/-er** to make the comparative form of most short adjectives and we use "more" **before/after** the adjective to make the comparative form of long adjectives.
c. The word **that/than** is used after the comparative form when we mention the other thing compared.

ninety-five 95

LISTENING COMPREHENSION

Presenting different kinds of oral texts with a diversity of language variation, this section aims at helping you fully understand the messages of the texts.

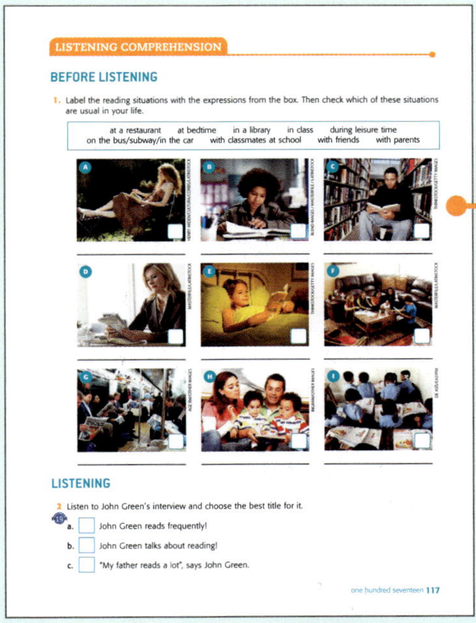

LISTENING COMPREHENSION

BEFORE LISTENING

1. Label the reading situations with the expressions from the box. Then check which of these situations are usual in your life.

at a restaurant	at bedtime	in a library	in class	during leisure time	on the bus/subway/in the car	with classmates at school	with friends	with parents

A ☐ ______ B ☐ ______ C ☐ ______
D ☐ ______ E ☐ ______ F ☐ ______
G ☐ ______ H ☐ ______ I ☐ ______

LISTENING

2. Listen to John Green's interview and choose the best title for it.

a. ☐ John Green reads frequently!
b. ☐ John Green talks about reading!
c. ☐ "My father reads a lot", says John Green.

one hundred seventeen 117

SPEAKING

Suggestions of contextualized situations for the use of theme-based, communicative and linguistic aspects presented in each unit. The objective of this section is to provide you with an opportunity to use what you learned in other contexts and/or communicative situations.

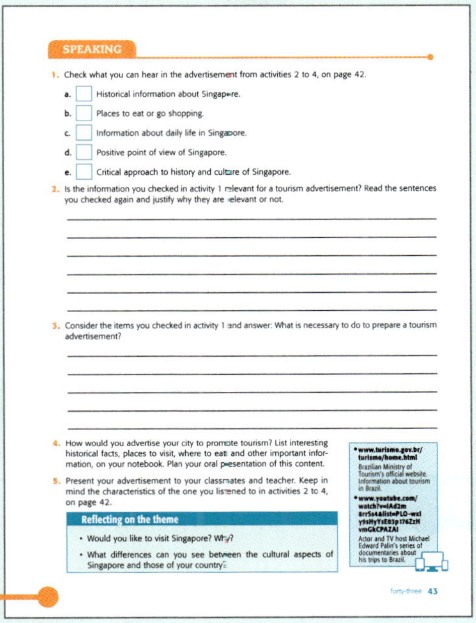

SPEAKING

1. Check what you can hear in the advertisement from activities 2 to 4, on page 42.

a. ☐ Historical information about Singapore.
b. ☐ Places to eat or go shopping.
c. ☐ Information about daily life in Singapore.
d. ☐ Positive point of view of Singapore.
e. ☐ Critical approach to history and culture of Singapore.

2. Is the information you checked in activity 1 relevant for a tourism advertisement? Read the sentences you checked again and justify why they are relevant or not.

______

3. Consider the items you checked in activity 1 and answer: What is necessary to do to prepare a tourism advertisement?

______

4. How would you advertise your city to promote tourism? List interesting historical facts, places to visit, where to eat and other important information, on your notebook. Plan your oral presentation of this content.

5. Present your advertisement to your classmates and teacher. Keep in mind the characteristics of the one you listened to in activities 2 to 4, on page 42.

Reflecting on the theme

- Would you like to visit Singapore? Why?
- What differences can you see between the cultural aspects of Singapore and those of your country?

- **www.turismo.gov.br/turismo/home.html**
Brazilian Ministry of Tourism's official website. Information about tourism in Brazil.
- **www.youtube.com/watch?v=lAd2m8rrSs4&list=PLO-wxly9sHyYsE03p176ZzHvmGkCPAZAI**
Actor and TV host Michael Edward Palin's series of documentaries about his trips to Brazil.

forty-three 43

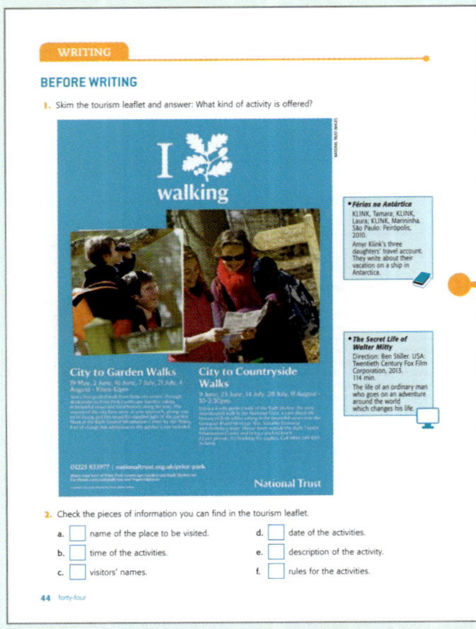

WRITING

BEFORE WRITING

1. Skim the tourism leaflet and answer: What kind of activity is offered?

• *Férias na Antártica*
KLINK, Tamara; KLINK, Laura; KLINK, Marininha. São Paulo: Peirópolis, 2010.
Amyr Klink's three daughters' travel account. They write about their vacation on a ship in Antarctica.

• *The Secret Life of Walter Mitty*
Direction: Ben Stiller. USA: Twentieth Century Fox Film Corporation, 2013. 114 min.
The life of an ordinary man who goes on an adventure around the world which changes his life.

2. Check the pieces of information you can find in the tourism leaflet.

a. ☐ name of the place to be visited.
b. ☐ time of the activities.
c. ☐ visitors' names.
d. ☐ date of the activities.
e. ☐ description of the activity.
f. ☐ rules for the activities.

44 forty-four

WRITING

This section proposes a writing task based on the theme and genre study of the unit as a closing activity. The task is divided in planning, production, evaluation and review of the work.

SELF-EVALUATION

This last section gives you the opportunity to evaluate your learning by checking your progress and difficulties with the objectives listed in the beginning of the unit.

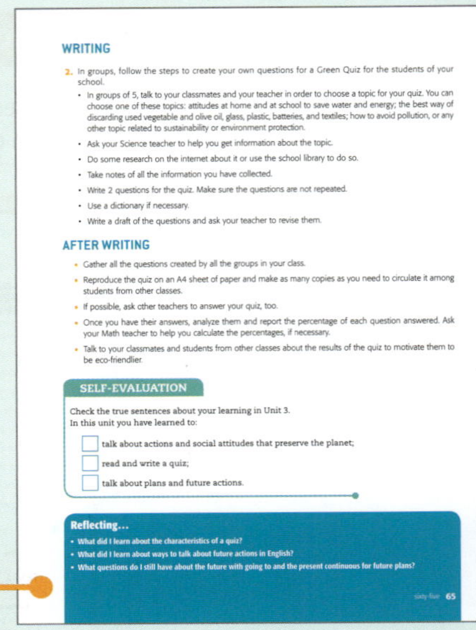

WRITING

2. In groups, follow the steps to create your own questions for a Green Quiz for the students of your school.

- In groups of 5, talk to your classmates and your teacher in order to choose a topic for your quiz. You can choose one of these topics: attitudes at home and at school to save water and energy; the best way of discarding used vegetable and olive oil, glass, plastic, batteries, and textiles; how to avoid pollution, or any other topic related to sustainability or environment protection.
- Ask your Science teacher to help you get information about the topic.
- Do some research on the internet about it or use the school library to do so.
- Take notes of all the information you have collected.
- Write 2 questions for the quiz. Make sure the questions are not repeated.
- Use a dictionary if necessary.
- Write a draft of the questions and ask your teacher to revise them.

AFTER WRITING

- Gather all the questions created by all the groups in your class.
- Reproduce the quiz on an A4 sheet of paper and make as many copies as you need to circulate it among students from other classes.
- If possible, ask other teachers to answer your quiz, too.
- Once you have their answers, analyze them and report the percentage of each question answered. Ask your Math teacher to help you calculate the percentages, if necessary.
- Talk to your classmates and students from other classes about the results of the quiz to motivate them to be eco-friendlier.

SELF-EVALUATION

Check the true sentences about your learning in Unit 3.
In this unit you have learned to:

☐ talk about actions and social attitudes that preserve the planet;
☐ read and write a quiz;
☐ talk about plans and future actions.

Reflecting...
- What did I learn about the characteristics of a quiz?
- What did I learn about ways to talk about future actions in English?
- What questions do I still have about the future with going to and the present continuous for future plans?

sixty-five 65

CONNECTIONS

This section presents texts, images and activities related to contents that you have learned in other subjects.

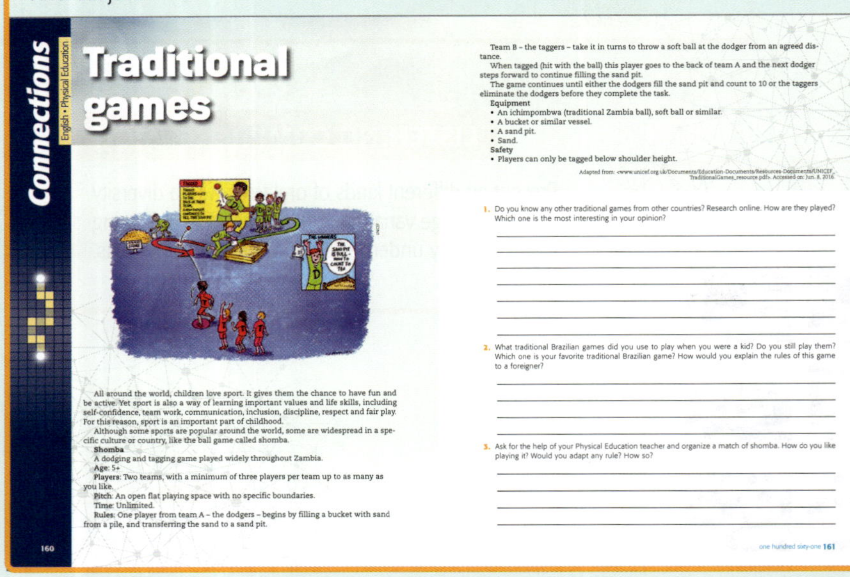

Connections — English • Physical Education

Traditional games

All around the world, children love sport. It gives them the chance to have fun and be active. Yet sport is also a way of learning important values and life skills, including self-confidence, team work, communication, inclusion, discipline, respect and fair play. For this reason, sport is an important part of childhood.

Although some sports are popular around the world, some are widespread in a specific culture or country, like the ball game called shomba.

Shomba
A dodging and tagging game played widely throughout Zambia.
Age: 5+
Players: Two teams, with a minimum of three players per team up to as many as you like.
Pitch: An open flat playing space with no specific boundaries.
Time: Unlimited.
Rules: One player from team A – the dodgers – begins by filling a bucket with sand from a pile, and transferring the sand to a sand pit.

Team B – the taggers – take it in turns to throw a soft ball at the dodger from an agreed distance.
When tagged (hit with the ball) this player goes to the back of team A and the next dodger steps forward to continue filling the sand pit.
The game continues until either the dodgers fill the sand pit and count to 10 or the taggers eliminate the dodgers before they complete the task.
Equipment
• An ichimpombwa (traditional Zambia ball), soft ball or similar.
• A bucket or similar vessel.
• A sand pit.
• Sand.
Safety
• Players can only be tagged below shoulder height.

1. Do you know any other traditional games from other countries? Research online. How are they played? Which one is the most interesting in your opinion?

2. What traditional Brazilian games did you use to play when you were a kid? Do you still play them? Which one is your favorite traditional Brazilian game? How would you explain the rules of this game to a foreigner?

3. Ask for the help of your Physical Education teacher and organize a match of shomba. How do you like playing it? Would you adapt any rule? How so?

160 — one hundred sixty-one 161

Besides the recurrent sections in each unit, the series offer other sections with activities for pronunciation practice, boxes with cultural or linguistic information, extra vocabulary, and reading and/or learning strategies.

PRONUNCIATION PRACTICE

9 Listen and practice the pronunciation of the standard form of **going to** and the contracted form **gonna**, which is normally used in informal speech.

standard form	contracted form
I'm **going to** have dinner at 9:00 pm.	I'm **gonna** (/'gɒnə/) have dinner at 9:00 pm.

10 Listen and write **going to** or **gonna**.

a. ______________________ c. ______________________

b. ______________________ d. ______________________

This book also contains several appendices which contribute to your learning experience. Read more about them below.

FURTHER PRACTICE

Extra activities covering the unit themes with texts and listening activities that review the most relevant linguistic aspects.

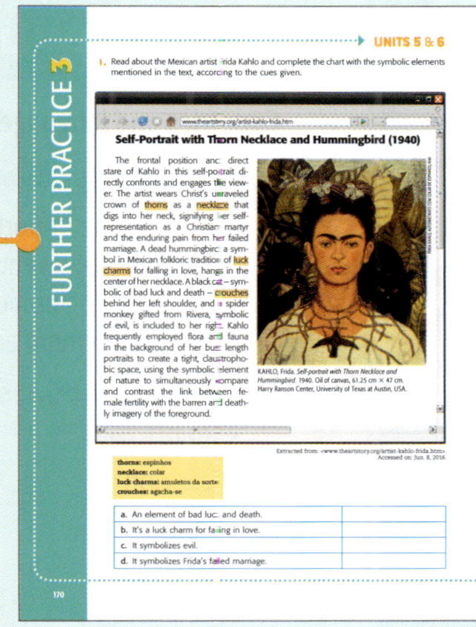

PROJECTS

Each book proposes two interdisciplinary projects with a wider scope. Based on a central theme and aimed at providing a deeper discussion about it, these projects culminate in a group closing activity.

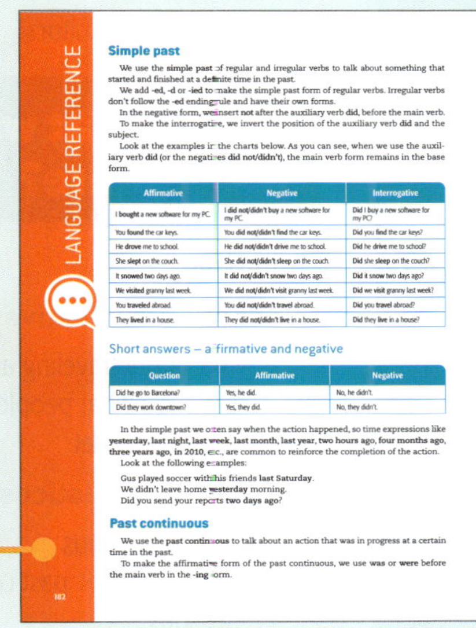

LANGUAGE REFERENCE

A summary of the linguistic aspects presented in the book. It can be used as reference material for studies.

AUDIO SCRIPTS

The transcriptions of the audios used in the "Listening Comprehension" section. They can be helpful while doing some activities or for future reference.

GLOSSARY

A list of the most important words from each volume translated according to the context in which they appear.

List of irregular verbs

In this section you will find a list of irregular verbs that are presented in books 8 and 9.

CONTENTS

1 Speaking English helps us... 10

Countries and languages

Funções comunicativas

Talk about the importance of English.
Talk about past events.
Create an infographic.
Express agreement and disagreement.

Conteúdos linguísticos

Simple past
Prefix **non**

Gênero discursivo

Infographic

Tema transversal

Pluralidade Cultural

2 What were you doing there? 28

Traveling

Funções comunicativas

Talk about traveling and tourist attractions.
Describe what people were doing.
Create a leaflet.

Conteúdos linguísticos

Past continuous
Simple past × past continuous
Seasons
Means of transportation

Gênero discursivo

Leaflet

Tema transversal

Pluralidade Cultural

3 What are you going to recycle? 48

Recycling

Funções comunicativas

Talk about environmental problems.
Talk about recycling.
Talk about future plans.
Write and answer a quiz.

Conteúdos linguísticos

Future with going to
Present continuous (future plans)

Gênero discursivo

Quiz

Tema transversal

Meio Ambiente

4 What do you know about her? 66

Professions

Funções comunicativas

Talk about relevant women in history.
Talk about future events.
Describe people's professions.
Create a biographical fact sheet

Conteúdos linguísticos

Simple future: will
Modals: must / have to
Modals: may / might
Professions

Gênero discursivo

Biographical fact sheet

Tema transversal

Trabalho

5 Which painting do you prefer? 86

Art

Funções comunicativas

Talk about art.
Describe and compare paintings.
Create front and back covers.

Conteúdos linguísticos

Adjectives
Comparative adjectives

Gênero discursivo

Front cover and
back cover

Tema transversal

Pluralidade Cultural

6 What's this story about? 104

Literature

Funções comunicativas

Talk about book genres.
Tell a fairy tale.
Describe book characters.
Talk about past events.

Conteúdos linguísticos

There to be (simple past)
Superlative adjectives
Book genres

Gênero discursivo

Fairy tale

Tema transversal

Pluralidade Cultural

7 A world of possibilities 124

Sports

Funções comunicativas

Identify Paralympic sports.
Talk about Paralympic athletes.
Write fast facts.

Conteúdos linguísticos

Relative pronouns
Modals: should
Paralympic sports

Gênero discursivo

Fast facts

Temas transversais

Pluralidade Cultural
Cidadania

8 Families 142

Family formations

Funções comunicativas

Talk about different family formations.
Talk about past events.
Write a testimonial.

Conteúdos linguísticos

Present perfect
Family formations

Gênero discursivo

Testimonial

Temas transversais

Pluralidade Cultural
Cidadania

Further practice, 162

Project, 178

Language reference, 182

Audio scripts, 190

Glossary, 196

List of irregular verbs, 206

Bibliography, 208

RICO

UNIT

1

Speaking English helps us...

Romanian artist Laurentiu Dimisca grew up under the communist regime and studied art from an early age up. He became PhD in painting in the University of Art and Design in Cluj-Napoca, in Romania. He began exhibiting in 2000 in his home country and abroad. The artist is part of the New Figurative, a movement between abstraction and figurative narrative, between "art brut" and "contemporary art". Mythology and the popular stories of his childhood and his country are present in his work.

Your learning objectives for this unit are...

- to talk about the importance of learning other languages;
- to talk about past actions;
- to read and write infographics.

EXCHANGING IDEAS

1. Look at the image on the left. What is in it?
2. This painting is called *Globalization*. What is the relation between the title and the painting?
3. A common language is necessary for people from different countries to communicate effectively. How important is English in this context?

- **www.dimiscartgallery.com/**
  Laurentiu Dimisca's official website with his biography and some works.

DIMISCA, Laurentiu. *Globalization*. 2010.
60 cm × 80 cm. Fundatia Outsider Art, Bucharest, Romania.

1 Speaking English helps us...

READING COMPREHENSION

TEXT 1

BEFORE READING

1. Imagine a world where people could speak a common language and still preserve their native language and culture. What would the benefits be? Explain.

READING

2. Skim the infographic and find a quote that summarizes it. Copy it here.

____

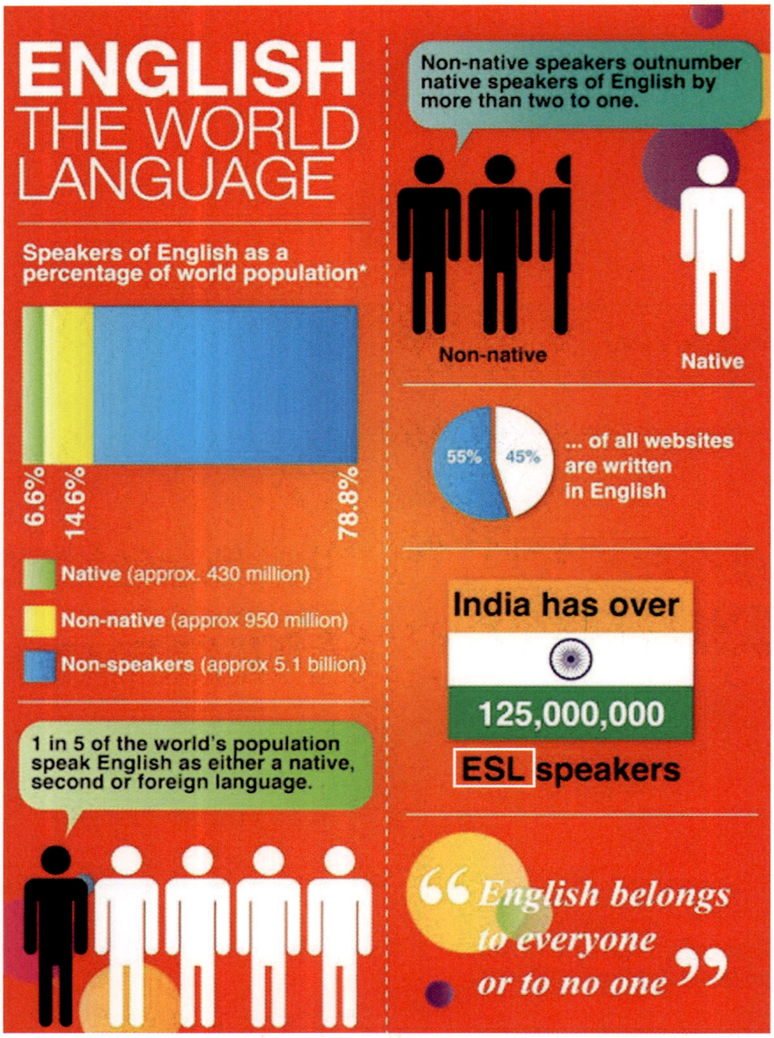

PAUL RAINE, 2012

- **www.vox.com/2015/3/3/8053521/25-maps-that-explain-english**
  Information about the origins of English, maps and other interesting facts about the language.

ESL (English as a Second Language): inglês como segunda língua

*Figures based on 2006 estimates | **Sources**: Saville-Troike, Muriel. *Introducing Second Language Acquisition*. Cambridge, UK: Cambridge UP, 2006.

http://unesdoc.unesco.org/images/0018/001870/187016e.pdf | http://en.wikipedia.org/wiki/English_language | Wardhaugh, Ronald.

Languages in Competition: Dominance, Diversity, and Decline. Oxford, UK: B Blackwell, 1987. This infographic ©Paul Raine 2012.

3. Read the text and check what these numbers refer to.

a. 125,000,000

☐ The population of India. ☐ ESL speakers in India.

b. 430 million

☐ Non-native English speakers.

☐ Estimated number of English native speakers.

c. 55%

☐ Websites written in languages other than English.

☐ Websites written in English.

4. Write **T** (true), **F** (false) or **NM** (not mentioned).

a. ☐ There are more non-native English speakers than native English speakers in the world.

b. ☐ English is India's first language.

c. ☐ Mandarin is the world's most widely spoken language.

d. ☐ One out of every five people in the world can speak English.

5. Read the dictionary entry below, go back to the infographic on page 12 and circle the correct option to complete each sentence.

infographic
noun [C]

a picture or diagram or group of pictures or diagrams showing or explaining information

Extracted from: <dictionary.cambridge.org/dictionary/british/infographic>. Accessed on: Jun. 6, 2016.

a. The information **is/isn't** presented clearly and quickly.

b. The visual part of the infographic consists of **statistics and facts/colors and graphics**

c. This is an effective infographic because people **cannot/can** receive a lot of information from the visual element.

AFTER READING

- What do people all over the world need English for?
- Why do you think English is the most common language in business, studies and entertainment?

TEXT 2

BEFORE READING

1. Look at the comic strips below. What do you think they are about?

READING

2. Read the comic strips and check what they are about.

☐ culture clash ☐ global communication ☐ tourism

1

YVES COTTEN

2

WWW.CHINESELEARNONLINE.COM

3. Read the dictionary entry for Globish and underline what you can infer.

Globish

noun

a simplified version of English used by non-native speakers, consisting of the most common words and phrases only

Extracted from: <www.collinsdictionary.com/dictionary/english/globish>. Accessed on: Jun. 6, 2016.

a. Globish is a simpler version of traditional English.

b. Globish can be used anywhere in the world.

c. It is not polite to speak Globish when talking to native speakers of English.

d. The term Globish is a combination of the words *Global* and *English*.

4. Match the parts to make meaningful sentences about the comic strips on page 14.

a. The man wearing the brown suit in the first strip

b. The phrase "Toilets, please"

c. The blonde guy thinks

d. The cook can speak enough English

e. Both cartoons show how

☐ can be easily understood by non-native speakers.

☐ efficient Globish can be in communication.

☐ to communicate with customers.

☐ does not ask the question in a simple way.

☐ his Chinese is terrible.

- ***English Vinglish***
  Direction: Gauri Shinde. India: Hope Productions, 2012. 134 min.
  A movie about an Indian woman who decides to learn English by taking an exchange course in the United States.
- ***The Terminal***
  Direction: Steven Spielberg. USA: Dream Works Home Productions, 2004. 128 min.
  A movie about a man whose admission in the United States is denied because of a problem in his country of origin. The airport becomes his temporary home and he has to deal with the fact that he does not speak the language and he is alone in a foreign country.

5. Answer the questions below. If necessary, go back to the comic strips.

Comic strip 1

a. What is the man's intention when he asks the Indian such a long question?

____

____

Comic strip 2

b. Does the cook seem angry at the customer who tries to speak Chinese?

____

____

AFTER READING

- Languages present varieties according to context, region, social group, age, occupation, etc. Knowing linguistic varieties allows people to communicate properly in different communicative situations. Share your opinion about this statement with your classmates and give examples of linguistic varieties.

FOCUS ON VOCABULARY

1. Match the words to their corresponding definitions.

a. foreign	☐	To be greater in number than someone or something.
b. native	☐	From a country that is not yours.
c. outnumber	☐	Your native language is the first language you learn as a child.
d. language	☐	The words used by the people of a country or region.

Adapted from: <dictionary.cambridge.org/us/>. Accessed on: Jun. 6, 2016.

Countries and languages

2. Read the texts and complete the chart below.

Germany

The official language of Germany is German, with over 95% of the population speaking German as their first language. Minority languages include Sorbian, spoken by 0.09% in the east of Germany and North Frisian spoken in Nordfriesland by around 10,000 people, or 0.01%, who also speak German.
Danish is spoken by 0.06%, mainly in the area along the Danish border. Romani, an indigenous language, is spoken by around 0.08%.
Immigrant languages include Turkish, which is spoken by around 1.8%, and Kurdish, by 0.3%.

Extracted from: <www.bbc.co.uk/languages/european_languages/countries/germany.shtml>. Accessed on: Jun. 6, 2016.

Spain

The official language is Spanish, also called Castilian, and is the first language of over 72% of the population. Galician is spoken in the region of Galicia and Basque by increasing numbers of the population of Euskadi, the Spanish Basque Country. Catalan is spoken in Catalonia and the Balearic Islands, and the closely-related Valencian in the Valencia region. All these languages have official regional status.
Other minority languages including Aragonese and Asturian are not officially recognised.

Extracted from: <www.bbc.co.uk/languages/european_languages/countries/spain.shtml>. Accessed on: Jun. 6, 2016.

Poland

98% of Poland's 39m population speak the official language of Polish. The remaining 2% speak minority languages including German, Ukrainian and Belarusian.

Extracted from: <www.bbc.co.uk/languages/european_languages/countries/poland.shtml>. Accessed on: Jun. 6, 2016.

country	official language	other languages
Germany		
Spain		
Poland		

Prefix **non**

3. Read the cartoon and do the activities.

"Can you spare a cup of non-fat milk, some no-calorie sweeteners, a cup of cottage cheese, a container of low-fat yogurt..."

sweeteners: adoçantes

a. What is the relationship between the two women?

____

b. Why is the woman at the door surprised?

____

c. Which word in the cartoon is formed the same way as a word in the infographic on page 12?

____

d. Look up this word in a dictionary and write down its meaning.

____

4. Check the correct alternative to complete the sentence below.

The prefix **non** has

- [ ] a negative meaning and indicates the absence of something.
- [ ] a neutral meaning in the context.

IT'S YOUR TURN!

In pairs, play the race word game. In 60 seconds write as many nationalities and/or languages as you can remember. Then compare your answers. The student who writes more words wins the game.

LANGUAGE IN USE

Simple past

1. Read this extract of the song "Who Knew" and check the correct alternatives.

Who **Knew**
Pink

You **took** my hand
You **showed** me how
You **promised** me you'd be around
Uh huh
That's right
I **took** your words
And I **believed**
In everything
You **said** to me
Yeah huh
That's right.
[...]

KEVORK DJANSEZIAN/GETTY IMAGES

Extracted from: <www.vagalume.com.br/pink/who-knew.html>. Accessed on: Jun. 6, 2016.

a. This part of the song is about

☐ things that happened in the past. ☐ things that are happening now.

b. The verbs in bold are in the

☐ negative form. ☐ affirmative form.

c. **Showed**, **promised** and **believed** are

☐ verbs that have different forms. ☐ regular verbs ending in **-ed.**

2. Now read the song extract again, pay attention to the verbs in bold and complete the table accordingly.

regular verbs		irregular verbs	
base form	simple past form	base form	simple past form
believe		know	
show		say	
promise		take	

3. In the word search find the simple past form of the verbs from the box and write them down. Then, use some of those verbs to complete the quotations about learning English.

be: ____________	have: ____________	start: ____________
come: ____________	help: ____________	take: ____________
go: ____________	live: ____________	understand: ____________

Q	Q	G	R	R	I	H	J	K	R	W	J	Y	J	W	D	P	H	H	V
O	O	V	F	L	T	C	Q	G	F	A	R	O	U	U	D	E	E	R	F
M	Y	V	E	W	H	A	D	B	Z	S	V	F	E	U	A	I	L	E	F
A	Y	R	X	C	J	P	C	T	I	G	Z	N	Q	F	Z	Y	P	R	N
A	C	O	I	W	D	N	J	L	B	N	N	R	U	P	D	H	E	E	I
T	N	E	W	E	K	D	Q	Z	K	J	O	I	P	J	F	K	D	C	R
J	Z	D	N	G	B	F	W	N	O	Z	U	S	F	F	T	N	Y	M	Y
G	M	E	M	A	C	E	V	U	S	Y	L	G	T	O	O	K	K	X	Y
O	D	H	C	V	S	T	V	Q	N	D	D	N	I	K	F	W	Z	X	F
C	H	O	L	K	M	J	K	N	L	K	M	R	J	L	H	W	O	H	D
T	P	Y	R	E	R	E	A	K	Z	D	V	N	P	F	S	Y	C	V	E
M	W	M	O	F	E	U	Q	O	E	I	I	B	N	B	F	K	Q	I	V
L	D	D	O	O	T	S	R	E	D	N	U	O	K	Y	M	J	G	B	I
P	H	J	D	Y	M	D	E	T	R	A	T	S	V	L	N	U	M	J	L
A	Q	H	U	O	C	D	P	B	O	I	O	D	L	P	D	P	W	T	A

a. "I ____________ in England to learn English. When I ____________ to England for the first time, it was like being on the Moon. I ____________ no friends, I couldn't speak the language. I ____________ very isolated."

Jean Alesi, French driver

Extracted from: <www.brainyquote.com/quotes/quotes/j/jeanalesi331985.html>. Accessed on: Jun. 6, 2016.

SPRINTPRESS/ULLSTEIN BILD/GETTY IMAGES

b. "I ____________ that without English I would never get far, so my dream was to become a receptionist, and so I ____________ to learn English from watching 'Sesame Street.'"

Anchee Min, Chinese athlete

Extracted from: <www.brainyquote.com/quotes/quotes/a/ancheemin614287.html>. Accessed on: Jun. 6, 2016.

PAT SULLIVAN/GETTY IMAGES

4. Based on the cartoon below, complete the sentences about the formation of the simple past tense in English.

to wet: molhar
soap: sabão

a. To ask a question in the simple past, use ______________ + subject + verb in the base form.

b. To form negative sentences in the simple past, use subject + ______________ (did not) + verb in the base form.

5. Read the extracts about the development of the English language and circle the time expressions. Do these expressions refer to the present or the past? Write **PR** for present and **PA** for past.

a. ☐ "It didn't happen really until the 1990s – English becoming a language that is spoken in every country in the world either as a first language, second language or as a significant foreign language in schools."

b. ☐ "You often go to a part of the world and you have difficulty understanding what has been said because you don't have the vocabulary in common because of the cultural differences.

c. ☐ "As I said, if people ADOPT language they ADAPT it, so there is always a fragmentation driven by this need for identity."

d. ☐ "So, English has already become a family of languages, like Latin and the Romance family of languages a thousand years ago."

Extracted from: <www.whichenglish.com/Author-Interviews/Interview-David-Crystal-04.html>. Accessed on: Jun. 6, 2016.

HANDS ON!

In your notebook, write down five questions to ask your classmates about things they did last week-end. You can use the verbs from the list on pages 206 and 207 and the time expressions presented in the **Language Reference**, on page 182. Walk around the classroom and interview three classmates. Take notes on their answers. Then, report the answers to the class.

Simple past

We use the **simple past** to talk about something that started and finished at a certain time in the past.

Affirmative

Irregular verbs can end in a variety of ways. Some verbs only change a vowel (ring – rang), while others change completely (go – went). There are also verbs that do not change at all (hit – hit). To learn them, consult a list.

Subject + **verb** (simple past) + complement

THINKSTOCK/GETTY IMAGES

Examples:

They **had** a conversation with me.

We **heard** a strange noise earlier.

I **knew** the answer to that question.

Negative

Subject + **did not (didn't)** + **verb** (infinitive) + complement

THINKSTOCK/GETTY IMAGES

Examples:

I **didn't see** you last night.

She **didn't like** the muffin.

We **didn't understand** the question.

Interrogative

Did + subject + **verb** (infinitive) + complement

ALAMY/FOTOARENA

Examples:

Did I **say** something wrong?

Did you **play** soccer last Saturday?

Did they **go** to the movies on the weekend?

1. Complete the table according to the examples.

Simple past		
affirmative	**negative**	**interrogative**
I went to the beach.	*I didn't go to the beach.*	______________
You saw a bird.	______________	______________
He studied French.	______________	______________
She said "Hello" in Spanish.	______________	*Did she say "Hello" in Spanish?*
It happened yesterday.	______________	______________
We bought eggs.	______________	______________
You ate pizza for dinner.	______________	______________
They drank coffee.	______________	______________

2. Rewrite the following sentences in the simple past tense.

a. They write beautiful poems.

____

b. Samuel plays basketball in the garage.

____

c. She doesn't speak Portuguese.

____

d. Do you see that car?

____

e. Does it cost more than 10 dollars?

____

f. We don't understand this exercise.

____

3. Complete the text with the verbs and instructions in parentheses.

My mother ______________ (cook) a special meal for us yesterday. It was a Spanish *paella*. She ______________ (learn) how to cook it with my great-grandmother Jimena. She ______________ (live) in Valencia. When my grandmother ______________ (get) married, the family ______________ (come) to Brazil. My great-grandmother ______________ (like – negative) her new life in Brazil and she ______________ (go) back to Valencia with my great-grandfather. My grandmother ______________ (want – negative) to go back to Valencia, so she ______________ (stay) in Brazil.

LISTENING COMPREHENSION

BEFORE LISTENING

1. Check the pictures that represent situations in which speaking English is important.

ILUSTRAÇÕES: RICO

have dinner

work

study abroad

make friends

communicate with customers

travel abroad

LISTENING

2. Listen to a Brazilian exchange student who has studied in the UK. Order the reasons she gives about the importance of speaking English.

2

> You do not have to understand all the words you hear to understand the general idea of a text. Pay attention to keywords and repeated words.

a. [ ] Speaking English helps people do business abroad.

b. [ ] Speaking English opened doors and gave her opportunities.

c. [1] Juliana decided to move and study in another country.

d. [ ] Clients would hire her because she could create content in English.

e. [ ] It was easier for her to adapt to another culture.

f. [ ] She could communicate with the foreign customers.

g. [ ] Speaking English helps us work with tourism and services.

3. Listen to Juliana again and write **T** (true) or **F** (false).

3

a. [ ] She is from Florianópolis.

b. [ ] She works as a marketing manager.

c. [ ] She thinks that speaking English isn't essential to having a successful career.

d. [ ] She studies in Birmingham, the United Kingdom.

e. [ ] She works as a digital marketing consultant.

f. [ ] She is in the United Kingdom to study English.

g. [ ] She says she can also speak German, French, Italian and Russian.

4. Complete part of Juliana's speech with the words from the box, according to the audio. Then read the audio script and check your answers.

4

events	host	opportunities	services

"Not to mention we are gonna ______________ two of the biggest world ______________ over the next three years and that will create loads of ______________ regarding tourism and ______________ and part of being prepared to seize these opportunities is speaking English. And you all want to be ready, don't you? Hope that helped you! Bye!"

AFTER LISTENING

5. Write two other reasons why speaking English is so important.

Speaking English helps us...

SPEAKING

1. In pairs, take turns reading your sentences from activity 5 in **After Listening** to a classmate. He/She has to say if he/she agrees or disagrees with you. Use the sentences below to express agreement or disagreement.

- I totally agree with you.
- I agree with you 100 percent.
- I couldn't agree more.
- You're right about that.
- You're absolutely right!
- Exactly.

- I'm afraid I disagree with you.
- I don't think so.
- I totally disagree.
- Not necessarily.
- That's not always true.
- I'm not so sure about that.

Reflecting on the theme

- Do you think that having a good knowledge of English can open up doors for your future? How?
- Is there any other language that you think is important to study? Which one? Explain.

BEFORE WRITING

1. Read the infographic and do the activities.

a. What language has the greatest number of speakers in the world?

____

b. How many people (in percentage) do not speak any of the languages mentioned in the infographic?

____

c. What is the title of this infographic?

____

____

d. What do the pie charts represent in the infographic?

☐ They represent the written information visually.

☐ They represent extra information about the topic.

- **www.nationsonline.org/oneworld/most_spoken_languages.htm**
  Information about the most spoken languages in the world.

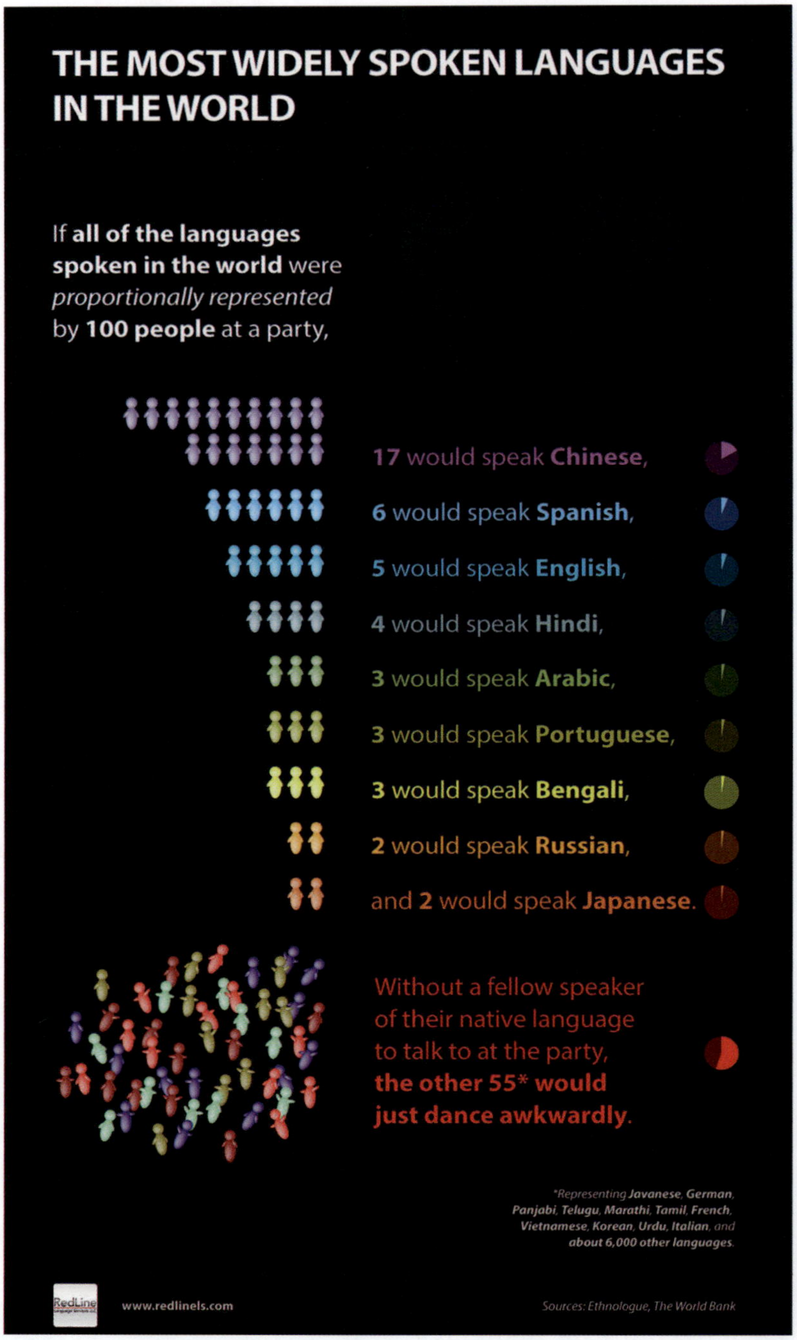

REDLINE LANGUAGE SERVICES LLC

WRITING

2. In small groups, you are going to create an infographic about the languages of the world. The infographic can be about different languages around the world, the most widely spoken languages, the origins of these languages, indigenous languages, curiosities about languages, linguistic varieties related to different regions, etc.
   - Choose a theme for the infographic.
   - Gather information about this theme. Research books or search the internet.
   - In your notebook, write down all the information you want to present and make a draft of your infographic.
   - Make a selection of images, graphs and charts to represent the verbal information.
   - Organize the verbal and non-verbal information to fit the page properly.
   - If necessary, use a dictionary to help you.
   - Ask your teacher to revise your work and make all necessary adjustments.

AFTER WRITING

- Produce the infographic on an adequate sheet, depending on its size: A2 or A3.
- Create a bulletin board to show all the infographics produced by you and your classmates. Then invite students from other classes to see the bulletin board.
- Create a page for the infographics on the school website and upload pictures of them or of the bulletin board.
- Alternatively, recreate and present your infographic on Prezi – Presentation Software (prezi.com). Follow the teacher's instructions for that.

SELF-EVALUATION

Check the true sentences about your learning in Unit 1.
In this unit you have learned to:

- [ ] talk about the importance of learning other languages;
- [ ] talk about past actions;
- [ ] read and write infographics.

Reflecting...

- **What did I learn about infographics?**
- **What did I learn about the simple past tense?**
- **What did I learn about the importance of learning other languages?**
- **What questions do I still have about the use of verbs in the simple past tense?**

UNIT

2

What were you doing there?

French painter, illustrator and professor Nicolas-Antoine Taunay, born in 1755, came to Brazil in the end of the Napoleonic empire as a member of the French Artistic Mission (Missão Artística Francesa). He arrived in Rio de Janeiro in 1816, at the age of 61, when he was already an experienced and renowned painter in France.

He became a member of the Royal School of Sciences, Arts and Crafts, later known as the Imperial Academy of Fine Arts (Academia Imperial de Belas Artes – Aiba). He was responsible for teaching landscape painting. He returned to France in 1821. Despite the short period of time he spent in Brazil, his paintings are extremely important in the history of Brazilian art in the 19th century.

MUSEU NACIONAL DE BELAS ARTES, RIO DE JANEIRO, BRASIL.

Your learning objectives for this unit are...

- to read information in a leaflet for tourists;
- to identify and recognize the seasons of the year and means of transportation;
- to read and write a leaflet for tourists.

EXCHANGING IDEAS

1. Look at the picture. It portrays a landscape in Rio de Janeiro. What elements are present in this painting?
2. Nicolas-Antoine Taunay's works show some sceneries from Rio de Janeiro in the 19th century. How do you imagine a painting of the same places nowadays? What new elements do you think would be portrayed in the picture?
3. We can get to know the history of a place by observing works of art or also visiting it. What city, country or place are you curious about? Why?

- **enciclopedia.itaucultural.org.br/en/pessoa24452/nicolas-antoine-taunay**
  Nicolas-Antoine Taunay's biography and some of his works.

TAUNAY, Nicolas-Antoine. *Entrada da baía e da cidade do Rio a partir do terraço do convento de Santo Antônio em 1816*. 1816. Oil on canvas, 45 cm × 56.5 cm. Museu Nacional de Belas Artes, Rio de Janeiro, Brasil.

2 What were you doing there?

READING COMPREHENSION

TEXT 1

BEFORE READING

1. Tourism can bring many social, economic and infrastructural benefits to a community. In pairs, mention and explain some of them.

READING

2. This tourism leaflet is from Punta Cana, Dominican Republic. Skim the text and list the languages used.

DOLPHIN ISLAND PARK

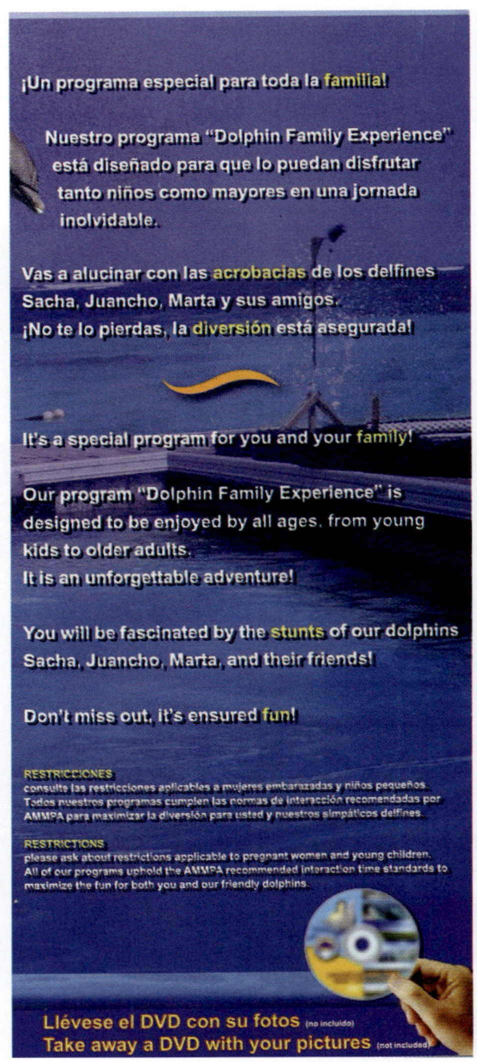

DOLPHIN ISLAND PARK

3. Join the parts and write meaningful sentences about the tourism leaflet.

they have to book by phone. If tourists want to visit the park,

It is a unique

Dolphin Island is experience.

a park.

Tourists can swim with dolphins.

a. ____

____

b. ____

____

c. ____

____

d. ____

____

4. Read the leaflet again. Check what we can infer.

a. ☐ Dolphins are docile and swim with humans.

b. ☐ People have to pay for the DVD photos.

c. ☐ Dolphin Island is an expensive tour.

d. ☐ There are interesting things to see when snorkeling.

e. ☐ Tourists can watch dolphins performance.

5. Who can participate in the activities with the dolphins?

____

____

AFTER READING

- Showcases with dolphins are harshly criticized, because animal defenders believe these performances take the animals out of their natural habitat and they suffer to perform the shows. Do you agree with the animal defenders? Should these shows be allowed? Why?
- Cities can have different attractions to attract tourists' attention. They can be historical patrimony, ecological reserves, places surrounded by natural beauties, places with amusement parks, museums. They can also be famous for their celebrations, traditions, cuisine, etc. Mention some Brazilian cities that receive many tourists and name what kind of tourism is available in those places.

TEXT 2

BEFORE READING

1. When people are a long way away they can communicate in many ways. E-mail is one of them. What other means of communication can be used to get in touch with people who are distant?

READING

In English, we say **at** for @ and **dot** for periods (.) when saying e-mail addresses.

2. Skim Mary's e-mail and check where she was some days before.

a. ☐ Savannah Island. b. ☐ South Carolina. c. ☐ Townhouse City.

From: Mary Smith <yyz786@mail.com>
To: Ella <girl162@mail.com>
Cc:
Subject: South Carolina trip

Hi Ella!

Maggie and I were away for 5 days. We visited Paul and his girlfriend Savannah. They were moving to a new townhouse he bought on Hilton Head Island, South Carolina, and we helped them.

We had a very nice time together – he is thinking it may be where he retires to in a few years.

We flew there and back – the ocean was too cold to swim in, but it was lovely walking along the shore.

Thought you would enjoy these – hope you and the family are well.

Hugs and lots of love,

Mary

RACHID DAHNOUN/CORBIS/LATINSTOCK

ALAMY/LATINSTOCK

shore: orla

A townhouse is "a house that has two or three levels and that is attached to a similar house by a shared wall."

JEFF GREENBERG/AGE FOTOSTOCK/AGB PHOTO

Extracted from: <www.merriam-webster.com/dictionary/town%20house>. Accessed on: Jun. 6, 2016.

3. Join the parts to make questions.

a. Who ☐ was the ocean?

b. How ☐ did Mary stay on the island?

c. How long ☐ did they do at the beach?

d. What ☐ is Savannah?

4. Now match the questions from activity 3 to the correct answers.

☐ It was too cold to swim.

☐ She stayed there for five days.

☐ They walked along the shore.

☐ She is Paul's girlfriend.

5. Read the e-mail again and write **T** (true) or **F** (false).

a. ☐ Maggie wrote this e-mail to Ella to tell her about her trip to the island.

b. ☐ Savannah bought a new townhouse in South Carolina.

c. ☐ Paul is thinking about living in South Carolina when he retires.

d. ☐ Mary and Maggie visited Paul together.

6. Using the words from the box, complete the sentences about some characteristics of e-mails.

body	bold	e-mail	greeting	language	subject

a. Headers always precede an ______________________.

b. Headers bring different pieces of information, such as the sender, the recipient, and the ______________________.

c. The ______________________ of an e-mail contains the text, that is, the actual message.

d. We can use special features in the body of an e-mail – ______________________, italics, underline and text color.

e. The ______________________ of an e-mail can be formal or informal. This depends on the subject of the e-mail as well as on the person we are writing to.

f. As in letters, e-mails usually begin with a ______________________ and end with a closing sentence.

AFTER READING

- In your opinion, what is the best way to communicate with family and friends when you are traveling? Why?

FOCUS ON VOCABULARY

1. Listen to the descriptions of some sea animals. Label the pictures using the names from the box.

5

dolphin	sea lion	shark	stingray

THINKSTOCK/GETTY IMAGES

THINKSTOCK/GETTY IMAGES

THINKSTOCK/GETTY IMAGES

THINKSTOCK/GETTY IMAGES

A ______ B ______ C ______ D ______

Seasons

2. Look at the paintings by Vincent van Gogh. They all have elements that are associated with a season of the year. Number the paintings accordingly.

1. autumn	2. spring	3. summer	4. winter

autumn (UK)
fall (USA)

COLEÇÃO PARTICULAR.

VAN GOGH, Vincent. *Landscape with snow*. 1888. Oil on canvas, 38.2 cm × 46.2 cm. Private collection.

J. PAUL GETTY MUSEUM, LOS ANGELES, CALIFÓRNIA, EUA.

VAN GOGH, Vincent. *Irises*. 1889. Oil on canvas, 74.3 cm × 94.3 cm. Jean Paul Getty Museum, California, USA.

KRÖLLER-MÜLLER MUSEUM, OTTERLO, HOLANDA.

VAN GOGH, Vincent. *Falling autumn leaves*. 1888. Oil on canvas, 73 cm × 92 cm. Kröller-Müller Museum, Otterlo, Netherlands.

KUNSTMUSEUM, WINTERTHUR, SUÍÇA.

VAN GOGH, Vincent. *Summer evening, wheatfield with setting sun*. 1888. Oil on canvas, 188 cm × 231 cm. Kunstmuseum, Winterthur, Switzerland.

Means of transportation

3. Read the texts below and find the names of some means of transportation. Write them under the corresponding picture.

CHRISTIAN BACH/ULLSTEIN BILD/GETTY IMAGES

____

RIA NOVOSTI/SPL/LATINSTOCK

____

JUAN ANTONIO ALONSO/EASYPIX

____

ROB WALLS/ALAMY/GLOW IMAGES

____

a. Japan is known for the bullet train, so it's no surprise that the Shinkansen train has a top speed of 275 mph. It is nicknamed the "Duck-Billed Platypus" for its odd-looking, aerodynamic nose.

Extracted from: <www.businessinsider.com/the-10-fastest-trains-in-the-world-2012-11?op=1>. Accessed on: Jun. 6, 2016.

b. Crowds aside, the extensive New York City subway system has to be among the world's best. In general, the system is easy to navigate with its color-coded and letter-or-number-named lines. Below ground, you'll find entertaining street (or should we say platform) performers, period tile work, funky art installations, and occasionally a newspaper/candy stand. [...]

Extracted from: <www.frommers.com/slideshows/818699-the-world-s-best-subways-10-top-cities#slide818705>. Accessed on: Jun. 6, 2016.

c. The Airbus A340-600 weighs 807,400 pounds and is 242 feet, 4 inches long with a wingspan of 208 feet, 2 inches. The plane was introduced in 1984 as an upgrade of earlier models and is a popular model still. It can carry 266 passengers with 240 in economy.

Extracted from: <www.forbes.com/2007/06/01/aviation-aerospace-planes-biz-cx_rm_0604bigplanes_slides1.html>. Accessed on: Jun. 6, 2016.

d. Our bus services allow you to take in the best Australia has to offer, and our wide variety of ticketing options allow you to travel at your own pace, hopping on and off as many times as your ticket allows. Or, you can simply choose your origin and destination and design your own trip along the way. [...]

Extracted from: <www.greyhound.com.au/about/about-greyhound>. Accessed on: Jun. 6, 2016.

mph: milhas por hora
Duck-Billed Platypus: ornitorrinco
newspaper/candy stand: banca de jornal e doces
in economy: na classe econômica
hopping on and off: subir e descer (do ônibus)

IT'S YOUR TURN!

Which means of transportation do you usually use when going to school? Explain your choices to a classmate. Change roles and compare your answers.

LANGUAGE IN USE

Past continuous

1. Read part of the e-mail Mary sent to Ella again and answer the questions below.

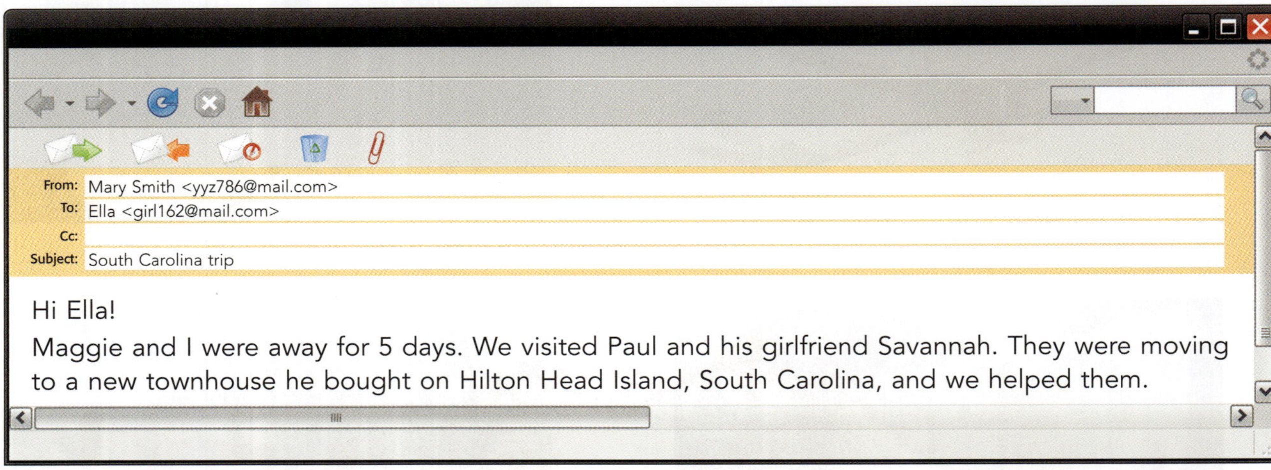
From: Mary Smith <yyz786@mail.com>
To: Ella <girl162@mail.com>
Cc:
Subject: South Carolina trip

Hi Ella!

Maggie and I were away for 5 days. We visited Paul and his girlfriend Savannah. They were moving to a new townhouse he bought on Hilton Head Island, South Carolina, and we helped them.

a. Where was Mary when she wrote this e-mail?

☐ She was at home. ☐ She was in South Carolina.

b. When did Mary and Maggie visit Paul and Savannah?

☐ After they had moved to the new house in South Carolina.

☐ While they were moving to their new house in South Carolina.

c. Why did Mary and Maggie visit them at this time?

☐ Because they wanted to help Paul and Savannah.

☐ Because they wanted to see Paul and Savannah's new house.

d. The verb form "were moving" in the e-mail indicates…

☐ that this action is in progress right now.

☐ that the action was in progress at a specific time in the past.

2. Refer to activity 1 and complete the rules of the past continuous.

a. The affirmative form of the past continuous is formed by

b. In the negative form,

c. In the interrogative form, we invert the position of the verb **to be** and the subject

☐ the verb **to be** in the past (**was/were**) + the main verb in the **-ing** form.

☐ and then we add the main verb in the **-ing** form.

☐ we use the verb **to be** in the past + **not** (**was not**, **wasn't/were not**, **weren't**) + the main verb in the **-ing** form.

Simple past × past continuous

worked out: faziam atividade física
fancy: sofisticado
sweaty: suado
laughed: riu

3. Read an excerpt of the story *The Turning Point*, circle the verbs in the simple past and underline the verbs in the past continuous.

RICHMOND PUBLISHING

Just then, I remembered my friends from old school.

They only worked out at that fancy fitness center in the shopping mall. And the guys here seemed to have a lot of fun just playing football in the street.

When I got back home, it was almost time for dinner. I was dirty and sweaty. When my mom saw me, she couldn't believe her eyes.

"Eric, is that you?", she asked.

"Of course, Mom. Why? Do I look so different?"

"You sure do! What were you doing?"

"I was playing football in the street with my friends. My team won the game but we had to play hard. The other team is really good. And I worked out without going to the gym. You see, I saved us some money."

Mom laughed. I was happy to see that her sense of humor was coming back.

Extracted from: TEODOROV, Veronica. *The Turning Point*. São Paulo: Richmond, 2004. p. 25.

4. Read another excerpt of the same book, pay special attention to the sentence in bold and do the activities.

> "And it really was easy. From that day on, I made my bed every day. Mom was proud of me. But in the beginning, Elizabeth was a little jealous. In the old days, she always made my bed for me. **One day, I was making my bed when Elizabeth opened the door**. She looked upset."

Extracted from: TEODOROV, Veronica. *The Turning Point*. São Paulo: Richmond, 2004. p. 18.

a. Which word is used to connect the actions?

b. Which part of the sentence indicates an action in progress?

c. The phrase "when Elizabeth opened the door" indicates...

☐ an action in progress.

☐ an action that interrupted another action in progress.

5. Read this text about Machu Picchu, Peru, and answer: What was Bingham searching for when he discovered the place?

> **Machu Picchu: Facts & History**
>
> by Owen Jarus, Live Science Contributor | August 31, 2012 12:32pm ET
>
> [...]
>
> In 1911, explorer Hiram Bingham III, a professor at Yale University, visited the site and published its existence for the first time. He found it covered with vegetation, much of which has now been removed. The buildings were made without mortar (typical of the Inca), their granite stones quarried and precisely cut.
>
> When Bingham discovered the site he was actually searching for Vilcabamba, the last capital of the Inca before their final defeat at the hands of the Spanish in 1572.
>
> The explorer found Machu Picchu largely intact, having apparently never been visited by the Spanish conquistadors. In fact, the only reference to the site at all in Spanish documents is a mention of the word "Picchu" in a 1568 document, the text implying that it belonged to the Inca emperor.

Extracted from: <www.livescience.com/22869-machu-picchu.html>. Accessed on: Jun. 6, 2016.

HANDS ON!

In pairs, study this painting for 1 minute and close your books. In your notebook, write down sentences about what was happening in the picture using the past continuous. Then, compare your answers in small groups and report them to the teacher.

GARDEN AT SAINTE-ADRESSE, CLAUDE MONET, 1867

MONET, Claude. *Garden at Sainte-Adresse*. 1867. Oil on canvas, 98.1 cm × 129.9 cm. The Metropolitan Museum of Art, New York, USA.

Past continuous

We use the **past continuous** to talk about an action that was in progress at a certain time in the past.

Affirmative

Subject + **to be** (past) + main verb in the -**ing** form

THINKSTOCK/GETTY IMAGES

Example:

I **was running** in the park.

Negative

Subject + **to be** (past) + **not** + main verb in the -**ing** form

SHUTTERSTOCK

Example:

They **weren't helping** me with my homework.

Interrogative

To be (past) + subject + main verb in the -**ing** form

JOSE LUIS PELAEZ INC/GETTY IMAGES

Example:

Was she **telling** you a secret?

Simple past × past continuous

When we talk about an action that interrupted another action in progress in the past, we use the **simple past**.

THINKSTOCK/GETTY IMAGES

Example:

I **was downloading** a file when my internet connection **dropped**.

- "I was downloading a file..." = the action that was in progress
- "... my internet connection dropped." = the action that interrupted the other action in progress

1. Complete this dialogue with the simple past or past continuous of the verbs in parentheses.

SHAY LEVY/ALAMY/FOTOARENA

Anne: ____________ you ____________ (watch) the match yesterday?

Claire: No, I ____________ (do). Who ____________ (win)?

Anne: Barcelona!

Claire: I ____________ (watch) it because my TV ____________ (break down).

Anne: Really? How awful! ____________ you ____________ (fix) it?

Claire: No. My father ____________ (take) it to the car when he ____________ (slip) and ____________ (twist) his ankle.

Anne: Wow, ____________ he ____________ (have) to go to a hospital?

Claire: Yes, he ____________ (do). We ____________ (take) him to the hospital, but when my mom ____________ (drive), a police officer ____________ (stop) us. And my mother ____________ (remember) that she ____________ (carry) her bag. And her driving license was in it.

Anne: No way! ____________ the police officer ____________ (give) your mom a ticket?

Claire: No, he ____________ (be) very cool. He ____________ (let) us go with a warning.

2. Match the verbs to the respective position in each sentence.

a. were playing

b. was studying

c. was running

d. started

e. called

f. arrived

I ☐ for the test when my friend ☐ me.

We ☐ when the rain ☐.

Her cat ☐ in the house when she ☐.

LISTENING COMPREHENSION

BEFORE LISTENING

1. Look at the pictures of some places in Singapore, Asia. Read the texts and match them to the pictures they represent.

A

MATTHEW WILLIAMS-ELLIS/ROBERT HARDING/DIOMEDIA

B

IMAGEBROKER RM/GTW/DIOMEDIA

C

DAVID LEFRANC/CORBIS/LATINSTOCK

D

ZOONAR/MTKANG/EASYPIX

☐ [...] The temple features many facets of Buddhist arts and culture of Singapore. It also houses what the Buddhists regards as the Sacred Buddha Tooth Relic in a stupa weighing 3.5 tonnes and composed of 320 kg of gold donated by devotees. [...]

Extracted from: <www.justgola.com/a/buddha-tooth-relic-temple-and-museum-1978046711>. Accessed on: Jan. 29, 2016.

☐ [...] There are more than 200 market stalls lining Pagoda, Terengganu and Sago streets, all of which offer a wide selection of old and new collectibles [...]. The Chinatown Street Market is especially vibrant and fun to visit during traditional holidays such as the Chinese New Year, with free live performances being offered every night, such as lion and dragon dances, martial arts displays, Chinese opera and stilt-walkers. [...]

Extracted from: <www.singaporeholidays.info/2015/06/chinatown-street-market.html>. Accessed on: Jan. 29, 2016.

☐ A cacophony of car horns, bicycle bells and vibrant chatter of its residents, Little India is one of the most vibrant and culturally authentic districts of Singapore. Take in the sights, sounds and smell as you immerse yourself in authentic Indian experience in Singapore. [...]

Extracted from: <sites.google.com/site/footprintbackpacker/misc/LittleIndia>. Accessed on: Jan. 29, 2016.

☐ The more than 150-year-old Singapore Botanic Gardens is a star visitor attraction for the sophisticated traveller and the local resident. The Gardens possess an array of botanical and horticultural attractions with a rich history and a wonderful plant collection of worldwide significance.

Extracted from: <www.nparks.gov.sg/gardens-parks-and-nature/singapore-botanic-gardens>. Accessed on: Jun. 6, 2016.

LISTENING

2. Listen to a woman talking about Singapore and check the correct sentences.

6

a. ☐ Singapore is one of the biggest and most densely populated countries in the world.

b. ☐ Singapore became a republic in 1965.

c. ☐ Singapore today is one of the most powerful countries in Asia.

d. ☐ Singapore was a British colony.

e. ☐ Singapore is in Asia.

3. Listen again and answer.

7

a. When it became a republic in 1965, many people think the country couldn't succeed. Why?

____

____

b. Singapore is called a great global city. What does the city still cherish from a time before the condition of a global city?

____

____

4. Listen further and answer: According to the audio, what are two Singaporean obsessions?

8

____

AFTER LISTENING

5. What is the audio you heard in activities 2 to 4?

a. ☐ Tourism advertisement.

b. ☐ A documentary about life in Singapore.

6. Considering your answer in activity 5, why do you think food and shopping are emphasized as Singaporean obsessions?

____

____

7. Do you think a documentary about life in Singapore would bring information the same way you heard in activities 2 to 4?

____

____

____

SPEAKING

1. Check what you can hear in the advertisement from activities 2 to 4, on page 42.

   a. ☐ Historical information about Singapore.

   b. ☐ Places to eat or go shopping.

   c. ☐ Information about daily life in Singapore.

   d. ☐ Positive point of view of Singapore.

   e. ☐ Critical approach to history and culture of Singapore.

2. Is the information you checked in activity 1 relevant for a tourism advertisement? Read the sentences you checked again and justify why they are relevant or not.

3. Consider the items you checked in activity 1 and answer: What is necessary to do to prepare a tourism advertisement?

4. How would you advertise your city to promote tourism? List interesting historical facts, places to visit, where to eat, and other important information, on your notebook. Plan your oral presentation of this content.

5. Present your advertisement to your classmates and teacher. Keep in mind the characteristics of the one you listened to in activities 2 to 4, on page 42.

Reflecting on the theme

- Would you like to visit Singapore? Why?
- What differences can you see between the cultural aspects of Singapore and those of your country?

- **www.turismo.gov.br/turismo/home.html**
  Brazilian Ministry of Tourism's official website. Information about tourism in Brazil.
- **www.youtube.com/watch?v=IAd2m8rrSs4&list=PLO-wxly9sHyYsE03p176ZzHvmGKCPAZAI**
  Actor and TV host Michael Edward Palin's series of documentaries about his trips to Brazil.

WRITING

BEFORE WRITING

1. Skim the tourism leaflet and answer: What kind of activity is offered?

NATIONAL TRUST IMAGES

- ***Férias na Antártica***
  KLINK, Tamara; KLINK, Laura; KLINK, Marininha. São Paulo: Peirópolis, 2010.
  Amyr Klink's three daughters' travel account. They write about their vacation on a ship in Antarctica.

- ***The Secret Life of Walter Mitty***
  Direction: Ben Stiller. USA: Twentieth Century Fox Film Corporation, 2013. 114 min.
  The life of an ordinary man who goes on an adventure around the world which changes his life.

2. Check the pieces of information you can find in the tourism leaflet.

a. ☐ name of the place to be visited.

b. ☐ time of the activities.

c. ☐ visitors' names.

d. ☐ date of the activities.

e. ☐ description of the activity.

f. ☐ rules for the activities.

3. Why do people read tourism leaflets?

____

WRITING

4. You are going to write a tourism leaflet about somewhere in your city or country. The ideia is to promote an activity, cultural spot or a place where young people have fun in your city.
   - Choose a place that might be interesting for young people. Think of the characteristics that might attract these readers.
   - If you need more information about the place or activity you choose, search on the internet or talk to the people who know more about it.
   - Describe the activity or place, highlighting aspects that might attract the readers' attention.
   - Choose pictures or drawings that represent this place or activity. Remember the picture must be attractive for the readers as well. So, make sure the picture you choose is relevant and characterizes the event.
   - Remember what information might help readers: date, time, place, description of the event.
   - In your notebook, make a draft of the leaflet. Show your teacher the draft you made.

AFTER WRITING

- Exchange your leaflet with a classmate and evaluate each other's writing:
  - Is the leaflet attractive for the intended reader?
  - Does the leaflet describe the activities?
  - Does the leaflet highlight the features of the place or activity?
  - Does the leaflet bring useful information for the intended reader?
- When the leaflets are ready, they can be distributed among other students at school and among people in your community.

SELF-EVALUATION

Check the true sentences about your learning in Unit 2.
In this unit you have learned to:

- [ ] read information in a leaflet for tourists;
- [ ] identify and recognize the seasons of the year and means of transportation;
- [ ] read and write a leaflet for tourists.

Reflecting...

- **What did I learn about the simple past and the past continuous?**
- **What did I learn about leaflets for tourists?**
- **What questions do I still have about the grammar points in this unit?**

Connections

English • Geography

UK's first driverless cars may be old acquaintances

Similar to the electric passenger shuttles in use at Heathrow Airport. That's how the first driverless cars to be tested on streets of the UK will look like. They will be the result of a £8m project cooperatively funded by the government agency Innovate UK and industry. The heathrow pods currently transport passengers from the car park to Terminal 5 at the airport. In their five-year history, they have already carried

CHARLES BOWMAN/ALAMY/FOTOARENA

1. Would you feel safe inside a moving car without a driver?

2. Answer **T** (true) or **F** (false).

a. ☐ The first driverless cars of UK are called Innovate.

b. ☐ The heathrow pods and the first driverless cars of UK will be similar.

c. ☐ The heathrow pods have been in use for five years.

d. ☐ Gateway stands for Greenwich Automobile Transportation Environment.

e. ☐ To avoid accidents, the driverless cars will not transit in residential areas.

f. ☐ The driverless cars can carry six passengers.

g. ☐ Although the driverless pods have traveled millions of kilometers on tracks, they have to be tested for use on streets.

1.5 million passengers and travelled 3 million kilometers.

The group behind the project, named The Greenwich Automated Transport Environment project (Gateway) confirmed that these driverless pods are being adapted for use on the roads, not on dedicated tracks. The carmaker Westfield Sportscars will be responsible for manufacturing and testing the pods. Heathrow Enterprise will design the software. Oxbotica will provide mapping and other safety sensors. The three companies are British.

ALAMY/FOTOARENA

ANDREW HOLT/ALAMY/FOTOARENA

The driverless pods will be tested in four locations in the UK. Although the exact routes are still being defined, they most certainly will include residential areas, an underground station, and businesses around the O2 Arena, in the Greenwich Peninsula. Invited users will be the first ones to test the pods, with the mandatory presence of a steward for the safety of the other five passengers, the probable maximum capacity. They will be followed by the general public, for a period of three months, which will hopefully provide enough data to "tell us whether people trust and accept these vehicles and how they would work as part of the urban landscape," according to Nick Reed, technical director for the Gateway project. He added: "This vehicle has millions of miles under its belt and now we have to take it outside of the track and modify it for use on pavements."

Based on: <www.bbc.com/news/technology-35432687>; <www.techweekeurope.co.uk/e-innovation/london-driverless-cars-greenwich-184915>. Accessed on: Mar. 3, 2016.

3. Which of the three companies mentioned in the text will probably be responsible for the following items?

1. Westfield Sportscars
2. Heathrow Enterprise
3. Oxbotica

- [ ] softwares to analyse data from the various sensors to manipulate the steering, acceleration and braking
- [ ] cameras to detect traffic lights, read road signs and keep track of other vehicles
- [ ] automated-steering technology
- [ ] proximity sensors to aid parking
- [ ] altimeters, gyroscopes and a tachometer
- [ ] softwares to build a 3D map based on the information collected by sensors
- [ ] mapping systems

UNIT

3

What are you going to recycle?

Brazilian artist based in New York, United States, Vicente José de Oliveira Muniz is considered extremely original. His originality comes from the use of recyclable material, hair, food, etc. His objective is to speak to audiences that do not usually go to art galleries.

Marat (Sebastião) is a piece based on a photo taken at a landfill in Rio de Janeiro of a waste collector named Sebastião. The photo was inspired by *The Death of Marat*, by Jacques-Louis David. Marat (1743-1793) was a doctor at the French Revolution who was murdered because of his efforts in causes on behalf of the people. *Marat (Sebastião)* was sold for 50,000 dollars in London and a portion of the money was donated to the waste collectors of Jardim Gramacho to be used to buy a truck to help their work in the recycling industry. Vik Muniz was the inspiration for the documentary *Waste Land (Lixo extraordinário)*, which was nominated for the 2011 Academy Awards for Best Documentary.

Your learning objectives for this unit are...

- to talk about actions and social attitudes that preserve the planet;
- to read and write a quiz;
- to talk about plans and future actions.

VIK MUNIZ, MARAT (SEBASTIÃO), 2008

EXCHANGING IDEAS

1. Look at the image on the left and describe it.
2. In art, the use of materials found in garbage modifies the original meaning of these objects. What do they represent in this Vik Muniz's piece?

- **www.vikmuniz.net**

  Vik Muniz's official website with his biography, news and some of his works.

- ***Waste Land***

  Direction: Lucy Walker; Karen Harley; João Jardim. Brazil/United Kingdom: Almega Projects/ O2 Filmes, 2010. 99 min.

  A documentary about the work of artist Vik Muniz on Jardim Gramacho, one of the largest landfills in the world, located in Rio de Janeiro.

MUNIZ, Vik. *Marat (Sebastião)*. 2008. Private collection.

3 What are you going to recycle?

READING COMPREHENSION

TEXT 1

BEFORE READING

1. The following article was extracted from a website that presents several schools that are aware of environmental problems. Why is this kind of school important to students' life?

READING

2. Skim the text and answer the question: What is the final product of the students' project?

www.greencommunityschools.org/

GREEN COMMUNITY SCHOOLS

Green Community Schools Initiative:
A Program of the MGR Foundation

Green Community Schools Initiative: A Program of the MGR Foundation

WWW.GREENCOMMUNITYSCHOOLS.ORG

(Charlotte, NC) MGR's Green Community Schools Environmental Justice Club and Leadership students at Charlotte-Mecklenburg Schools Vance recently completed their 6 month, Arts in Action project: a life-size, recycled tree.

Inspiration for this project came from the desire to educate their peers about the amount of waste coming out of their cafeteria and classrooms on a daily basis. The tree is made completely from recycled items found around the school (with the exception of chicken-wire to sculpt the trunk). Materials included: old milk crates, string, paper from classroom recycling bins, cardboard boxes, Styrofoam lunch trays, etc. EJC Senior, Katie Foster, said, "the tree taught me that if we work together to recycle and cherish the environment, others will follow."

These students proved that you can truly make something amazing out of what others view as trash. The tree is now showcased in the middle of the cafeteria, reminding students of the importance of practicing the words "Reduce, Reuse, Recycle."

Extracted from: <www.greencommunityschools.org/>. Accessed on: Mar. 3, 2015.

peers: colegas
trunk: tronco
Styrofoam: isopor
cherish: valorizar

• ***The 11th Hour***
Direction: Leila Conners; Nadia Conners. EUA: Warner Bros., 2007. 95 min.
A documentary about the state of planet Earth and how we can make it a better place.

3. Complete the chart with the appropriate information about the school project.

Project name	
Duration	
Inspiration	
The foundation and people involved	

Green Community Schools (GCS) is a program from the MGR Foundation to promote environmental awareness and responsibility in schools.

4. Read the text on page 50 again, complete the questions using the words from the box, and then answer them.

chicken-wire	items	only	recycled	tree

a. What were the ________________ items used to make the tree?

____

____

b. Where did the ________________ to build the tree come from?

____

c. What was the ________________ item used to build the tree that was not recycled?

____

d. What was the ________________ used for?

____

e. Where was the ________________ displayed? Why?

____

____

AFTER READING

- One of the students said "the tree taught me that if we work together to recycle and cherish the environment, others will follow." Do you agree with her? Why?

TEXT 2

BEFORE READING

1. What's the title of the quiz below? What kind of questions do you expect to answer?

READING

2. Skim the text and answer: Are the questions of the quiz directed to the readers or to their family members?

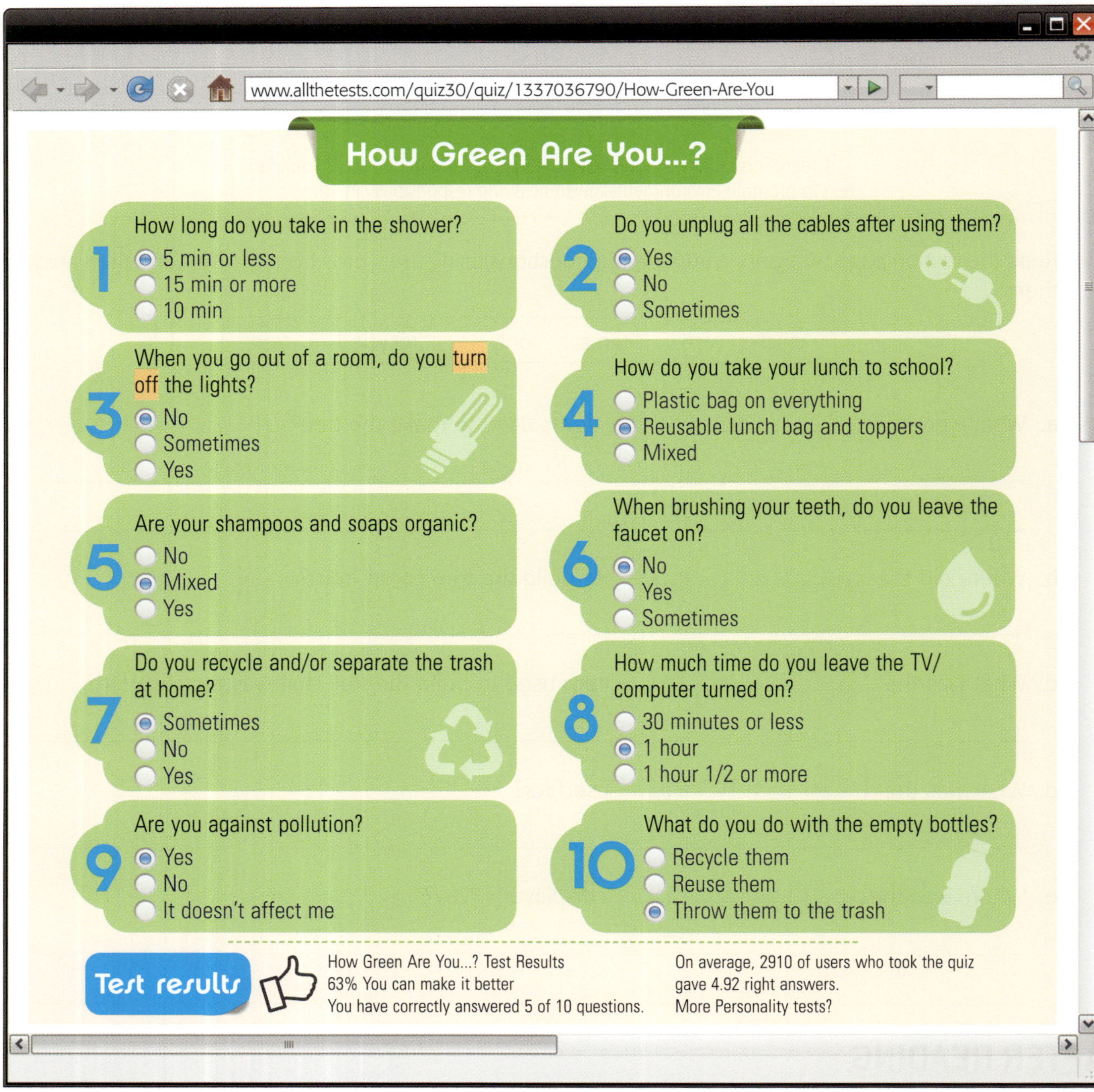

www.allthetests.com/quiz30/quiz/1337036790/How-Green-Are-You

How Green Are You...?

1. How long do you take in the shower?
   - (•) 5 min or less
   - ( ) 15 min or more
   - ( ) 10 min

2. Do you unplug all the cables after using them?
   - (•) Yes
   - ( ) No
   - ( ) Sometimes

3. When you go out of a room, do you turn off the lights?
   - (•) No
   - ( ) Sometimes
   - ( ) Yes

4. How do you take your lunch to school?
   - ( ) Plastic bag on everything
   - (•) Reusable lunch bag and toppers
   - ( ) Mixed

5. Are your shampoos and soaps organic?
   - ( ) No
   - (•) Mixed
   - ( ) Yes

6. When brushing your teeth, do you leave the faucet on?
   - (•) No
   - ( ) Yes
   - ( ) Sometimes

7. Do you recycle and/or separate the trash at home?
   - (•) Sometimes
   - ( ) No
   - ( ) Yes

8. How much time do you leave the TV/ computer turned on?
   - ( ) 30 minutes or less
   - (•) 1 hour
   - ( ) 1 hour 1/2 or more

9. Are you against pollution?
   - (•) Yes
   - ( ) No
   - ( ) It doesn't affect me

10. What do you do with the empty bottles?
    - ( ) Recycle them
    - ( ) Reuse them
    - (•) Throw them to the trash

Test results

How Green Are You...? Test Results
63% You can make it better
You have correctly answered 5 of 10 questions.

On average, 2910 of users who took the quiz gave 4.92 right answers.
More Personality tests?

Extracted from: <www.allthetests.com/quiz30/quiz/1337036790/How-Green-Are-You>. Accessed on: Feb. 28, 2015.

turn off: desliga

3. Read the sentences related to the quiz and write **T** (true) or **F** (false).

a. ☐ All the questions are related to everyday habits.

b. ☐ The quiz was specially written for adults.

c. ☐ The user can check the results after answering the quiz.

d. ☐ Most of the questions are about water pollution.

e. ☐ Some of the questions are about food habits.

f. ☐ There are questions about recycling.

- ***Avatar***

  Direction: James Cameron. EUA: Twentieth Century Fox Film Corporation, 2009. 162 min.

  A movie about the different ways people relate to the environment: as the exploiters or as a community.

4. Check what you can infer about being "green".

☐ It's basically to avoid wasting food and water.

☐ It's a lifestyle focused on preserving the planet and its natural resources.

☐ It's the preservation of the neighborhood environment we live in.

5. Answer these questions about the test results.

a. According to the quiz, how many questions did he/she answer correctly?

____

b. Is that a good result?

____

c. Did most of the users give correct answers?

____

d. In your opinion, is the person who took the quiz green? Why?

____

____

6. Match the parts to form meaningful sentences about some characteristics of quizzes.

a. The quiz presents a title	☐	simple and direct.
b. There are questions and	☐	based on the user's answers.
c. The questions are	☐	that makes the topic clear to the reader.
d. There is immediate feedback	☐	a few options of answers.

AFTER READING

- What actions can you take in your daily life to preserve the environment?

FOCUS ON VOCABULARY

1. Look at the pictures and check the ones that represent the materials used in the recycled tree mentioned in text 1. Then match the pictures to their corresponding words or expressions.

THINKSTOCK/GETTY IMAGES

THINKSTOCK/GETTY IMAGES

THINKSTOCK/GETTY IMAGES

THINKSTOCK/GETTY IMAGES

STOCK PHOTOS/GLOW IMAGES

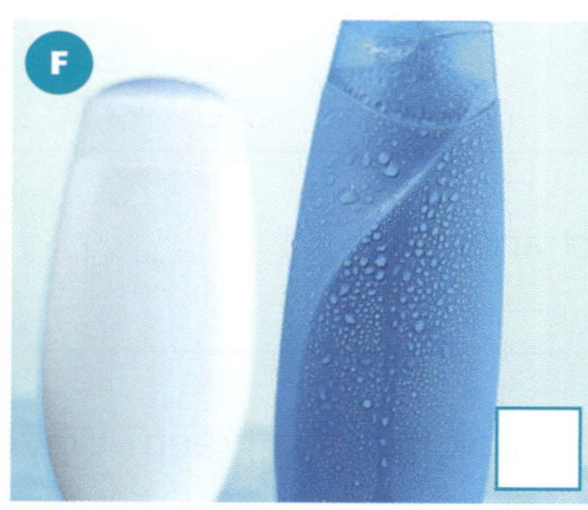

THINKSTOCK/GETTY IMAGES

THINKSTOCK/GETTY IMAGES

THINKSTOCK/GETTY IMAGES

- [ ] aluminum cans
- [ ] batteries
- [ ] cardboard boxes
- [ ] chicken-wire
- [ ] milk crate
- [ ] shampoo bottles
- [ ] string
- [ ] Styrofoam lunch trays

2. Complete the sentence below using some words or expressions from activity 1.

The materials that were not used in the tree are ______________________________, ______________________________, and ______________________________.

3. Match the pictures to their corresponding questions from the quiz on page 52.

ILUSTRAÇÕES: RICO

Recycling

4. Read some interesting facts about environment preservation and complete the sentences using the words or expressions from the box.

cloth bag	glass	newspapers	recycled paper	reusable lunch box	shopping bags

a. For your school lunch, use a ____________________ and thermos. Wash it at night and it's ready to go for tomorrow.

b. ____________________ only creates 25% of the pollution that new paper creates when making it into new products.

c. Recycling a single ____________________ bottle will save enough energy to power a light bulb for four hours.

d. All ____________________ in the United Kingdom are 100% recycled paper.

e. In one person's lifetime, using a ____________________ will save over 22,000 plastic bags!

f. Only 1% of plastic ____________________ are recycled.

Extracted from: <gogreencyclopedia.blogspot.com.br/2013/09/50-facts-about-your-environment-for-kids.html>. Accessed on: Jun. 6, 2016.

IT'S YOUR TURN!

Do you usually recycle at school or at home? In pairs, tell a classmate the things you normally do to recycle and reuse things. Think about at least 2 more things you can do to help the environment and tell him or her.

LANGUAGE IN USE

Future with going to

1. Read Carl Sagan's quote and check the correct alternatives.

"Anything else you're interested in is not going to happen if you can't breathe the air and drink the water. Don't sit this one out. Do something. You are by accident of fate alive at an absolutely critical moment in the history of our planet."

Carl Sagan

SANTI VISALLI INC/GETTY IMAGES

Extracted from: <www.andiquote.co.za/authors/Carl_Sagan.html>. Accessed on: Jun. 6, 2016.

don't sit this one out: não perca esta oportunidade
fate: destino

Carl Sagan was an American scientist and astronomer who dedicated his life to the study of Astronomy and the dissemination of science.

a. What **is going to happen** to you if you can't breathe the air and drink the water?

- [ ] We **are going to die** and our interests **are not going to matter** anymore.
- [ ] We **are going to take action** and do something about that.

b. The sentence "Anything else you're interested in **is not going to happen**..." expresses

- [ ] an obligation you **are going to fulfill**.
- [ ] a future plan that **is not going to come true**.

c. What **is going to happen** if you sit this one out?

- [ ] Things are going to be different.
- [ ] Things are not going to change.

2. Refer back to activity 1 and circle the best options to complete the statements about the verb forms in bold.

a. The verb form **going to** indicates **orders/plans or intentions** for the **past/near future**.

b. To form the future with **going to**, we use the verb **to have/to be** + going to + the base form of the verb.

c. In the **negative/affirmative** form, we use **not** between the verb **to be** and the **going to** form.

d. In the interrogative form, we invert the position of the **subject and the main verb/subject and the verb to be**.

3. Underline the correct verb form to complete the quote below.

"The only way forward, if we **are going to improve/going to improve** the quality of the environment, is to get everybody involved."
Richard Rogers

ANCOIS GUILLOT/AFP

Extracted from: <www.brainyquote.com/quotes/quotes/r/richardrog228217.html?src=t_environmental>. Accessed on: Jun. 6, 2016.

Richard Rogers is a British modernist architect with an active participation in urban and political issues in England.

4. Read the comic strip and write **T** (true) or **F** (false).

© MAURICIO DE SOUSA PRODUÇÕES - BRASIL/2011
MAURICIO DE SOUSA EDITORA LTDA.

gonna: going to (informal speech – American English)
yá: you (informal subject pronoun you)

a. ☐ Smudge knows that Jimmy Five can draw very well.

b. ☐ Jimmy Five is sure he is good at drawing.

c. ☐ The phrase "you're gonna be an artist" indicates a plan for the future.

d. ☐ "... when yá grow up!" is a time phrase that refers to the present.

e. ☐ The standard form for the colloquial "you're gonna be an artist" is "you going to be an artist".

PRONUNCIATION PRACTICE

9 Listen and practice the pronunciation of the standard form of **going to** and the contracted form **gonna**, which is normally used in informal speech.

standard form	contracted form
I'm **going to** have dinner at 9:00 pm.	I'm **gonna** (/'gɒnə/) have dinner at 9:00 pm.

10 Listen and write **going to** or **gonna**.

a. ____________________ c. ____________________

b. ____________________ d. ____________________

Present continuous (future plans)

5. Read *Calvin and Hobbes* comic strip and match the columns accordingly.

CALVIN & HOBBES, BILL WATTERSON © 1989 WATTERSON/ DIST. BY UNIVERSAL UCLICK

a. Calvin's mother isn't [ ] because he didn't want her to go out.

b. Calvin took his mother's shoes [ ] his parents are not leaving him with the babysitter.

c. According to Calvin's plan, [ ] leaving home because she can't find her shoes.

6. Look at the last panel of the comic strip again and use the information from the box to complete the text.

CALVIN & HOBBES, BILL WATTERSON © 1989 WATTERSON/DIST. BY UNIVERSAL UCLICK

future	present continuous	time	tonight

Besides the future with **going to**, we can also use the ____________ to talk about ____________ plans. We normally use it when we know the date, the time, and the place something is happening. We can use some future ____________ expressions, such as **next** (**week**, **month**, **class**), **tomorrow**, ____________ , **this** (**after-noon**, **evening**), **in** (**a year**, **a month**).

HANDS ON!

Finish the sentences by writing your own true plans using **going to**. Then, tell your classmates about your plans and listen to theirs as well. Are you going to be busy?

Tonight ____________

Tomorrow morning ____________

Next weekend ____________

In 10 days ____________

Future with going to

We use the future with **going to** to indicate a plan or an intention.

THINKSTOCK/GETTY IMAGES

THINKSTOCK/GETTY IMAGES

PETEK ARICI/GETTY IMAGES

Affirmative

Subject + verb **to be** + **going to** + infinitive
Examples:
I **am going to** travel to Australia next year.
They **are going to** have dinner together.

Negative

Subject + verb **to be** + **not** + **going to** + infinitive
Examples:
He **isn't going to** tell you my secret.
They **are not going to** help me with my homework.

Interrogative

Verb **to be** + subject + **going to** + infinitive
Examples:
Is she **going to** buy that skirt?
Are we **going to** play video game at night?

Present continuous (future plans)

We can use the **present continuous** to talk about arrangements or specific future plans. We usually know when something is happening.

Affirmative

Subject + verb **to be** + **main verb** in the **-ing** form
Examples:
I **am running** the marathon tomorrow at 8.
They **are having** dinner at 9 tonight.

Negative

Subject + verb **to be** + **not** + **main verb** in the **-ing** form
Examples:
He **isn't flying** to Denver at 9 because there was a delay.
They **aren't playing** soccer at 9 tomorrow because of the event.

Interrogative

Verb **to be** + subject + **main verb** in the **-ing** form
Examples:
Is she **arriving** at the station at 7 on Wednesday?
Are we **serving** lunch at 12 today?

1. Complete these sentences with the future with **going to**. Use the verbs in parentheses.

a. Paula ______________________________ me at 7 tonight. (call)

b. We ______________________________ our new video game after class. (play)

c. My cousin ________________________ the new *Star Wars* movie tomorrow at 9. (watch)

d. You ____________________ a surprise party for your mother next Saturday night. (prepare)

e. We __________________________ to the bus stop in five minutes. (walk)

f. Mark and you _________________ some friends at the library this afternoon. (meet)

g. I ____________________ this package to the post office after work this afternoon. (take)

2. Rewrite the sentences from activity 1 according to the instructions in parentheses.

a. ____ (negative)

b. ____ (interrogative)

c. ____ (negative)

d. ____ (negative)

e. ____ (interrogative)

f. ____ (interrogative)

g. ____ (negative)

3. Check the sentences in which the present continuous is used to talk about future plans.

a. ☐ Somebody is calling me on the phone.

b. ☐ If you need to talk to me next week, I am staying at the Hilton Hotel in Miami.

c. ☐ My mother and I are doing some shopping this afternoon.

d. ☐ I am waiting for a friend. I think he is late.

e. ☐ She is walking her dog around the block.

f. ☐ My father is giving me a car next month.

g. ☐ We are watching our favorite TV show.

h. ☐ We are leaving when the sun rises!

LISTENING COMPREHENSION

BEFORE LISTENING

1. The pictures below show actions that people can take to help the planet. Match them to the corresponding sentences.

UNITED ARCHIVES/DIOMEDIA

ALBERTO BISCARO/MASTERFILE/LATINSTOCK

SCIENCE SOURCE/RICH/DIOMEDIA

THINKSTOCK/GETTY IMAGES

DENKOU IMAGES/DIOMEDIA

THINKSTOCK/GETTY IMAGES

THINKSTOCK/GETTY IMAGES

IMAGEBROKER RM/DIOMEDIA

a. Brush without running water.

b. Buy local.

c. Fly with an e-ticket.

d. Go vegetarian once a week.

e. Plant a tree.

f. Recycle aluminum and glass.

g. Turn off computers at night.

h. Use rechargeable batteries.

LISTENING

2. Listen to the beginning of the program *Curiosity Quest Goes Green* and answer the questions.

11

a. Who is Joel Greene?

____

b. What is the episode going to be about?

____

c. Where is he recording the show?

____

3. Listen to another part of the program and check the picture that matches the subject they are talking about.

12

SIMPLY NATURAL MOM

JULIEN PEREIRA/FOTOARENA

4. In your own words, answer: What is a trash-free lunch for the kids in Grand View Elementary?

____

____

____

____

____

5. What are the benefits of a trash-free lunch, according to the kids in Grand View Elementary? Check the correct options.

a. ☐ You don't produce any trash out of it, so it helps protect the environment.

b. ☐ It's healthier than lunch that produces trash.

c. ☐ You don't have to spend time throwing trash away.

d. ☐ You can have juice.

AFTER LISTENING

6. Could a trash-free lunch be implemented at your school? What would the benefits be?

SPEAKING

1. In pairs, make a list with five habits people have at your school that are bad for the environment.

2. What are possible solutions for the problems listed in activity 1?

3. Make plans to aware the school community to change these habits in order to help the planet. Then report to class.
   Don't forget to mention:
   - How you are going to show people the problem.
   - How everyone can help solve them.
   - The benefits these actions can bring to your school.

Reflecting on the theme

- Do you know any Brazilian program similar to the one you heard?
- Does the government of your city encourage people to recycle or reuse things?
- What actions can you take in your neighborhood/city to help reduce, reuse and recycle?

BEFORE WRITING

1. Read the extract of the quiz below and compare it to the one on page 52. Then check the true sentences.

Green Quiz

You tell people you care about the planet, but are your actions matching your words? Take this fun quiz to find out how well you're doing now, and also get some ideas of more things you can do on your own. Once you know how you score, move on to Projects to find out how to do a service-learning project with a team.

1 In order to learn more about the environment, I...

- ◯ perk up when biology teacher mentions anything about ecology.
- ◯ watch TV shows or read about endangered wildlife or at-risk ecosystems.
- ◯ take an elective environmental science course in my high school.

Check all that apply | Question 1 of 10 | Next Question

2 To have a positive impact on my local environment, I...

- ◯ attend Earth Day Celebrations.
- ◯ am a member of an environmental club (local, national, or international) or a zoo or aquarium.
- ◯ write letters to elected Environmental Science Course in my high school.

Check all that apply | Question 2 of 10 | Next Question

3 I recycle...

- ◯ paper.
- ◯ plastic bottles.
- ◯ aluminum cans.
- ◯ glass bottles.

Check all that apply | Question 3 of 10 | Next Question

4 After high school I plan to...

- ◯ continue doing what I already do for the environment.
- ◯ go to college and major in Science.
- ◯ plan on a career in Conservation Science, Wildlife Biology, Environmental Education, etc.

Check all that apply | Question 4 of 10 | Next Question

5 When I am going to meet my friends, I...

- ◯ walk to meet them.
- ◯ carpool.
- ◯ take my bike.
- ◯ use mass transit.

Check all that apply | Question 5 of 10 | Next Question

[...]

Extracted from: <www.teensforplanetearth.org/page/green-quiz>. Accessed on: Mar. 3, 2015.

a. ☐ Both quizzes present titles.

b. ☐ Both quizzes have the same number of possible answers.

c. ☐ Both quizzes require the user to write complete answers.

d. ☐ Both quizzes use multiple-choice questions.

e. ☐ Only the quiz on page 52 presents questions.

WRITING

2. In groups, follow the steps to create your own questions for a Green Quiz for the students of your school.

- In groups of 5, talk to your classmates and your teacher in order to choose a topic for your quiz. You can choose one of these topics: attitudes at home and at school to save water and energy; the best way of discarding used vegetable and olive oil, glass, plastic, batteries, and textiles; how to avoid pollution, or any other topic related to sustainability or environment protection.
- Ask your Science teacher to help you get information about the topic.
- Do some research on the internet about it or use the school library to do so.
- Take notes of all the information you have collected.
- Write 2 questions for the quiz. Make sure the questions are not repeated.
- Use a dictionary if necessary.
- Write a draft of the questions and ask your teacher to revise them.

AFTER WRITING

- Gather all the questions created by all the groups in your class.
- Reproduce the quiz on an A4 sheet of paper and make as many copies as you need to circulate it among students from other classes.
- If possible, ask other teachers to answer your quiz, too.
- Once you have their answers, analyze them and report the percentage of each question answered. Ask your Math teacher to help you calculate the percentages, if necessary.
- Talk to your classmates and students from other classes about the results of the quiz to motivate them to be eco-friendlier.

SELF-EVALUATION

Check the true sentences about your learning in Unit 3.
In this unit you have learned to:

- [ ] talk about actions and social attitudes that preserve the planet;
- [ ] read and write a quiz;
- [ ] talk about plans and future actions.

Reflecting...

- **What did I learn about the characteristics of a quiz?**
- **What did I learn about ways to talk about future actions in English?**
- **What questions do I still have about the future with going to and the present continuous for future plans?**

UNIT

4

What do you know about her?

Sao Paulo-born Eduardo Kobra is considered one of the most distinguished neo-avant-garde artists. His art aims at transforming the urban scenario by means of interferences and overlapping of remarkable scenes and characters from the 20th century with impressive results.

In 2014, Eduardo Kobra painted the façade of MAAM (Museo dell'Altro e dell'Altrove) in Rome, as a tribute to young activist Malala Yousafzai. Malala is known worldwide for her struggle for a better education to all, for which she was shot in the head by the Taliban, a radical militant group. She survived and won the Peace Nobel Prize in 2014.

Your learning objectives for this unit are...

- to read and write a biographical fact sheet;
- to identify the names of some occupations;
- to make future predictions, talk about obligations, prohibitions and possibilities.

EXCHANGING IDEAS

1. By depicting Malala on the façade of an important museum, Kobra gave more than an artistic meaning to the piece. Which meaning is this?
2. Do you know any women who stand out for their actions in politics, education, environmental issues, sports, social activism, etc.? If so, talk about them with your classmates.

EDUARDO KOBRA, MALALA YOUSAFZAI, 2014

- **www.eduardokobra.com**
  Eduardo Kobra's official website with his biography and some of his works.
- **www.malala.org**
  The official website for the Malala Fund with Malala Yousafzai's story and information about this organization's work.

KOBRA, Eduardo. Mural on the Museo dell'Altro e dell'Altrove (MAAM), Rome, Italy. 2014.

4 What do you know about her?

READING COMPREHENSION

TEXT 1

BEFORE READING

1. Do you know who the first African woman to receive a Nobel Peace Prize was? She had an important role in environmental preservation matters. How important is receiving an international prize to promote a cause?

READING

scholar: acadêmica
grass-roots movement: movimento popular
broader: mais ampla

2. Read the biographical fact sheets and answer the questions.

A

www.nobelprize.org/nobel_prizes/peace/laureates/2004/maathai-facts.html

Wangari Maathai – Facts

RICHARDSEN, TOR/EPA/EFEVISUAL

Wangari Muta Maathai
Born: 1 April 1940, Nyeri, Kenya
Died: 25 September 2011, Nairobi, Kenya
Residence at the time of the award: Kenya
Prize motivation: "for her contribution to sustainable development, democracy and peace"
Field: humanitarian work
Prize share: 1/1

Sustainable Development, Democracy and Peace

Wangari Maathai was the first African woman to receive the Nobel Peace Prize. She was also the first female scholar from East and Central Africa to take a doctorate (in biology), and the first female professor ever in her home country of Kenya. Maathai played an active part in the struggle for democracy in Kenya, and belonged to the opposition to Daniel arap Moi's regime.

In 1977 she started a grass-roots movement aimed at countering the deforestation that was threatening the means of subsistence of the agricultural population. The campaign encouraged women to plant trees in their local environments and to think ecologically. The so-called Green Belt Movement spread to other African countries, and contributed to the planting of over thirty million trees.

Maathai's mobilisation of African women was not limited in its vision to work for sustainable development; she saw tree-planting in a broader perspective which included democracy, women's rights, and international solidarity. In the words of the Nobel Committee: "She thinks globally and acts locally."

Extracted from: <www.nobelprize.org/nobel_prizes/peace/laureates/2004/maathai-facts.html>. Accessed on: Jun. 6, 2016.

a. Where was Wangari Maathai from?

____

____

b. Besides being the first professor in her country, what else was she the first woman to achieve?

____

____

c. What was the result of the grass-roots movement that she started in 1977?

____

____

d. What happened to the Green Belt Movement?

____

____

e. What was the Nobel Committee's opinion about her?

____

____

B

www.ovguide.com/zilda-arns-9202a8c04000641f80C0000013a3a5ce

Zilda Arns

Biography: Zilda Arns Neumann was a Brazilian pediatrician and aid worker. A sister of Cardinal Dom Paulo Evaristo Arns, the former Archbishop of São Paulo known for his efforts against the Brazilian military dictatorship, Zilda Arns became internationally known by founding a Catholic pastoral care for poor children. Her humanitarian work, which also included the poor and the elderly, spanned over three decades. Arns died on January 12, 2010 as a result of the 2010 Haiti earthquake.

Born: August 25, 1934, Forquilhinha

Died: January 12, 2010 (age 75), Port-au-Prince

Occupation: Pediatrician, Health Professional

RODOLFO BUHRER/AE

Extracted from: <www.ovguide.com/zilda-arns-9202a8c04000641f8000000013a3a5ce>. Accessed on: Jun. 6, 2016.

Archbishop: Arcebispo
spanned: estendeu-se

In 2010, a large-scale earthquake struck Haiti, killed more than 300,000 people, and left 1,500,000 homeless.

Based on: <g1.globo.com/mundo/noticia/2015/01/fotos-mostram-dificil-reconstrucao-do-haiti-5-anos-depois-de-terremoto.html>. Accessed on: Jun. 6, 2016.

a. What was Zilda Arns's occupation?

____

____

b. Who was her brother?

____

____

c. What was her brother known for?

____

____

d. Besides children, who did she help through her humanitarian work?

____

____

e. When and why did she die?

____

____

3. Read the sentences and check the correct columns.

	Wangari Maathai	Zilda Arns
a. She devoted her life to helping poor children.		
b. She became the first professor in her country.		
c. She won a very important prize.		
d. She was internationally known for her humanitarian work.		
e. She founded a Catholic pastoral care for poor children.		
f. She had a broader perspective including democracy, women's rights, and international solidarity.		
g. She had formal education.		
h. She was Brazilian.		

AFTER READING

- In your opinion, what legacy did these two women leave behind?

TEXT 2

BEFORE READING

1. Do you think that women and men must have the same rights? Give examples and explain.

READING

2. Skim the quotes and answer: What are they about?

3. Write **T** (true) or **F** (false) according to the quotes you have just read.

RALF JUERGENS/GETTY IMAGES

Gender equality is more than a goal in itself. It is a precondition for meeting the challenge of reducing poverty, promoting sustainable development and building good governance.

Kofi Annan

Extracted from: <www.brainyquote.com/quotes/quotes/k/kofiannan401690.html>. Accessed on: Jun. 6, 2016.

SANJEEV VERMA/GETTY IMAGES

In the future, there will be no female leaders. There will just be leaders.

Sheryl Sandberg, *Lean In: Women, Work, and the Will to Lead*

Extracted from: <www.goodreads.com/quotes/tag/womens-rights>. Accessed on: Jun. 6, 2016.

ISSEI KATO/REUTERS/CORBIS/LATINSTOCK

African women in general need to know that it's OK for them to be the way they are – to see the way they are as a strength, and to be liberated from fear and from silence.

Wangari Maathai

fear: medo

Extracted from: <www.brainyquote.com/quotes/quotes/w/wangarimaa166688.html>. Accessed on: Jun. 6, 2016.

a. ☐ According to Kofi Annan, fighting for gender equality is directly related to important social issues.

b. ☐ According to Sandberg, it doesn't matter if a leader is a man or a woman.

c. ☐ Wangari Maathai says that all African women aren't self-confident.

4. Complete these sentences. Use the words and expressions from the box.

impacting	point of view	reflection

a. Quotes express the author's ________________ about something or somebody.

b. They usually present ________________ short sentences.

c. Quotes lead the reader to a ________________ about the issue.

AFTER READING

- In your opinion, what actions could be taken by young people to preserve the ecuality for men and women's rights?

FOCUS ON VOCABULARY

1. Use the words or expressions from the box to complete the extracts below.

aid workers	democracy	sustainable development

a.

[...]

All definitions of ______________________ require that we see the world as a system – a system that connects space; and a system that connects time.

When you think of the world as a system over space, you grow to understand that air pollution from North America affects air quality in Asia, and that pesticides sprayed in Argentina could harm fish stocks off the coast of Australia.

[...]

Extracted from: <www.iisd.org/sd/>. Accessed on: Jun. 6, 2016.

b.

[...]

"______________________" are defined as the employees and associated personnel of not-for-profit aid agencies (both national and international) that provide material and technical assistance in humanitarian relief contexts. [...]

Extracted from: <https://aidworkersecurity.org/about>. Accessed on: Jun. 6, 2016.

c.

[...]

______________________ requires that citizens' interests be heard, deliberated and legislated on. Women are half of the world's population, and as such their voice should be heard in the democratic process. [...]

Extracted from: <www.un.org/en/globalissues/democracy/women.shtml>. Accessed on: Jun. 6, 2016.

2. Match the pictures below to the corresponding texts in activity 1.

ANN SUMMA/CORBIS /LATINSTOCK

STRINGER/AFP

BLEND RF/KIDSTOCK/DIOMEDIA

Professions

3. Read the texts and identify the people in the pictures. Write **SW** for Social Worker or **CS** for Conservation Scientist.

What is a Conservation Scientist?

Also known as: Environmental and Conservation Biologist, Environmental and Conservation Scientist, Conservation Biologist.

A conservation scientist is someone who manages the overall land quality of forests, parks, rangelands and other natural resources. They work with landowners and all levels of government to devise ways to use and improve the land while safeguarding the environment. They advise farmers, farm managers, and ranchers on how they can improve their land for agricultural purposes and to help control erosion.

A Conservation Scientist is a specialized type of Scientist.

Extracted from: <www.sokanu.com/careers/conservation-scientist/>. Accessed on: Jun. 6, 2016.

What does a Social Worker do?

A social worker helps people cope with challenges in every stage of their lives. They help with a wide range of situations, such as adopting a child or being diagnosed with a terminal illness. Social workers work with many populations, including children, people with disabilities, and people with addictions.

[...]

Extracted from: <www.sokanu.com/careers/social-worker/>. Accessed on: Jun. 6, 2016.

BEBE CROUSE

DAVID MCNEW/GETTY IMAGES

THINKSTOCK/GETTY IMAGES

JOHN BIRDSALL/EASYPIX

JUPITERIMAGES/GETTY IMAGES

IT'S YOUR TURN!

In pairs, write at least two more responsibilities you think a Social Worker and a Conservation Scientist could have to help your community or your school. Then share your suggestions with the whole group.

LANGUAGE IN USE

Simple future: will

1. Read the quotes carefully. Then, read the statements, write **T** (true) or **F** (false) and correct the false statements.

> *"Women **will be** no longer made the slaves of, or dependent upon men...They **will be** equal in education, rights, privileges and personal liberty."* (Robert Owen, Welsh social reformer)

Extracted from: <www.robertowen2008.coop/equal.htm>. Accessed on: March 6, 2015.

> *"My manager's biggest dream is for me to be on Letterman. She says, 'Oh, Maggie, **will** you **promise** me you**'ll** be on Letterman?' What can I say? I just tell her I can't promise, but I**'ll** try my best."* (Maggie Q, American actress, model and Animals Right activist)

Extracted from: <www.brainyquote.com/quotes/quotes/m/maggieq495758.html>. Accessed on: Jun. 7, 2016.

'll: will

a. ☐ According to Owen's quote, women are slaves of men.

____

b. ☐ We can infer from Owen's quote that he doesn't believe in a change concerning the future of women.

____

c. ☐ Maggie Q promised her manager she would be on *Letterman*.

____

d. ☐ According to Owen's quote, women are equal in education and rights, but not in privileges or personal liberty.

____

e. ☐ Maggi Q's manager is a woman.

____

2. Now match the columns to find out the different uses of **will** in the quotes from activity 1.

a. "...They will be equal in education, rights, privileges and personal liberty."

b. "... but I'll try my best."

☐ expresses a promise to do something in the future.

☐ indicates a prediction about the future.

- **www.youtube.com/watch?v=ayj9EVc2ZLI**

ATKINS, Ros. *All That Stands in the Way*. BBC. 2014.

A documentary about four teenage girls from different parts of the world and their opinions about gender gap and how women are brought up.

3. Refer back to activities 1 and 2 and write the appropriate words or expressions to complete the rules for the simple future. The first letter of each word is given to help you out.

a. We use **will** to make p_______________ or promises about the f_______________.

b. In the affirmative form, we use **will** (or **'ll**) + verb base form without **to**.

c. To form the negative, we use **will not** (or **w**_______________) + verb base form without **to**.

d. In the interrogative form, we invert the position of **w**__________ and the subject of the sentence.

Modals: must / have to

4. Read the quotes and pay attention to the verb forms in bold. Then, underline the correct alternatives to complete the rules below.

*"Whenever people say, 'We **mustn't be** sentimental,' you can take it they are about to do something cruel. And if they add, 'We **must be** realistic,' they mean they are going to make money out of it."* (Brigid Brophy, novelist, critic and crusader)

Extracted from: <www.goodreads.com/quotes/169257-whenever-people-say-we-mustn-t-be-sentimental-you-can-take>. Accessed on: Jun. 7, 2016.

*"Everyone has the potential to become an encourager. You **don't have to** be rich. You **don't have to** be a genius. You **don't have to** have it all together. All you **have to** do is care about people and initiate."* (John C. Maxwell, author, speaker and leadership expert)

Extracted from: <www.brainyquote.com/quotes/quotes/j/johncmaxw600870.html>. Accessed on: Jun. 7, 2016.

a. **Must** and **have to** are modal verbs used to express **an order/an obligation**. Use **must** in formal situations.

b. **Mustn't** is used to express **possibility/prohibition**.

c. **Don't have to/Must** is used to say that there is no obligation.

5. Circle the correct verb forms to complete the quote below.

"Perhaps everything that frightens us is, in its deepest essence, something helpless that wants our love. So you **have to/mustn't** be frightened, if a sadness rises in front of you, larger than any you have ever seen; if an anxiety, like light and cloud-shadows, moves over your hands and over everything you do. You **must/mustn't** realize that something is happening to you, that life has not forgotten you, that it holds you in its hand and **have to/will not** let you fall."

Extracted from: <www.goodreads.com/quotes/523573-perhaps-everything-that-frightens-us-is-in-its-deepest-essence>. Accessed on: Jun. 7, 2016.

Modals: may / might

6. Read this excerpt from UN Women Goodwill Ambassador Emma Watson's speech at a special event for the *HeForShe* campaign, in New York, and check the correct alternatives to complete the sentences.

"[...] These rights I consider to be human rights but I am one of the lucky ones. My life is a sheer privilege because my parents didn't love me less because I was born a daughter. My school did not limit me because I was a girl. My mentors didn't assume I would go less far because I might give birth to a child one day. These influencers were the gender equality ambassadors that made me who I am today. They may not know it, but they are the inadvertent feminists who are changing the world today. And we need more of those. [...]"

UNITED NATIONS

Extracted from: <www.unwomen.org/en/news/stories/2014/9/emma-watson-gender-equality-is-your-issue-too>
Accessed on: Jun. 7, 2016.

a. In *"I **might give** birth to a child one day"*, the verb form in bold indicates that

- ☐ Emma Watson is expressing an obligation.
- ☐ Emma Watson is expressing a possibility.

b. In *"They **may not know** it"*, Emma Watson means

- ☐ she is not sure whether they know it or not.
- ☐ she is sure they know it.

c. We use **may** and **might** to

- ☐ indicate we are sure that something will happen in the future.
- ☐ indicate possibility, something that has the chance of happening.

HANDS ON!

Ask a classmate: *What may/might happen if women don't stand up for their rights in the labor market*? Then change roles and tell him/her what you think may/might happen as well. Finally, report your opinions to the class.

Simple future: will

We use **will** to indicate a prediction and to express a promise to do something in the future.

Affirmative

Subject + **will** + main verb

Examples:

You **will** love this new Greek restaurant!

I **will** travel to France one day.

THINKSTOCK/GETTY IMAGES

Negative

Subject + **will** + **not** + main verb

Examples:

She **will not** come to school today.

They **will not** bring the cake for the party.

THINKSTOCK/GETTY IMAGES

Interrogative

Will + subject + main verb

Examples:

Will they give it back to me when it is finished?

Will we take something for seasickness before we embark?

KUMAR SRISKANDAN/ALAMY/FOTOARENA

Modals

Modal verbs belong to a group of verbs that usually follow the same structural rules and that are used to express different ideas; for example, possibility, obligation, ability, permission.

Affirmative

Subject + **modal verb** + main verb

Negative

Subject + **modal verb** + **not** + main verb

Interrogative

Modal verb + subject + main verb

modal verb	expresses	example
may	possibility	You **may** be lucky and buy the winning ticket.
might	possibility	I **might** become a father someday.
must	obligation	He **must** be over 18 to have a driver's license.
mustn't	prohibition	They **mustn't** keep your documents without your permission.
To express lack of obligation, use **don't have to**. Example: We **don't have to** wear a uniform at school.		

1. Choose the appropriate verb in the box to complete each sentence. Use **will**.

be	feel	get	help	please	turn	win

a. I forgot my notebook in the classroom. I ________________ it.

b. I believe my candidate ________________ the next election for president.

c. Stella is moving out and I ________________ her pack her things.

d. I ________________ very surprised if I pass this test.

e. It's hot today. I ________________ on the air conditioner.

f. If you eat another piece of cake, you ________________ sick later.

g. The director says his next movie ________________ his fans. (negative)

2. Choose the alternative that completes each sentence correctly.

a. It's very hot today, so you _____ drink some water.

☐ may ☐ must ☐ might

b. He likes you, so he _____ accept your offer.

☐ must ☐ might ☐ have to

c. Dad is working late, so he _____ not come home for dinner.

☐ may ☐ must ☐ have to

d. I am not good at Math, but I _____ be able to help you with this problem.

☐ must ☐ might ☐ have to

e. I _____ not go to the party.

☐ may ☐ mustn't ☐ have to

f. My mom said I _____ be back home before 11. It's a rule!

☐ may ☐ must ☐ might

g. She _____ play around the stove. It's too dangerous!

☐ may ☐ mustn't ☐ have to

h. It's a secret. You _____ tell anybody!

☐ may ☐ mustn't ☐ have to

i. I think we have to wait here. But I don't speak Italian, so I _____ be wrong.

☐ must ☐ might ☐ have to

j. The doctor said I _____ take this medicine for 2 weeks.

☐ may ☐ must ☐ might

LISTENING COMPREHENSION

BEFORE LISTENING

1. Do you know UN Women? According to the organization's official website: "UN Women focuses on priority areas that are fundamental to women's equality, and that can unlock progress across the board." Look at the following topics and check the ones you think that UN Women is related to.

a. ☐ Leadership and political participation.

b. ☐ Economic empowerment.

c. ☐ End of violence against women.

d. ☐ Peace and security.

e. ☐ Humanitarian action.

f. ☐ HIV and AIDS.

2. Why is there an organization that takes action in so many different areas in order to guarantee and broaden women's rights?

____

____

____

____

LISTENING

3. Listen to the introduction of a speech and identify which woman made it.

13

BARRY CHIN/BOSTON GLOBE/GETTY IMAGES

Sheryl Sandberg, Chief Operating Officer of Facebook

JUAN VITA/GETTY IMAGES

Michelle Bachelet, UN Women Executive Director

4. What was being celebrated when the speech was delivered?

____

____

____

____

5. Listen to the continuation of the speech and check the themes she addresses.

14

a. ☐ Benefits of guaranteeing women's rights around the world.

b. ☐ Names of people who are famous for fighting for women's rights.

c. ☐ How she became the leader of UN Women.

d. ☐ What has changed since the first International Women's Day.

e. ☐ UN Women's vision.

6. Listen again and write down at least one sentence that justifies each of the items you checked in activity 5.

15

____

____

____

____

____

____

____

____

____

7. According to Michelle Bachelet's speech, who benefits from having women's rights guaranteed around the world?

____

____

____

____

____

____

____

AFTER LISTENING

8. In pairs, discuss if you agree with this part of Michelle's speech.

> "I'm determined that UN Women will live up to the hopes of those who worked so hard to establish it, and will generate new energy bringing together people from every country, society and community in a shared endeavour."

Extracted from: <www.youtube.com/watch?v=4SZUUUS46qk>. Accessed on: Jun. 7, 2016.

SPEAKING

1. Choose an important woman to talk about. Follow these guidelines:

- The woman must be from your country.
- The woman can be alive or dead.
- The woman must have at least one big achievement in her life.

2. Work in small groups. Make a combined list of great women. Is there anything in common among the lists?

3. With your group, choose one woman from the combined list to talk about. You can use some of the sentences below to justify your choice or ask your classmates about their choices:

- We may choose… because she is/was famous for…
- I think we must talk about… because she…
- What do you know about her?
- What are/were her achievements?

4. Discuss with your group what you are going to present about the woman you chose in activity 3. Take notes on the topics you are going to cover.

____

____

____

____

____

____

5. Choose one person in the group to speak to the class about the woman you have chosen.

Reflecting on the theme

- Are there any important women in your city or state? Why are they important?
- Who are the most important women in Brazil? Why?

WRITING

BEFORE WRITING

1. Read the biographical fact sheet and answer the questions in your notebook.

http://famousfemalescientists.com/jane-goodall

Jane Goodall

Born: Apr. 3, 1934 in London, United Kingdom

Nationality: British

Famous For: Welfare of animals, conservation, study of chimpanzees

MITSUAKI IWAGO/BIOSPHOTO/AFP

Jane Goodall was born in London, England in 1934. She is famous for her study of chimpanzees in Tanzania. Goodall discovered primate behaviors that have continued to define the course of this science field. She is the world's foremost authority on these animals as she closely observed their behavior for about a quarter of a century. Goodall is a highly respected figure in the scientific community and is a strong advocate of ecological preservation.

[...]

Achievements and Contributions

Her research at the Gombe National Park is well known for uprooting two long standing beliefs; one being that humans were the only animals that could construct and utilize tools, and the other that chimps were passive-vegetarians.

Leakey and Jane began a crucial study of the chimpanzees in 1960 by the Lake Tanganyika in the Gombe Stream Reserve. The wild chimpanzees slowly revealed interesting habits. Such habits included eating meat. She also noted that the wild animals made certain tools from the bark of a tree that they used for extraction of termites. This was among the most important discoveries of her study because during that time, many people assumed that only human beings could make tools.

Extracted from: <famousfemalescientists.com/jane-goodall>. Accessed on: Jun. 7, 2016.

a. What is Jane Goodall's area of expertise?

b. What were Jane Goodall's two main discoveries?

c. Why were these discoveries important to Science?

2. Compare Jane Goodall's biographical fact sheet to the ones on pages 68 and 69. Then answer **T** (true) or **F** (false).

a. ☐ The biographical fact sheets present personal information about famous women.

b. ☐ The biographical fact sheets present the reasons that made these women famous worldwide.

c. ☐ The biographical fact sheets present an opinion about the actions taken by these women.

d. ☐ The main purpose of biographical fact sheets is to present a summary of each woman's life.

WRITING

3. In pairs, write a biographical fact sheet about a Brazilian woman who is famous for her social actions or achievements.
   - You may choose women from different areas: education, sports, culture, social work, animal protection, environmental protection, etc.
   - The person you choose does not have to be famous all over the country or worldwide. You can write about someone who is famous in your neighborhood, in your school, in your city or even in your family.
   - Research in books or websites and gather information about this woman. Remember to mention her birthplace and birthdate among other personal data.
   - If you choose to write about a woman from your community, city, school or family, you can interview people who know her and ask about her achievements or actions.
   - Don't forget to add the main information a biographical fact sheet reader expects to find in this kind of text: personal data and actions taken that made this person special or famous.
   - Write a draft of the fact sheet in your notebook.
   - You may use a dictionary if necessary.
   - Show your draft to your teacher.
   - Make the necessary adjustments and write the final version.

AFTER WRITING

- Exchange your biographical fact sheet with your classmates and check if:
  - the chosen person has done something important;
  - the reasons why she is famous are clear in the text.
- After you have finished, you can publish your work at the school website or blog. You can also share it on the classroom bulletin board.

SELF-EVALUATION

Check the true sentences about your learning in Unit 4.
In this unit you have learned to:

- [ ] read and write a biographical fact sheet;
- [ ] identify the names of some occupations;
- [ ] make future predictions, talk about obligations, prohibitions and possibilities.

Reflecting...

- **What did I learn about the use of verbs in the simple future?**
- **What did I learn about the modal verbs must / have / may / might?**
- **What questions do I have about the verbs we learned in this unit?**

Gender inequality

Gender inequality is still a reality around the world. Women earn 33% less than men and are concentrated in jobs with poor working conditions; 700 million women are victims of physical and/or sexual violence each year; men own and manage just under 70% of all businesses and women sit on only 19% of board seats globally; and two thirds of the 774 million illiterate adults worldwide are female.

YouGov, a company specialized in statistics, collected public opinion data on gender equality from 24 countries and the result of the survey is a clear picture of gender inequality. But it also highlights where gender equality is close to becoming a reality.

Global gender equality attitude ranking

Average net responses to ten agree/disagree statements, from representative adult populations in the following countries. **Higher scores show progressive attitudes to gender equality**

	Total	Men	Women
Sweden	72	70	73
Finland	68	65	72
Denmark	62	56	68
Australia	59	56	63
Norway	59	53	66
France	59	59	59
Britain	58	54	61
Germany	57	52	61
USA	49	46	51
China	44	35	55
Hong Kong	42	31	52
Singapore	41	31	51
Thailand	39	34	44
Indonesia	31	20	42
Malaysia	30	23	39
Lebanon	38	-	-
UAE	33	-	-
Tunisia	16	-	-
Iraq	14	-	-
Saudi Arabia	14	-	-
Jordan	10	-	-
Morocco	7	-	-
Egypt	6	-	-
Algeria	-11	-	-

Sweden

Sweden has repeatedly appeared at the top – or towards the top – of the World Economic Forum's Gender Gap Index and has been known as a place where gender equality is almost reality. It has one of the highest employment rates for women and steps have been made to split childcare responsibilities more equally, as both men and women have the right to 480 days of parental leave.

Finland

Women in Finland were the first in the world to fully exercise the right to vote and to be a candidate in elections. Now, the country ranks number one in terms of the percentage of women parliamentarians, where every 10 posts out of 18 is held by women.

Denmark

The YouGov survey found that 85% of Danish respondents said they believed women and men are equally intelligent – considerably higher than in the 18 Middle East and north African countries, where the figure was 48%.

Australia

Australia has taken a stance against female genital mutilation (FGM) and for the first time in the country's history, a court has found two women guilty of carrying out FGM on two young girls.

Norway

Norway is considered to be one of the most gender equal countries in the world, with paternity leave introduced in 1993 as a successful equality policy measure to change attitudes towards women. No Norwegian government has been formed with less than 40% women since the 1980s.

France

In 2014, France introduced sweeping gender equality laws that eased restrictions on abortion, encouraged fathers to take paternity leave and promoted gender parity at home.

Britain

Larger numbers of women are only now entering the workplace. But despite the Equal Pay Act being introduced 45 years ago, women still earn less than men in Britain today – so there is still a long way to go before Britain can be called a gender equal country.

Germany

Germany is leading the way in bridging the gender gap in science. Over the five years from 2010, the number of female researchers has risen more rapidly than the number of men, increasing by 25%.

USA

America ranks high globally in economic opportunities for women but it suffers from a shortage of women in power – and there are large regional disparities in regards to employment and earning, as southern women are the worst off. The status of women differs even further by race and ethnicity, with Hispanic women having the lowest median annual earnings compared to other women.

China

According to the YouGov research, Chinese people are more likely to prefer a female boss than respondents in Indonesia or Malaysia. Around 60% of respondents in China disagreed that "a wife's first role is to look after her husband" – compared with 27% in Indonesia and 31% in Malaysia.

Adapted from: <https://yougov.co.uk/news/2015/11/12/global-gender-equality-report/> and <www.ibtimes.co.uk/equal-rights-10-best-worst-countries-attitudes-towards-gender-equality-1528452>. Accessed on: Jan. 4, 2016.

1. How many of the top 10 countries in the list are located in Europe?
2. Which Scandinavian countries appear on the list?
3. Which countries are the top 10 worst countries for attitudes towards gender equality, based on the list?

UNIT

5

Which painting do you prefer?

Spanish artist Pablo Picasso (1881–1973) was not only an accomplished painter, but also a skilled sculptor, graphic artist and ceramist. He is considered one of the greatest artists of the 20th century.

In 1949, photographer Gjon Mili visited Picasso in France. Mili showed Picasso some of his photographs of ice skaters with light beams attached to their skates. Picasso was so impressed by the effect that he allowed Mili to photograph him in a dark room while making drawings of centaurs, buffalos and his own signature. This series of 30 photos became known as *Light Drawings*, and since then they have toured the world.

Your learning objectives for this unit are...

- to identify elements of a book front and back cover;
- to describe a work of art;
- to read and create front and back covers for a book.

EXCHANGING IDEAS

1. The image below is a photo of Picasso making a work of art and, by analyzing it, it is possible to recognize his artistic process. Which elements of the photo help us identify how Picasso created this piece?
2. Look at the light lines and describe them.

THE LIFE PICTURE COLLECTION/GETTY IMAGES

PICASSO, Pablo. *Light Drawing*. 1949. Photo by Gjon Mili/The LIFE Picture Collection/Getty Images, Vallauris, France.

- **www.picasso.com**
  Pablo Picasso's artwork on his official website.

- ***The Boy Who Bit Picasso***
  PENROSE, Antony. London: Thames and Hudson Ltd, 2010.
  Stories told by Antony Penrose about his childhood memories with the great artist Pablo Picasso.

5 Which painting do you prefer?

READING COMPREHENSION

TEXT 1

BEFORE READING

1. Famous paintings are displayed in art galleries and museums around the world and people admire them for lots of reasons. The text below presents a painting by Diego Velázquez. Look at the picture and answer: Which features are going to be presented in the text?

READING

2. Scan the text and find the original name of the painting.

THE MAIDS OF HONOR

By Diego Velázquez

DIEGO VELÁZQUEZ, THE MAIDS OF HONOUR, 1656. MUSEO NACIONAL DEL PRADO, MADRID, SPAIN.

Spain, 1656, oil paint on canvas, 10 ft 5 in x 9 ft 1 in (3.18 m x 2.76 m) – making the picture itself about lifesize.

This unusual portrait gives you a peek at royal life behind the scenes. It shows a young Spanish Princess, Margarita, surrounded by the everyday bustle of courtiers and servants – including the artist himself. "Maids of Honor" (In Spanish, *Las Meninas*) are the Queen's personal attendants.

Mirror image

At first glance, the princess seems to be the focus of attention. The other figures are neatly arranged around her, and the shadowy background shows off her pale, pretty hair and dress perfectly. But if you study their faces, she and several others are gazing out of the picture at something. What is it?

The answer lies in the mirror on the wall behind. It reveals a couple overlooking the scene – the King and Queen. King Philip disliked having his portrait painted as he grew older, but the artist cleverly found this way of including him anyway, creating a portrait not just of the princess, but of her parents too.

Look for touches of red across the picture. There is a red cup being offered to the princess on a golden tray.

There is also a red cross on the artist chest: this was probably added a few years later to commemorate an award the King gave him.

A little courtier dressed in red tries to rouse a sleeping dog with his foot.

Although it is still hazy, you can see the reflection of the King and Queen, standing under a red curtain, more clearly in this close-up.

Extracted from: DICKINS, Rosie. *The Usborne Book of Famous Paintings*. Pages 20-21. United Kingdom: Usborne, 2009.

3. Check the best alternatives to complete the sentences.

a. The environment in the painting is clearly rich because of the presence of

☐ luxurious clothes, servants, and courtiers in a big room.

☐ many paintings on the wall and a nun in the big room.

b. The little blonde girl in the white dress is a

☐ servant. ☐ princess.

c. The other people in the painting are

☐ princesses and artists.

☐ courtiers and servants.

d. The king didn't like to have his portrait painted because he was

☐ old. ☐ shy.

- **www.google.com/culturalinstitute/project/art-project?hl=pt-BR#**
  Google Art Project is a website that offers virtual tours of museums and art galleries around the world.

4. Join the parts to make true sentences about the painting.

a. The girl on her knees is offering	☐	at the King and the Queen.
b. Some people are gazing out	☐	a red cup to the princess on a golden tray.
c. The artist is the man	☐	talking to a courtier.
d. The sister seems to be	☐	rouse a sleeping dog with his foot.
e. The courtier is trying to	☐	with a red cross on his chest.

5. Use the sentences in activity 4 to answer the questions below.

a. What is the girl down on her knees doing?

____

b. Who are some people in the painting gazing at?

____

c. Which of the people in the painting is the artist?

____

d. Who is the sister talking to?

____

AFTER READING

- Choose a painting and present it to your classmates. You may choose one from a virtual visit to a museum or from an art book available in a library.
- After showing the chosen painting to your classmates, present the artist who created it. Remember to explain why you chose this painting.

TEXT 2

BEFORE READING

1. The painting reproduced on the following cover is one of the most famous in the world. Do you know its title and who painted it?

____

READING

2. Look at the cover, read the back cover of the book and check the correct answer.

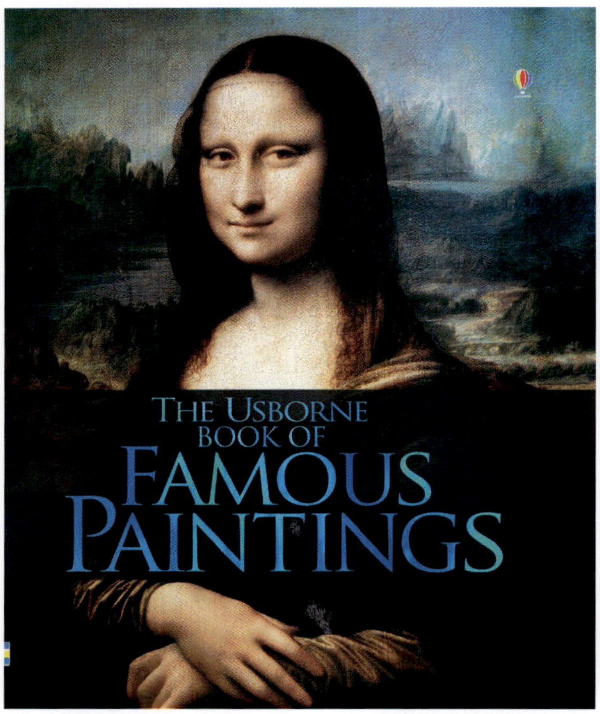

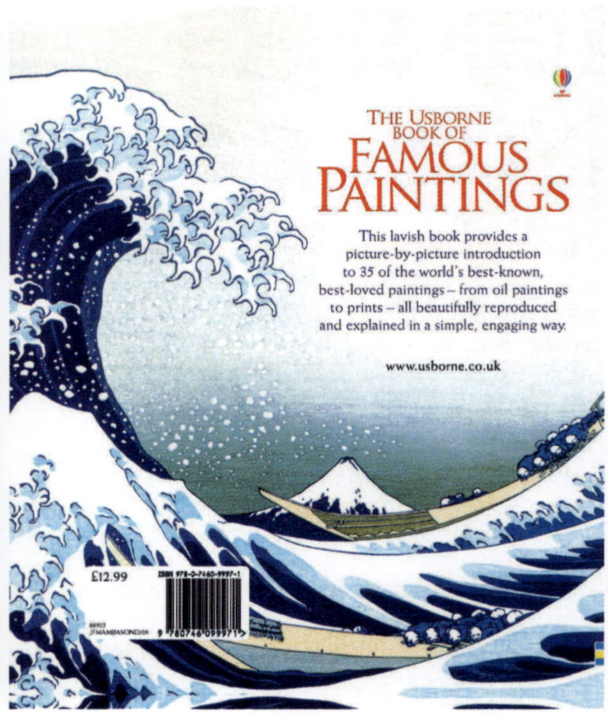

REPRODUCED FROM *THE USBORNE BOOK OF FAMOUS PAINTINGS* BY PERMISSION OF USBORNE PUBLISHING, 83-85 SAFFRON HILL, LONDON EC1N 8RT, UK. WWW.USBORNE.COM. COPYRIGHT © 2009 USBORNE PUBLISHING LTD.

Extracted from: DICKINS, Rosie. *The Usborne Book of Famous Paintings*. Front cover and back cover. United Kingdom: Usborne, 2009.

Why do you think these paintings were chosen to illustrate the front and the back covers?

a. ☐ Because they are famous masterpieces.

b. ☐ Because they belong to the author of the book.

3. Complete the chart with the information required.

Title	
Book genre	
Publishing house	
Price	

4. Look at the book cover again and, in pairs, answer these questions.

a. Do you think it captures the readers' attention? Why?

____

____

b. What kind of readers will the book capture the attention of?

____

____

c. Does it reflect the book's content? Explain.

____

____

d. Why are there two sizes of letters in the title?

____

____

____

5. Complete the following text with the words and expressions from the box.

back cover	convince	details	front cover	opportunity	paragraphs

Back Cover Elements

If you've gained a reader's attention with your ______________, they will most likely turn to the ______________ to gain more ______________ and make a decision about purchasing the book.

- Nonfiction books usually feature a few ______________ about the book's topic and may use bullet points or a list to cover specific subjects in the book.
- Fiction books usually feature an excerpt of the text and a brief plot synopsis. This text is the best ______________ for an author to ______________ shoppers to purchase their book. It deserves careful thought and attention.

[...]

Extracted from: <www.iuniverse.com/ExpertAdvice/DesignAndIllustration/CoverDesign.aspx#A>. Accessed on: Jun. 7, 2016.

AFTER READING

- Imagine you are writing a book. What characteristics should a book cover have to attract the readers' attention (kind of image, title)?
- What is the importance of the back cover to the reader?

FOCUS ON VOCABULARY

1. In "This unusual portrait gives you a peek at the royal life behind the scenes," which word qualifies the noun "portrait"?

____

2. Go back to the text on page 88, circle all the words that describe nouns and write them in the correct column of the chart below.

quality/opinion	size	age	color	nationality
unusual				
pretty				

3. Why do you think the author used those words in the text about the painting *The Maids of Honor*?

____

____

> To better understand a text, take into account the context and the purpose to which it was written.

4. Read the description of *The Great Wave*, which is printed on the back cover of *The Usborne Book of Famous Paintings*, and underline the words that describe the nouns.

The Great Wave

By Katsushika Hokusai

Japan 1829-33, ink and color on paper, 10 in × 15 in (26 cm × 38 cm)

Made nearly 200 years ago, this dramatic scene shows a huge wave about to crash over three tiny boats, with Japan's Mount Fuji just visible in the distance. A print rather than a painting, it has become one of the best-known examples of Japanese Art. [...]

KATSUSHIKA HOKUSAI, *THE GREAT WAVE*, C. 1831. LIBRARY OF CONGRESS, WASHINGTON D.C., USA.

Extracted from: DICKINS, Rosie. *The Usborne Book of Famous Paintings*. United Kingdom: Usborne, 2009. p. 30.

5. Use some of the words underlined in activity 4 to complete these sentences.

A

GUY BELL/REX FEATURES/KEYSTONE BRASIL

WIGAN, Willard. *Microscopic Art Exhibition*. 2015. Royal Thames Yacht Club, London, England.

These __________________ artworks by artist Willard Wigan prove that small can be incredibly beautiful.

Extracted from: <www.dailymail.co.uk/news/article-2893671/Small beautiful-Artist-create-micro-sculptures-sit-INSIDE-eyes-needles.html>. Accessed on: Jun. 7, 2016.

B

EGENE KOO, RED NARCISSIST1, 2014

KOO, Egene. *Red Narcissist 1*. 2014. Oil on canvas. 110 cm × 80 cm. Private Collection.

EGENE KOO, RED NARCISSIST2, 2014

KOO, Egene. *Red Narcissist 2*. 2014. Oil on canvas. 110 cm × 80 cm. Private Collection.

Looking at the paintings of Korean artist Egene Koo is like piecing together a puzzle. Her ______________________ red portraits of anthropomorphic characters are meant to be allegorical. [...]

Extracted from: <hifructose.com/2015/01/23/egene-koo-hides-allegory-in-dramatic-red-paintings/>. Accessed on: Jun. 7, 2016.

anthropomorphic characters: personagens antropomórficos (semelhantes ao homem)

C

PAUL MAROTTA/GETTY IMAGES

OSGEMEOS. Mural at the Boston Rose Fitzgerald Greenway. 2013. Boston, USA.

This August the ICA presents the first solo exhibition in the United States of Works by the Brazilian Brothers Otavio and Gustavo Pandolfo. ______________________ as Os Gemeos, the twins are a major force in graffiti and urban art. The twins have a deep bond; they are tireless collaborators and say that they often experience the same dreams.

Extracted from: <www.icaboston.org/exhibitions/os-gemeos>. Accessed on: Jun. 7, 2016.

ICA: The Institute of Contemporary Art (Boston, USA)

IT'S YOUR TURN!

Do some research in art books or on the internet and choose a painting you like very much. Write one or two sentences about the painting using the words you learned on the previous pages. Then share your sentences with a classmate.

LANGUAGE IN USE

Adjectives

1. Read the text from the back cover of *The Usborne Book of Famous Paintings* again and pay attention to the highlighted words. Then match the parts to form meaningful sentences.

> This lavish book provides a picture-by-picture introduction to 35 of the world's best-known, best-loved paintings – from oil paintings to prints – all beautifully reproduced and explained in a simple, engaging way.

a. Adjectives are used to describe

b. In English, adjectives don't have plural forms

c. In most cases, adjectives are positioned

d. A compound adjective corresponds to two or more words that

e. When we have more than one adjective to describe a noun,

☐ or gender distinctions.

☐ can be connected by hyphens.

☐ or qualify nouns (things, people or places).

☐ we order them from the most general to the most specific.

☐ before the nouns they describe.

Comparative adjectives

2. Read the texts and answer the questions that follow.

damages: danos
concealed and hidden: ocultados e escondidos
rather than: em vez de

TEXT 1

Kintsugi, The Japanese Art of Fixing Broken Pottery With Gold

Most people would like damages to their broken items to be concealed and hidden by repair making the object look like new. But the Japanese art of Kintsugi follows a different philosophy. Rather than disguising the breakage, Kintsugi restores the broken item incorporating the damage into the aesthetic of the restored item, making it part of the object's history. Kintsugi uses lacquer resin mixed with powdered gold, silver, platinum, copper or bronze, resulting into something more beautiful than the original. [...]

Tea bowl fixed in the Kintsugi method.

Extracted from: <www.amusingplanet.com/2014/05/kintsugi-japanese-art-of-fixing-broken.html>. Accessed on: Jun. 7, 2016.

a. Does this art of restoring make the broken items look the same as they were before being broken?

____

b. Copy the part of the text that states the result of the comparison between the broken object and the original one.

____

TEXT 2

formerly: antigamente
likenesses: semelhanças

The Hyperrealistic Sculptures of Ron Mueck

ALAN TAYLOR

London-based sculptor Ron Mueck, formerly a model maker and puppeteer for children's television and films, has been creating fine art sculptures since 1996. Using resin, fiberglass, silicone, and many other materials, Mueck constructs hyperrealistic likenesses of human beings, while playing with scale. The detailed sculptures are captivating when viewed up close, as they may be many times larger or smaller than expected.

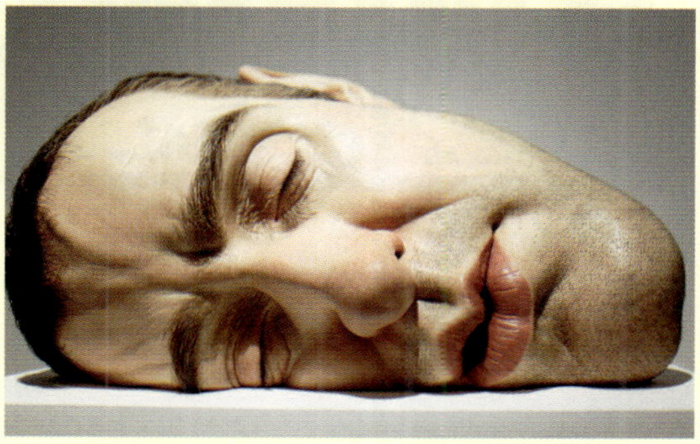
HENRY ROMERO/REUTERS/LATINSTOCK

A sculpture entitled *Mask II* by sculptor Ron Mueck, at the San Ildefonso Museum in Mexico City, on September 20, 2011.

Extracted from: <www.theatlantic.com/photo/2013/10/the-hyperrealistic-sculptures-of-ron-mueck/100606/>. Accessed on: Jun. 7, 2016.

a. Do Ron Mueck's sculptures have the same shape as human beings?

____

b. Are all the sculptures the same size?

____

c. Copy the part of the text that states the sculptures have different sizes.

____

3. Read these excerpts from text 1 and text 2 again and pay attention to the expressions in bold. Then underline the best alternatives to complete the sentences.

*"The detailed sculptures are captivating when viewed up close, as they may be many times **larger** or **smaller than** expected."*

*"Kintsugi uses lacquer resin mixed with powdered gold, silver, platinum, copper or bronze, resulting into something **more beautiful than** the original."*

a. The structures "larger" or "smaller than" and "more beautiful than" are used **to talk about unique things/to make comparisons**.

b. We add **more/-er** to make the comparative form of most short adjectives and we use "more" **before/after** the adjective to make the comparative form of long adjectives.

c. The word **that/than** is used after the comparative form when we mention the other thing compared.

4. Look at two of the most valuable paintings in private hands. Read the sentences that compare them and write **T** (true) or **F** (false). Then, in your notebook correct the false statements.

SANDRO BOTTICELLI, FESTA NO CASAMENTO DO CAVALEIRO NASTAGIO DEGLI ONESTI, 1483

Author: Sandro Botticelli
Work: "The Story of Nastagio degli Onesti (fourth episode)", c.1483 tempera on panel, 83 × 142 cm.
Private collection, Florence
[...]
(*) $70-100 million
[...]
(*) Open market valuation. However, due to Italian export restriction the painting can not be sold to a foreign buyer.

VAN GOGH, SELF-PORTRAIT WITH BAN, 1889

Author: Vincent van Gogh
Work: "Self-portrait with bandaged ear", 1889 oil on canvas, 60.5 × 50 cm.
Niarchos collection
[...]
$100-140 million
[...]

> • ***Starry Starry Night***
> Lyrics by Don McLean
> A tribute to Vincent van Gogh; the song describes *The Starry Night*, one of the Dutch artist's most famous paintings.

Extracted from: <www.theartwolf.com/articles/most-valuable-private-art.htm>. Accessed on: Jun. 7, 2016.

a. ☐ The painting *The Story of Nastagio degli Onesti (fourth episode)* is more recent than the painting *Self-portrait with bandaged ear*.

b. ☐ The painting *Self-portrait with bandaged ear* is larger than the painting *The Story of Nastagio degli Onesti (fourth episode)*.

c. ☐ The painting *Self-portrait with bandaged ear* is estimated to be more expensive than the painting *The Story of Nastagio degli Onesti (fourth episode)*.

5. Check the alternative that best completes the quotes below.

a. "It is not the language of painters but the language of nature which one should listen to, the feeling for the things themselves, for reality, is ______________________ the feeling for pictures." – Vincent van Gogh

b. "On the floor I am more at ease. I feel ____________, more a part of the painting, since this way I can walk around it, work from the four sides and literally be in the painting." – Jackson Pollock

Extracted from: <www.dionarchibald.com/ArtQuotes/art.htm>. Accessed on: Jun. 7, 2016.

☐ more important / near

☐ more important than / nearer

HANDS ON!

Take a classroom survey. Ask four classmates different questions about their favorite kinds of art. You can use, for example: *What's your favorite kind of art? Why do you think this is more interesting than...?* Then report the results of the survey to your classmates and teacher.

Adjectives

We use **adjectives** to describe or qualify nouns. In English, adjectives don't have plural or gender distinction.

THINKSTOCK/GETTY IMAGES

He is a very **hard-working** teacher.

THINKSTOCK/GETTY IMAGES

This artwork looks very **intriguing**.

Comparative adjectives

The **comparative form of adjectives** is used for comparing one person or thing with another.

ERICK NGUYEN/ALAMY/FOTOARENA

The purple house is **smaller than** the blue house.

RICHARD LEVINE/ALAMY/FOTOARENA

The TV on the right is **more expensive** than the TV on the left.

With short adjectives, add **-er** to the adjective to form its comparative.

adjective	comparative form
long	long**er**
old	old**er**
small	small**er**

When short adjectives end in **vowel + consonant**, double the final consonant before **-er**.

adjective	comparative form
big	bi**gger**
fat	fa**tter**
thin	thi**nner**

When short adjectives end in **-y**, remove the **-y** and add **-ier**.

adjective	comparative form
angry	angr**ier**
busy	bus**ier**
happy	happ**ier**

Some adjectives are **irregular**, so they don't follow any of these rules.

adjective	comparative form
bad	worse
far	farther/further
good	better

To form the comparative of long adjectives, add **more** before the adjective.

adjective	comparative form
careful	**more** careful
expensive	**more** expensive
interesting	**more** interesting

1. Find and underline the adjectives in the sentences below.

a. I think her attitude was inconsequential; she should be more careful next time.

b. Look at this room! It is so messy! You should clean it up right now!

c. I love rainy days, they are so relaxing, and I can just read and watch TV all day!

d. I can't believe she won the first prize! She is so lucky!

e. She is very experienced and talented; I think she is perfect for the job.

2. Use the comparative form of the adjectives in parentheses to complete the sentences.

a. This loaf of bread was made this morning, so it's ________________ than the others. (fresh)

b. You need to keep medicine in a ________________ cabin, so the kids can't reach it. (high)

c. They preferred to see the horror movie because they thought it was ________________________ than the comedy. (entertaining)

d. Things usually seem ______________________________ than they really are. (complicated)

e. If you enjoy the summer, you should go to Rio because it's ___________________ there! (hot)

f. My room is never messy and it's always ________________ than my sister's. (tidy)

g. In my opinion, Japanese food is ________________ than Chinese food. (good)

3. Look at OSGEMEOS' mural and Wigan's artwork on page 93 again. Compare them using the adjectives below.

a. (colorful) ____

____

____

b. (old) ____

____

____

c. (big) ____

____

____

d. (creative) In my opinion, ____

____

____

LISTENING

BEFORE LISTENING

1. Look at the paintings below. Which one is your favorite? Why?

A

DEREK O'CONNOR, MELT, 2006

O'CONNOR, Derek. *Melt*. 2006. Oil on canvas. 121 cm × 244 cm. National Gallery of Australia, Canberra, Australia.

B

THE BRIDGEMAN ART/LIBRARY/KEYSTONE BRASIL

PISSARRO, Camile. *White Frost*. 1873. Oil on canvas. 65 cm × 93 cm. Musée d'Orsay, Paris, France.

C

CLAUDE MONET, WOMEN IN THE GARDEN, 1866

MONET, Claude. *Women in the Garden*. 1866. Oil on canvas. 255 cm × 205 cm. Musée d'Orsay, Paris, France.

- **Portinari**
  TRZMIELINA, Nadine. São Paulo: Callis, 2009.
  A book about Candido Portinari's life, with images of his artwork.

D

CANDIDO PORTINARI, MORRO, 1933

PORTINARI, Candido. *Hill*. 1933. Oil on canvas. 144 cm × 145.7 cm. Museum of Modern Art, New York, USA.

E

LASAR SEGALL, PAISAGEM BRASILEIRA, 1925

SEGALL, Lasar. *Paisagem Brasileira*. 1925. Oil on canvas. 64 cm × 54 cm. Museu Lasar Segall, São Paulo, Brazil.

F

VIK MUNIZ, SHANGHAI POSTCARD (POSTCARDS FROM NOWHERE), 2014

MUNIZ, Vik. *Shanghai Postcard* (Postcards from Nowhere). 2014. Digital c-print. 180.3 cm × 256 3 cm. Ben Brown Fine Arts, London, United Kingdom.

LISTENING

2. Listen to an artist talking about one of his paintings and answer.

16

a. Who is the artist?

____

b. What's the name of the painting he is describing?

____

c. What is the painting about?

____

d. What inspired him to paint this?

____

3. Listen to a description of the colors he used in this painting. What were they? Circle the correct ones.
17 Then write their names.

SHUTTERSTOCK

____

____

____

____

____

4. Listen to the last part of the audio. Where is it possible to see the painting *Melt*?

18 ____

5. Based on what Derek said about how important the purchase of his painting was, answer: What are the benefits of art galleries?

____

AFTER LISTENING

6. Derek mentions his inspiration for *Melt* came from a series of photographs and a film he watched. Do you think all the artists get inspiration the same way?

7. How can what we watch, listen to, or do, influence or inspire us? Have you ever felt inspired to do something because of something else? Discuss and share your experiences with your classmates and teacher.

SPEAKING

1. What aspects of the painting did you hear Derek describe?

a. ☐ Colors and equipment he used.

b. ☐ How long it took him to paint it.

c. ☐ The size of the canvas he used.

d. ☐ What inspired him to paint it.

e. ☐ Where the painting is exposed.

f. ☐ The techniques he applied.

2. Are the aspects you didn't check in activity 1 also possible to be included in a painting description? Are there any other aspects you would include?

____

____

____

____

____

3. Go back to page 99 and look at the paintings again. Choose one of them and do research to find the information listed in activity 1 about the painting you chose. You can search on the internet or in books. You don't have to find all the items listed and you can take notes on other different and interesting information you find. Make your notes below.

____

____

____

____

____

____

4. Make groups with the people who did the research about the same painting you did. Share the information you found and prepare a group presentation about it. Divide the presentation into parts and decide what each student is going to talk about. Listen to Derek again (tracks 16,17, and 18) and then do your own presentation. Remember to include greetings and a closure.

Reflecting on the theme

- In this unit we presented some artworks that use the painting technique as a way of expression. Do research on websites or in museums about other forms of art expression. Then present it to your classmates.
- Who are the most famous Brazilian exponents in visual arts? What are their most famous paintings? Do research on that and present it to your classmates.

BEFORE WRITING

1. Look at the pictures and write down which one is the *front cover* and which is the *back cover*.

______________________ ______________________

2. Compare the elements from these front and back covers to the ones on page 90. Then read the statements and write **FC** (front cover) and/or **BC** (back cover).

a. ☐ This cover can present one or more images.

b. ☐ It is very common to find here a short description of the book and/or some other information about the book or the author.

c. ☐ It presents the title of the book, its subtitle – if there is one – and, sometimes, the author's and coauthor's full names.

d. ☐ It usually shows the publisher's name and/or logo.

e. ☐ The publisher's or the author's website, when divulged, is printed on this cover.

f. ☐ For this cover, the title of the book is not necessary, but it is recommended.

g. ☐ This cover includes a bar code and a unique ISBN number.

> The International Standard Book Number (ISBN) is an international numeric commercial book identifier. With the ISBN, it's possible to identify the book's title, author, publisher, and country of origin.

WRITING

3. In groups, follow the steps to create new covers for *The Usborne Book of Famous Paintings*.
    - In your notebook, make a checklist of all the elements your covers should have.
    - Write a draft of the text for the new covers – front and back – of *The Usborne Book of Famous Paintings*.
    - Include a new title and a description to go on the back cover.
    - Share your work with a classmate and revise it together.
    - Ask the teacher to revise your work.
    - Then correct your work as needed and include your teacher's suggestions.
    - On an appropriate piece of paper, produce the covers.
    - You can make some drawings or glue appropriate images to illustrate them.
    - Verify if your covers present the elements from the checklist.

AFTER WRITING

- Show your covers to your classmates.
- All the students vote for the best covers.
- Pin the best covers to the bulletin board in your classroom.
- If possible, invite students from other classes to see your work.

SELF-EVALUATION

Check the true sentences about your learning in Unit 5.
In this unit you have learned to:

- [ ] identify elements of a book front and back cover;
- [ ] describe a work of art;
- [ ] read and create front and back covers for a book.

Reflecting

- **What did I learn about the use of adjectives?**
- **What questions do I still have about the creation of front and back covers?**
- **Which artwork did I like best? Why?**
- **Which artwork did I dislike? Why?**

UNIT

6

What's this story about?

English painter Seymour Joseph Guy (1824-1910) became famous during the mid-nineteenth century as one of the best painters of children. He was very respected for his technical ability and knowledge of the science of painting, but with the emergence of a younger generation of European artists in the 1880s, Guy's paintings of children began to fall out of fashion. In recent decades his art and talent have been reappraised by museums, scholars, and collectors of early American art.

Your learning objectives for this unit are...

- to read and identify elements of a fairy tale;
- to describe places;
- to tell a story, describing characters and places;
- to write a new ending for a fairy tale.

EXCHANGING IDEAS

1. The image below is entitled *An Interesting Book*. What elements of the painting illustrate this title?
2. What kind of book do you think it is?
3. What kinds of books do you like reading? When do you usually read?

SEYMOUR JOSEPH GUY, AN INTERESTING BOOK, 1852

GUY, Seymour Joseph. *An Interesting Book*. 1852. Oil on canvas, 21.59 cm × 26.04 cm. Private collection.

6 What's this story about?

READING COMPREHENSION

TEXT 1

BEFORE READING

1. Do you know the story "Beauty and the Beast"? If so, share it with your classmates. If not, imagine what the story is about and talk to the whole class.

READING

2. Skim the illustrations and the text. Who might these characters be?

____

ONCE there was a rich man who had a lot of ships. He lived in a big white house by the sea. He had three daughters and three sons. His daughters were all beautiful. But the most beautiful was the youngest daughter, and because she was so beautiful, everyone called her 'Beauty'.

Beauty was a kind and clever girl. She loved reading. Her two older sisters were not as nice as Beauty. They were often nasty to her. And they laughed at her, because she loved books. They only liked to wear fine clothes and go to parties.

ILLUSTRATED BY CLAIRE POUND/OXFORD UNIVERSITY PRESS

Extracted from: ARENGO, Sue. "Beauty and the Beast". *Classic Tales*, Elementary 1, Oxford. England: Oxford University Press, 1995. p. 2.

3. Read the excerpt from the fairy tale on the previous page and check the true statements.

a. ☐ There are seven people in Beauty's family.

b. ☐ Beauty and her sisters have the same likes.

c. ☐ Beauty's sisters are older than she is.

d. ☐ The family lives in a very simple house.

e. ☐ The two sisters are superficial and vain.

- **fairytalesoftheworld.com/**
  Fairy tales from around the world. It's possible to narrow the search by story, author or country of origin.
- **www.storynory.com/archives/fairy-tales/**
  A selection of text and audio of classic and modern fairy tales.
- **www.youtube.com/user/teatrodecontosdefada/featured**
  The classic series *Contos de Fadas*, originally broadcasted by TV Cultura.

4. Answer these questions.

a. Which characters are mentioned in the excerpt?

b. What do Beauty's sisters do when they see her reading books?

c. What adjectives are used in the text to describe Beauty?

d. What kind of image does the text transmit about Beauty?

5. Read another page from the same fairy tale and do the activities that follow.

And Beauty was happy. She and her prince had a wonderful wedding. Her three brothers came and so did her father.

'Oh, dear Father!' she said. 'Now you can come and live with me always!'

But Beauty's two older sisters and their husbands did not come.

'I have sent them far away,' said the good fairy, 'because they were nasty and unkind. They will never find their way to this palace. You will never see them again, until, perhaps, one day ... if they learn to be kind.'

'I will wait for that day,' said Beauty.

ILLUSTRATED BY CLAIRE POUND/OXFORD UNIVERSITY PRESS

Extracted from: ARENGO, Sue. "Beauty and the Beast". *Classic Tales*, Elementary 1, Oxford. England: Oxford University Press, 1995. p. 27.

6. Answer the questions according to the story.

a. Who are the main characters?

____

b. Who attended the wedding?

____

7. Read the excerpt on page 107 again and correct the sentences below. You can use a dictionary to help you if necessary.

a. Beauty doesn't get married. She ends up living with her family.

____

____

b. The prince becomes Beauty's friend.

____

____

c. The good fairy casts a spell and Beauty's sisters become good people.

____

____

d. Beauty has no hope of seeing her sisters again.

____

____

8. Check some of the common characteristics of fairy tales.

	YES	NO
a. They are usually set in a dreamtime that is far from reality.		
b. Talking creatures are not common.		
c. Good is rewarded and evil is punished.		
d. The princesses are mean.		
e. There is a happy ending.		
f. There is a good fairy to help and protect the protagonist.		

AFTER READING

- What other fairy tales do you know?
- What do they have in common with "The Beauty and the Beast" story?

TEXT 2

BEFORE READING

1. Look at the cartoons, but don't read the texts yet. Can you predict what they are about just by looking at them?

READING

2. Match the cartoons to their corresponding sentences.

☐ According to the fairy tale, Pinocchio was a puppet made of wood and brought to life by a good fairy. His biggest dream was to become a real boy. His wish came true, but now he feels bored again.

☐ Frogs are endangered because they become princes when they are kissed, like the ones in fairy tales.

3. What do both cartoons have in common?

____

____

____

In both cartoons about fairy tales there is a creation of a text based on another well-known text. This literary device is known as intertextuality.

AFTER READING

- By bringing famous fairy tale characters into another context, we give a new meaning to them. What is the purpose of the cartoons?

FOCUS ON VOCABULARY

1. Complete the words below. Then match these words to their corresponding pictures.

a. F _____ _____ R Y

b. P _____ L _____ C _____

c. P R _____ N C _____

d. W _____ D D _____ N G

MARY EVANS PICTURE LIBRARY/OTHER IMAGES

MARY EVANS PICTURE LIBRARY/OTHER IMAGES

TIM ROOKE/REX FEATURES/GLOW IMAGES

ROBERT HARDING/DIOMEDIA

2. Look at the pictures and read the texts. Then use the words from the box to complete them.

bored	endangered	makeover	tint

a. Whales are at the top of the food chain and have an important role in the overall health of the marine environment. Unfortunately their large size and mythical aura does not protect them; seven out of the 13 great whale species are classified as _________________ or vulnerable, even after decades of protection. [...]

Extracted from: <www.worldwildlife.org/species/whale>. Accessed on: Jun. 7, 2016.

ALEXANDER SAFONOV/GETTY IMAGES

b. [...] Hair _________________ is a hair dye designed to permanently change the colour of your hair. [...]

Extracted from: <www.hair-styles-and-tips.com/hair-tint.html>. Accessed on: Mar. 8, 2015.

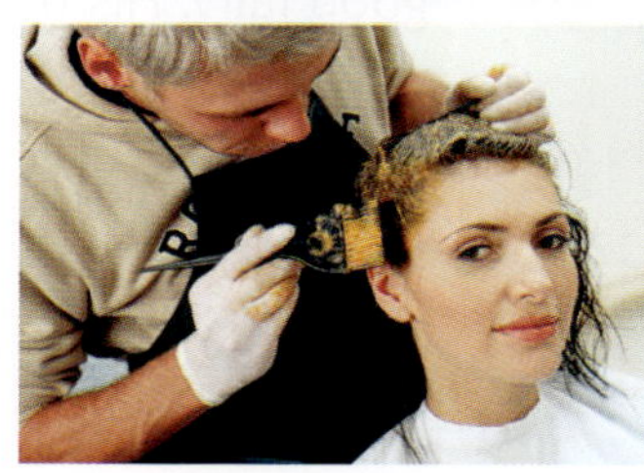

AGE FOTOSTOCK/AGB PHOTO

c. [...] _________________ teens are more likely to eat, particularly junk food, according to the Women's and Children's Health Network. As they sit around wondering what to do, they might mindlessly snack, which combined with a lack of exercise can result in unhealthful weight gain. [...]

Extracted from: <everydaylife.globalpost.com/happens-teens-bored-5096.html>. Accessed on: Jun. 7, 2016.

THINKSTOCK/GETTY IMAGES

d. [...] If your bedroom feels bland and you think it could use some major upgrading, you may want to give it a _________________! You can make your bedroom look its best simply by tidying up and giving it some beautifying flair. [...]

Extracted from: <www.wikihow.com/Makeover-Your-Bedroom>. Accessed on: Jun. 7, 2016.

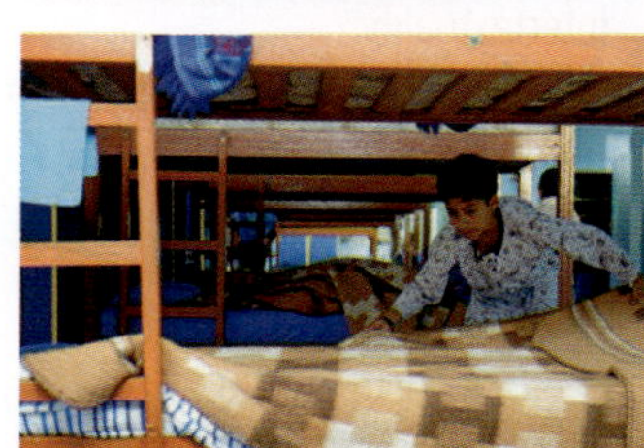

FLORIAN KOPP/ALAMY/LATINSTOCK

Book genres

3. Label the pictures with the words from the box. Then read the definitions and write the corresponding book genre. Use a dictionary if necessary.

autobiography comic book fable fantasy mystery poetry science fiction tragedy

A

REPRODUÇÃO

____

B
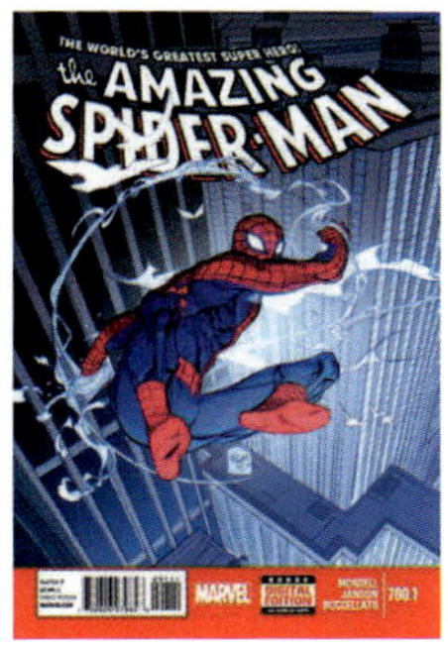

MARVEL

____

C
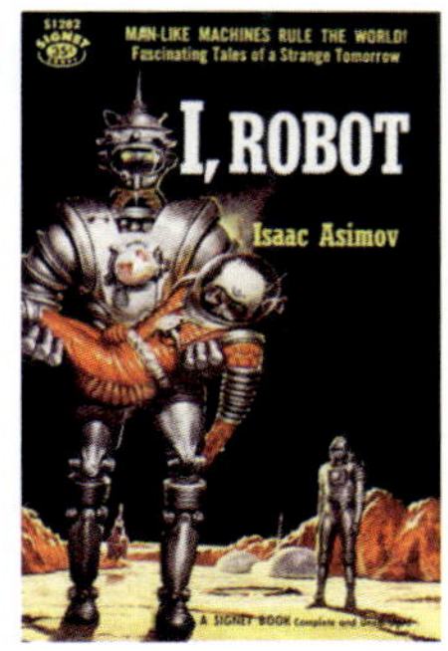

SIGNET BOOK

____

D

REPRODUÇÃO

____

E
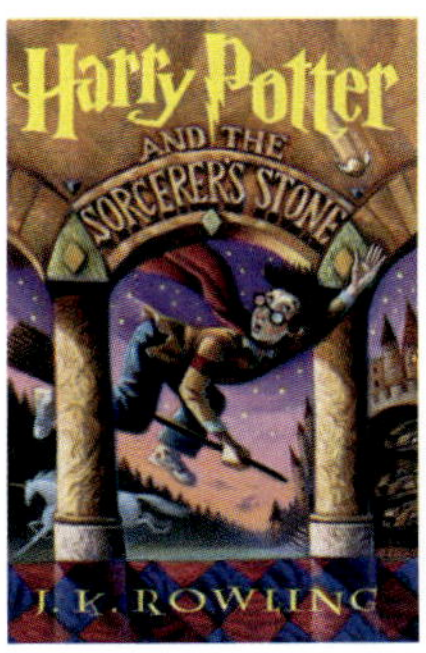

POTTERMORE LIMITED

____

F

ASHLEY BRYAN

____

G

SOVEREIGN

____

H
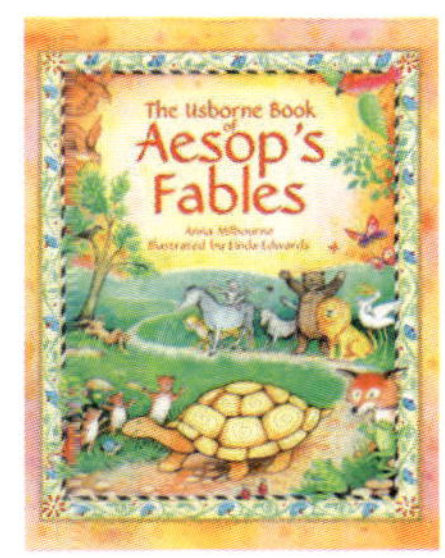

THE USBORNE BOOK

____

Definitions	Book genres
a. A story about a murder, in which you are not told who the murderer is until the end.	
b. A publication that tells a story using comic strips.	
c. A story about events in the future which are affected by imaginary developments in science, for example, travelling in time or to other planets with life on them.	
d. A book in which someone writes about their own life.	
e. A story set in a magic world.	
f. A literary composition written in verse.	
g. A play in which the main characters are overcome by sad events or die at the end.	
h. A traditional short story that teaches a moral lesson, especially a story about animals.	

Adapted from: <www.ldoceonline.com/>. Accessed on: Jun. 7, 2016.

IT'S YOUR TURN!

In pairs, ask a classmate about the kind of books he/she likes reading. You can ask: *What kind of books do you like reading?* Take turns. Then report the information to the whole group.

There to be (simple past)

1. Read the beginning of the fairy tale "Goldilocks and the Three Bears" and check the correct answers to the questions.

This is the story of three bears and a little girl called Goldilocks.
The three bears lived in a house in the forest. There was a father bear, a mother bear and a baby bear.
Father bear was the biggest bear. He was very big. Mother bear was smaller than father bear. And the smallest bear was baby bear. He was a very little bear.

ANTON BRAND/SHUTTERSTOCK

HAGAQUEZART ESTÚDIO

In the bears' house there were three chairs: a very big chair for father bear, a smaller chair for mother bear and a little chair for baby bear.

There were three bowls on the table: a very big bowl for father bear, a smaller bowl for mother bear and a little bowl for baby bear.
And upstairs in the bedroom there were three beds: a very big bed for father bear, a smaller bed for mother bear and a little bed for baby bear.

Extracted from: ARENGO, Sue. "Goldilocks and the Three Bears". *Classic Tales*, Elementary 1, Oxford. England: Oxford University Press, 1996. pages 2 and 3.

a. Who lived in a house in the forest?

☐ Goldilocks. ☐ The three bears.

b. How many baby bears were there in father bear's family?

☐ There was only one baby bear. ☐ There were two baby bears.

c. Was there a bowl for Goldilocks on the table?

☐ Yes, there was. ☐ No, there wasn't.

d. Were there beds for the three bears?

☐ Yes, there were. ☐ No, there weren't.

2. Go back to activity 1 and circle the correct words or expressions to complete these sentences.

a. We use **there was** and **there were** to talk about the existence of someone or something in the **present/past**. The verb form **there was/there were** is used in the singular and **there was/there were** is used in the plural.

b. In the interrogative form, we use **was there and were there/there was and there were**. In the negative form, we use **there was not (there wasn't)** and **there were not (there weren't)**.

c. When we have a list of things and the first item of that list is singular, we use **there to be** in the **singular/plural** form.

3. Read the opening lines from the fairy tales "The Tale of Peter the Rabbit" and "The Elves and the Shoemaker" and complete them with **there was** or **there were**.

a. Once upon a time ____________________ four little Rabbits, and their names were Flopsy, Mopsy, Cotton-tail, and Peter. They lived with their Mother in a sand-bank, underneath the root of a very big fir-tree. […]

Extracted from: <etc.usf.edu/lit2go/148/peter-rabbit-and-other-stories/4923/the-tale-of-peter-rabbit/>. Accessed on: Jun. 7, 2016.

b. ____________________ once a shoemaker, who worked very hard and was very honest: but still he could not earn enough to live upon; and at last all he had in the world was gone, save just leather enough to make one pair of shoes. […]

Extracted from: <www.authorama.com/grimms-fairy-tales-39.html>. Accessed on: Jun. 7, 2016.

underneath: embaixo
fir-tree: pinheiro
leather: couro

Superlative adjectives

4. This is an excerpt from the fairy tale on page 112. Pay attention to the structures in bold and answer the questions.

[…]

Father bear was **the biggest** bear. He was very big. Mother bear was smaller than father bear. And **the smallest** bear was baby bear. He was a very little bear. […]

a. In *"Father bear was **the biggest** bear"* and *"And **the smallest** bear was baby bear"*, does the author compare father bear to baby bear or to the whole family?

____

b. Who do you think is **the most important** bear in the family? Justify your answer.

____

____

c. Look at the pictures of the three chairs on page 112. In your opinion, which one is the best chair?

____

____

Irregular superlative forms:
good: the best
bad: the worst

5. Use the words and expressions from the box to make meaningful sentences about superlatives.

-est	group	the most	to compare	vowel

a. The superlative is used when we want ____________ people, things or actions to other people, things or actions that also belong to the same ____________.

b. To form the superlative of short adjectives, we add ____________ at the end of the word. For adjectives ending in **e**, we add **-st**.

c. For short adjectives ending in **consonant** + ____________ + **consonant**, we double the last consonant before adding **-est** at the end.

d. Before long adjectives, we use ____________ or **the least**.

6. Read the comic strips and choose the alternatives that best complete the speech bubbles.

A

☐ the greatest / the bravest / the smartest

☐ greater than / the bravest / smart

B

☐ The worst / worse

☐ The best / the worst

HANDS ON!

Complete the sentences below according to your personal opinion. Then, share your sentences with your classmates and your teacher. Compare your ideas to your friends. Does anybody have similar answers?

The most interesting classic tale I know is ____________.

The saddest book I've read is ____________.

The best movie based on a book is ____________.

There to be (simple past)

We use **there to be** in simple past to say that something existed or didn't exist.

Affirmative

There was + singular noun	**There was** a fly in my soup, so I returned it.
There were + plural noun	**There were** many people at the concert yesterday.

Interrogative

Was there + singular noun	**Was there** a girl with red hair in our class last year?
Were there + plural noun	**Were there** shoe stores at the mall you visited?

Negative

There wasn't + singular noun	**There wasn't** anyone here last weekend.
There weren't + plural noun	**There weren't** balloons in the party, only wall decoration.

Superlative adjectives

Superlative adjectives are used for saying that a person or thing has more of a quality than a whole group of people or things.

	adjectives	superlative form
With short adjectives, add **-est** to the adjective to form its superlative.	long, old, small	long**est**, old**est**, small**est**
When one-syllable adjectives end in **consonant + vowel + consonant**, double the final consonant before **-est**.	big, fat, thin	big**gest**, fat**test**, thin**nest**
When short adjectives end in **-y**, remove the **-y** and add **-iest**.	angry, busy	angr**iest**, bus**iest**
Some adjectives are irregular, so they don't follow any of these rules.	bad good	worst best
To form the superlative of long adjectives (three or more syllables), add **most** or **least** before the adjective.	careful, expensive	**most** careful, **least** expensive

1. How different were cities 50 years ago? Write 5 sentences using **there to be** to describe what existed or didn't exist back then. Use affirmative and negative sentences.

ARQUIVO/ESTADÃO CONTEÚDO/AE/

a. ______________________________

b. ______________________________

c. ______________________________

d. ______________________________

e. ______________________________

2. Choose the correct option to complete the sentences.

a. The bookstore opened ______________________ usual today.

☐ later than ☐ the latest

b. The third book was ______________________ of the trilogy.

☐ sadder ☐ the saddest

c. It's ______________________ to do online shopping.

☐ more convenient ☐ the most convenient

d. Don't be afraid! What's ______________________ thing that can happen?

☐ worse ☐ the worst

e. Skydiving was ______________________ experience of my life.

☐ more exciting ☐ the most exciting

LISTENING COMPREHENSION

BEFORE LISTENING

1. Label the reading situations with the expressions from the box. Then check which of these situations are usual in your life.

at a restaurant	at bedtime	in a library	in class	during leisure time
on the bus/subway/in the car	with classmates at school	with friends	with parents	

HENRY ARDEN/CULTURA/CORBIS/LATINSTOCK

____

BLEND IMAGES / MASTERFILE / LATINSTOCK

____

THINKSTOCK/GETTY IMAGES

____

MASTERFILE/LATINSTOCK

____

THINKSTOCK/GETTY IMAGES

____

MASTERFILE/LATINSTOCK

____

AGE RM/OTHER IMAGES

____

INGRAM/OTHER IMAGES

____

DE ASÍS/EASYPIX

____

LISTENING

2 Listen to John Green's interview and choose the best title for it.

19

a. ☐ John Green reads frequently!

b. ☐ John Green talks about reading!

c. ☐ "My father reads a lot", says John Green.

3. Listen to John Green's interview again. Check all the reasons why he enjoyed his reading moments as a kid. 20

a. ☐ During his reading moments with his parents, they talked about interesting subjects.

b. ☐ John's reading moments with his parents were special one-on-one times for John.

c. ☐ He read *Kon-Tiki* all by himself and it was an exciting experience.

d. ☐ Reading and talking to his parents made John feel he wasn't just a child.

e. ☐ His parents used to read with John and his brother.

f. ☐ Those reading moments were the best quality time he had with his parents.

4. Use the words and expressions from the box to complete John Green's sentences according to the audio. Then check your answers with the audio script.

active participant	alive	awesome	journey	fairy tales	share

a. "... the story of a guy's ________________ across the ocean on this little raft..."

b. "... because I didn't have to ______________ it with my brother – which was ______________ –..."

c. "... so I was able to kind of feel like I was an ________________ in the conversation,..."

d. "We especially read a lot of ________________..."

e. "... and it was just so exciting and real and ________________."

5. Match the pictures with the corresponding parts of the interview you have just heard.

A

B

ILUSTRAÇÕES: RICO

C

D

☐ "I remember when I was pretty little, I read this book, *Kon-Tiki* with my dad. [. .] and it was really special for me."

☐ "Reading was really important in our house growing up."

☐ "[...] we got to talk about stuff that really interested both of them and me."

☐ "When I was a little kid, the reading time I had with my parents was in many ways, like, the best quality time I had with them [...]."

AFTER LISTENING

6. What kind of reading experiences did you have when you were a kid? Write one sentence that summarizes that. Share it with the whole group.

____

SPEAKING

1. In pairs, tell a classmate the story of your favorite book. Do not forget to describe the characters and compare them, whenever possible. Include details of where the story takes place as well. Then make a drawing that represents the story you have heard. Change roles.

BIS

Reflecting on the theme

- What do you think of having reading as a hobby?
- How do you think making reading a habit can help you as a person, a student, and a professional in the future?

BEFORE WRITING

Both *dwarfs* and *dwarves* are correct plural forms of the noun *dwarf*.

1. Read the fairy tale "Snow White and the Seven Dwarfs" and do the activities.

SNOW WHITE AND THE SEVEN DWARFS

Once upon a time there was a beautiful little princess named Snow White. She grew up and became even more beautiful. Her stepmother was very jealous. She could not stand the fact that Snow White was more beautiful than her.

So, one day she ordered a huntsman to take Snow White to the forest and kill her. But the huntsman was not that cruel and freed her instead – "Snow White, find somewhere to hide and don't leave that place".

Snow White followed the huntsman's advice. When she was hanging around the forest she found a little house and decided to go inside. There was nobody there, only seven tiny beds in the bedroom. She slept on one of the beds. The seven dwarfs arrived home and found Snow White asleep.

The stepmother, who was actually a witch, found out that Snow White was still alive and living with the seven dwarfs in the woods. One day she disguised herself as an old woman and went to the little house in the woods. Snow White was alone and the witch was able to trick her and give her a poisoned red apple.

When the seven dwarfs arrived, they found Snow White lying on the floor. They were very upset.

Little did they know that only a kiss from a prince would wake her up.

____

____

a. What is a fairy tale?

- [ ] It is a story written especially for little children that frequently teaches a moral lesson.
- [ ] It is a story, usually written for children, about fantasy and make-believe elements.

b. What are the characteristics of a fairy tale? Check all that apply.

- [ ] The story presents humor centered on the protagonist.
- [ ] There are kings, queens, princesses, and princes.
- [ ] There are magical creatures.
- [ ] Sometimes, there are personified objects as main characters.
- [ ] There are good and evil characters in the stories.
- [ ] Fairy tales most often have happy endings.

- ***Shrek***

  Direction: Andrew Adamson; Vicky Jenson. USA. Dreamworks, 2001, 90 min.

  The movie is a modern and innovative fairy tale, full of intertextuality among well-known classic fairy tales.

- ***Brave***

  Direction: Mark Andrews; Brenda Chapman. USA. Pixar, 2012, 93 min.

  A Disney animated movie which tells the story of Princess Merida and her attempts to avoid marriage. A fairy tale featuring the Scottish culture.

2. In pairs, read the "Snow White and the Seven Dwarfs" tale again and check the correct ending for the story. Then write it down at the end of the text on page 120.

a. ☐ One day, the witch felt sorry for what she did and woke Snow White up with a spell. Snow White forgave her, and they became friends.

b. ☐ And so, one day, a prince found Snow White and kissed her. And they lived happily ever after.

WRITING

3. Write a new ending for the fairy tale "Beauty and the Beast" on page 107. Follow the steps.
- Write down your ideas for a new ending for the story.
- Remember to use the characteristics of a fairy tale.
- Write a draft of the ending of the fairy tale "Beauty and the Beast".
- Ask the teacher to revise your work.
- Then correct it as needed.

AFTER WRITING

- Rehearse by reading the ending of your story aloud to yourself.
- Read the ending you wrote to your classmates and teacher.
- If possible, try to perform it as a narrator.
- All the students then vote for the best ending and the best narrator.

SELF-EVALUATION

Check the true sentences about your learning in Unit 6.
In this unit you have learned to:

☐ read and identify elements of a fairy tale;

☐ describe places;

☐ tell a story, describing characters and places;

☐ write a new ending for a fairy tale.

Reflecting...

- **What questions do I still have about the use of there to be in the past?**
- **What questions do I still have about the use of the superlative?**
- **What did I learn about fairy tales?**
- **Which fairy tales did I already know?**
- **Which fairy tale did I like best? Why?**

Connections

English • Math • Arts

Da Vinci's Vitruvian Man turned to action figure

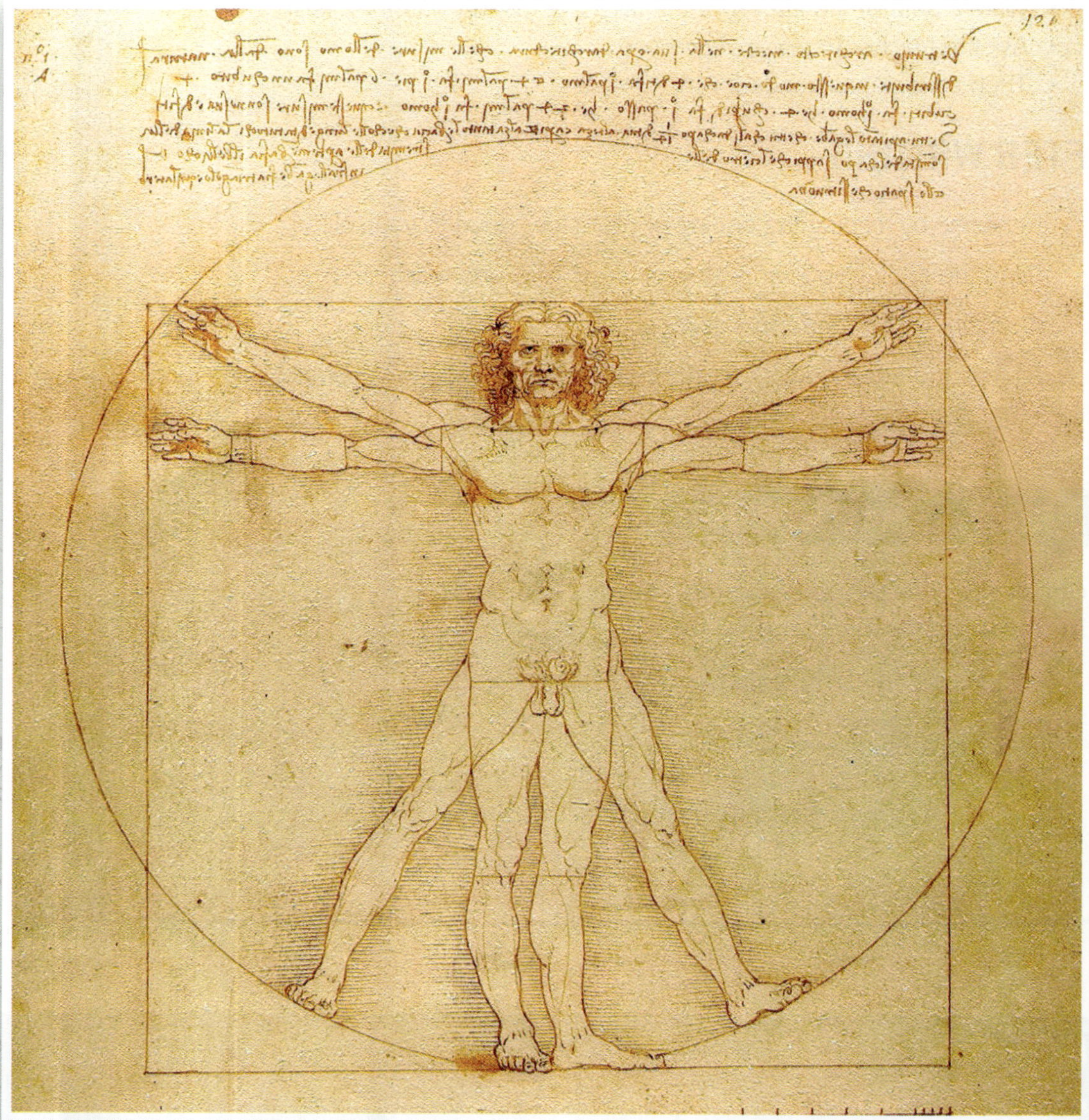

LEONARDO DA VINCI, VITRUVIAN MAN, C1492

DA VINCI, Leonardo. *Vitruvian Man*. 1492. Drawingpen, ink and wash on paper. Gallerie dell'Accademia, Venice, Italy.

Leonardo da Vinci's "Vitruvian Man" has come alive after more than half a millennia since it first appeared. It is now possible to get one of the world's most famous illustrations as a fully poseable action figure, thanks to Max Factory, which decided to include it as one of the Figma models, a popular line of Japanese action figures produced and distributed by Good Smile Company.

The Vitruvian Man action figure was uncovered at the Wonder Festival Exhibition, a seasonal event held in Chiba City, Japan. This exhibition shows off resin and plastic models from the anime and video game worlds.

The striking figure caught the attention of visitors due to its correspondence in appearance to the original drawing. Also, its amazing moveable body can clearly demonstrate the beauty of anatomical symmetry. The smart design allows some of the legs and arms to be detached. That detail gives it the capability of striking poses with any combination of two, three or four limbs, whose smoothness of movement around the body is provided by ball joints.

Completed in 1490, Leonardo Da Vinci's "Vitruvian Man" found inspiration from the connection between geometry and ideal human proportions found in the studies of Roman architect Vitruvius (c.80-70BC). This anatomical drawing represents the figure of a naked man with his arms and legs spread in two overlapping positions, within both a circle and a square, displaying a symbol of symmetry.

Max Factory is yet to confirm the figure's sale price and its release date, so it might take some time before you are able to play with da Vinci's beautiful proportions with your own hands.

Adapted from: <en.rocketnews24.com/2016/02/08/leonardo-da-vincis-vitruvian-man-comes-to-life-as-eight-limbed-action-figure-in-japan>. Accessed on: Feb. 18, 2016.

1. The "Vitruvian Man" is a world-renowned drawing created by Leonardo da Vinci. It is based on the correlations of ideal human proportions with geometry. Da Vinci wrote notes about the proportions of the male human body. Here are some examples:
   - the length of a man's outspread arms is equal to his height
   - the distance from the top of the head to the bottom of the chin is one-eighth of a man's height
   - the length of the hand is one-tenth of a man's height
   - the length of the ear is one-third of the length of the face

   Check these proportions by measuring them on your body (or a friend's body). Ask for the help of a Math teacher.

2. Are these proportions accurate? Discuss the results with your classmates.

UNIT

7

A world of possibilities

The movie *Buddies* was the first Brazilian movie to feature actors with Down syndrome as main characters. Three young people go on an adventurous road trip in search for their dreams.

The director's objective was not to discuss the importance of inclusion. He wanted the viewers to get involved in the adventure and forget the fact that the actors have Down syndrome. He claims that if he reaches his objective, it means that Brazilians will have taken a major step towards social inclusion.

Your learning objectives for this unit are...

- to identify the main characteristics of fast facts and write a text with them;
- to get to know Paralympic sports;
- to use relative pronouns.

EXCHANGING IDEAS

1. What characteristics from the group of actors did the director want to draw the viewer's attention to?
2. Marcelo Galvão, the director, said in an interview that it was hard to find a sponsor for the movie production. What reasons could people have not to support the production of this movie?

GATACINE

- ***Buddies***

  Direction: Marcelo Galvão. Brazil: Gatacine, 2012. 103 min.

  The movie shows the simple things in life from the innocent and poetic perspective of three young people with Down syndrome, who decide to go on an adventurous road trip in search for their dreams.
- ***I am Sam***

  Direction: Jessie Nelson. USA: New Line Cinema, 2001. 132 min.

  The movie tells the story of a mentally handicapped father who fights for custody of his 7-year-old daughter.

GALVÃO Marcelo. *Buddies*. Brazil: Gatacine, 2012. 103 min.

7 A world of possibilities

READING COMPREHENSION

TEXT 1

BEFORE READING

1. Do you know any para-athlete? Who? What sports does he/she play?

READING

2. Skim the fast facts below and answer the questions: Who are the fast facts about? What is his occupation?

www.paralympic.org/Athletes/Biographies

BATISTA DOS SANTOS Claudiney			
Sport	Athletics	**Born**	13 Nov 1978
NPC	Brazil	**Height**	1.73 m
Gender	Men	**Weight**	68 kg

Human Interest

Impairment Information	
Classification	F57
Further Personal Information	
Residence	Brazil
Occupation	Athlete
Sport Specific Information	
When and where did you begin this sport?	He began participating in para-athletics events in 2007, two years after his accident.
Why this sport?	While he was in hospital recovering from his accident, he received a visit from some para-athletics who invited him to a local athletics club. He resisted the invitation for two years before he began para-athletics.
Club / Team	Clube Amigos dos Deficientes (CAD): São José do Rio Preto, BRA
General Interest	
Memorable sporting achievement	Winning a silver medal in the F57/58 javelin at the 2012 Paralympic Games in London (diarioweb.com.br, 11 Sep 2012)
Awards and honours	He was named 201 Paralympic Performer of the Year in the athletics at the 2014 Brazilian Paralympic Awards in Copacabana. (rio2016.com, 10 Dec 2014)
Ambitions	To win a medal at the 2016 Paralympic Games in Rio de Janeiro. (diarioweb.com.br, 11 Sep 2012)
Impairment	He was involved in a road accident in May 2005 and part of his left leg needed to be amputated as a result of his injuries. (cad.org.br, 23 Apr 2013)

recovering: recuperando-se
javelin: arremesso de dardo

Extracted from: <www.paralympic.org/Athletes/Biographies>. Accessed on: Jun. 7, 2016.

The Paralympic Games, which takes place right after the Olympic Games, is an international multi-sport event involving athletes with a range of physical disabilities. The sports are adapted to cater for the athletes limitations.

3. What do the years in the chart refer to?

Year	Event
1978	
2007	
2012	
2014	
2005	

4. Match the parts to form questions and answers.

a. What		after the accident did he join the athletics club?		It's an athletic modality.
b. Where		does he weigh?		In 2007.
c. How tall		did he begin in para-athletics?		He is 1.73 m.
d. Where		is Claudiney Batista dos Santos from?		68 kg.
e. How long		did he choose athletics?		Two years after.
f. How much		is the javelin?		In Brazil.
g. When		is he?		He is from Brazil.
h. Why		does he live?		Because he was invited by the local athletics club.

5. Write **T** (true), **F** (false) or **NM** (not mentioned).

a. ☐ At first, he didn't accept the para-athletes' invitation.

b. ☐ His family and friends convinced him to practice the javelin.

c. ☐ He doesn't play for any club.

d. ☐ The 2014 Brazilian Paralympic Awards took place in Rio de Janeiro.

e. ☐ He didn't win any medal at the 2012 Paralympic Games.

f. ☐ The 2012 Paralympic Games took place in London.

g. ☐ He lost part of his leg in a road accident in São José do Rio Preto – SP.

h. ☐ He began participating in para-athletics events in 2005.

- **www.cpb.org.br**
  The official website of the Brazilian Paralympic Games committee.

6. Answer the questions below.

a. What was his memorable achievement?

____

____

b. Can we affirm that Claudiney Batista dos Santos has made plans for his future in sports? Why?

____

____

7. Check the correct options to complete the sentence about Claudiney's fast facts.

The fast facts present

a. ☐ general, but relevant information.
b. ☐ the author's opinion about some events.
c. ☐ information organized in topics.
d. ☐ a detailed bio.
e. ☐ the main topics in bold.
f. ☐ brief texts.
g. ☐ important dates.
h. ☐ a brief bio.
i. ☐ detailed information about the events.

8. In pairs, answer the questions below.

a. Who would be interested in reading fast facts?

____

____

b. Where can we find fast facts?

____

____

AFTER READING

- How do you imagine the routine of para-athletes?
- What paralympic sport would you like to follow?
- If you met Claudiney, what would you like to ask him? Why?

TEXT 2

BEFORE READING

1. The following text is about a para-athlete and it was published in *The Better India* website. This website brings happy stories of unknown heroes and presents them to the world. What information do you think you'll find in the text?

READING

2. Read the text about the Indian para-athlete Malathi Krishnamurthy Holla and match the columns to form true sentences.

www.thebetterindia.com/16449/famous-indians-with-disability/#sthash.iSWSshYn.dpuf

This international para-athlete from Bangalore was paralyzed completely at the tender age of one after a high fever. A regular electric shock treatment for two years got the strength of her upper body back, but below the waist her body remained weak. Holla decided to live life in the best possible way and chose sports to excel in. She started participating in various games at college, and today she has taken part in various international events including the Para-Olympics. She won Gold in 200m, shot put, discus and javelin throw at the 1989 World Masters' Games in Denmark. She has over 300 medals in her kitty, and is also the proud recipient of the Arjuna Award and Padma Shri. She runs the Mathru Foundation to help disabled children from rural India.

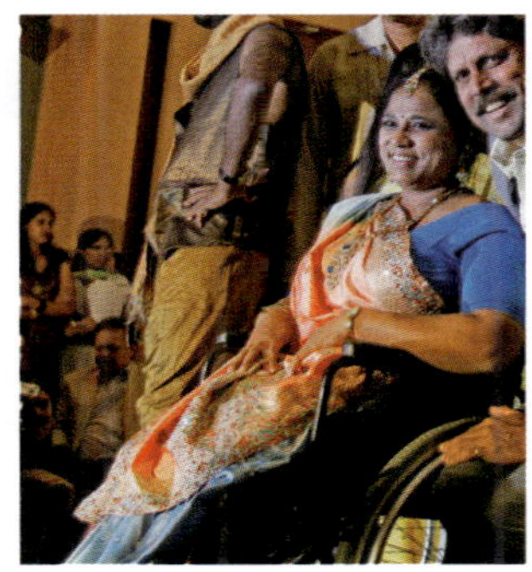

AIJAZ RAHI/AP PHOTO/GLOW IMAGES

Malathi Krishnamurthy Holla

waist: cintura
excel in: destacar-se

Extracted from: <www.thebetterindia.com/16449/famous-indians-with-disability/#sthash.iSWSshYn.dpuf>. Accessed on: Jun. 7, 2016.

a. Because of a high fever, the athlete	☐	hundreds of medals and some awards too.
b. Her upper body	☐	was paralyzed when she was only one year old.
c. Malathi has won	☐	a foundation which helps disabled children.
d. The athlete manages	☐	is stronger than the part below her waist.

3. Check the correct answers to the questions.

a. What was the electric shock treatment used for?

☐ To make her walk again. ☐ To make her body strong.

b. When did Malathi start competing?

☐ When she was at college. ☐ When she was in Denmark.

AFTER READING

- What do Malathi and Claudiney have in common?
- What is your opinion about *The Better India* website? Do you know stories of unknown heroes that could be published in this website? Share them with your classmates.

FOCUS ON VOCABULARY

1. Read the fast facts on page 126 again and find the words that correspond to the definitions below. Write them down. The first letter is given to you.

a. h________________: the degree to which something is high or someone is tall

b. w________________: a measurement of how heavy a person or thing is

c. i________________: the fact that a part of your body is unable to do something fully

d. a________________: a particular thing that you have achieved

Extracted from: <www.macmillandictionary.com>. Accessed on: Jun. 7, 2016.

2. Using the words from the box, complete these texts about some Paralympic athletes.

disabled	high fever	strength

A

www.paralympic.org/feature/portugal%E2%80%99s-talented-youngster-dreams-london-2012

Portugal's Talented Youngster Dreams of London

Swimmer Emanuel Gonçalves claimed silver in the 5,000m Open Water event at the European Championships this year.

[...]

"I had a ________________ and couldn't leave home. I only started training on the day of my arrival in Berlin."

[...]

IMAGO SPORTFOTODIENST/ KEYSTONE

Extracted from: <www.paralympic.org/feature/portugal%E2%80%99s-talented-youngster-dreams-london-2012>. Accessed on: Jun. 7, 2016

B

www.paralympic.org/feature/no-46-jack-all-trades-fernandes

No. 46: Jack-of-all-trades Fernandes

The No. 46 moment in Paralympic sport of 2012 is when Brazilian Fernando Fernandes won his third para-canoe world crown.

[...]

"Since I had the accident, I have been using sport to communicate to the world, and want to change the physically fragile image ________________ people have," Fernandes said.

[...]

ROLAND WEIHRAUCH/AP IMAGES

Extracted from: <www.paralympic.org/feature/no-46-jack-all-trades-fernandes>. Accessed on: Jun. 7, 2016.

• ***Estrelas tortas***

CARRASCO, Walcyr. São Paulo: Moderna, 2003.

Marcella was a young athlete until an accident left her paralyzed from the waist down. From that moment on, her life changed completely.

Jack-of-all-trades: "pau para toda obra"

C

www.paralympic.org/feature/hong-kong%E2%80%99s-chong-eyes-wheelchair-fencing-gold

Hong Kong's Chong Eyes Wheelchair Fencing Gold

[...]

"Keeping my body balance on the wheelchair is very important, as for a B class fencer it is not the easiest, so I will need to put more effort on that. My ______________ and conditioning programme help me a lot," she said.

[...]

IMAGO SPORTFOTODIENST/KEYSTONE

Extracted from: <www.paralympic.org/feature/hong-kong%E2%80%99s-chong-eyes-wheelchair-fencing-gold> Accessed on: Jun. 7, 2016.

3. Look at the pictures and check the medals mentioned in the texts you have read in activity 2.

a. ☐ bronze and gold

MARCO ANDRAS/LATINSTOCK

b. ☐ silver and gold

MARCO ANDRAS/LATINSTOCK

gold medal: 1st place
silver medal: 2nd place
bronze medal: 3rd place

- **www.paralympic.org/**
The official website of the international Paralympic Games committee.

Paralympic sports

4. Unscramble the letters to form the names of some Paralympic sports and then label the pictures.

A  C H E A R Y R ______________

B  5-a-side A L O O T F B L ______________

C  M I S W G M I N ______________

D  wheelchair E T N I N S ______________

E  D O U J ______________

F  L L O A L B G A ______________

G  T C S I A H T L E ______________

H  wheelchair A A L L T E B S K B ______________

I  wheelchair I N N E C G F ______________

J  sitting L A B L O V E L Y L ______________

IMAGENS: RIO 2016

IT'S YOUR TURN!

Choose a Paralympic sport from activity 4 you would like to see athletes competing. Then talk to a classmate and explain to him or her why you would like to see these athletes in action. Take turns.

Relative pronouns

1. Read the fast facts about Maria J. Alves and write **T** (true) or **F** (false).

www.paralympic.org/Athletes/Biographies

ALVES Maria J.	
Sport	Athletics
NPC	Brazil
Gender	Women
Born	10 Mar 1977 in Sobradinho, BRA

Human Interest

Impairment Information	
Type of Impairment	Visual impairment
Origin of Impairment	Congenital – Genetic
Further Personal Information	
Residence	Brazil
Occupation	Athlete, Student
Languages	Portuguese, Spanish
Higher education	Journalism – Superior Luterano de Santa Catarina: Santa Catarina, BRA
Sport Specific Information	
When and where did you begin the sport?	Started when she was seven years old. She went to the Benjamin Constant Institute where she came in contact with all sports.
Club / Team	Associação Joinvilense para Integração dos Deficientes Visuais (AJIDEVI): Joinville, BRA
General Interest	
Nicknames	Zeze (Athens 2004)
Hobbies	Listening to music and reading (Athens 2004)
Competition Highlights (historical) **World Championships**	
Rank	5
Year	2006
Event	200m T12
Result	27.19

Extracted from: <www.paralympic.org/Athletes/Biographies>. Accessed on: Jun. 7, 2016.

a. ☐ Maria J. Alves is a Brazilian athlete **who** is visually impaired.

b. ☐ The Benjamin Constant Institute is the place **where** Maria's impairment was diagnosed.

c. ☐ Maria, **whose** nickname is Zeze, was born in Sobradinho.

d. ☐ 1977 is the year **when** she was born.

e. ☐ Portuguese and English are the languages **which** Maria speaks.

2. Read the statements in activity 1 again and pay attention to the words in bold. Then check the correct alternatives to complete the sentences.

a. Relative pronouns are used when we want

- [ ] to introduce additional information about a person, a thing, a place, etc.
- [ ] to talk about someone's obligations.

b. The relative pronouns **who**, **where**, **whose**, **when**, and **which** refer to the words

- [ ] athlete, place, Sobradinho, she, and Maria respectively.
- [ ] athlete, place, Maria, year, and languages respectively.

> The relative pronoun **that** is often used instead of **who** and **which**, but it s more informal.

c. When we refer to people we use ________________, and to refer to things, animals, or ideas we use ________________.

- [ ] which / who
- [ ] who / which

d. We use **where** for ________________ and **when** for ________________.

- [ ] places / time
- [ ] people / things

e. The relative pronoun **whose** is used to indicate ________________. It is always followed by a noun.

- [ ] possession
- [ ] reason

3. Read about the Mexican artist Frida Kahlo. Then circle the correct relative pronouns to complete the text.

Frida Kahlo

July 6, 1907 – July 13, 1954

Disability: Polio

Frida Kahlo was a renowned Mexican painter **which/who** created striking paintings, most of them being self-portraits reflecting her pain and sorrow. She painted using vibrant colors **where/that** were influenced by the cultures of Mexico. She was the first Mexican artist of 20th century **when/whose** work was purchased by an international museum. Kahlo contracted polio at age six, **which/whose** left her right leg thinner than the left, **which/when** Kahlo disguised by wearing long, colorful skirts.
[...]

FRIDA KAHLO, AUTORRETRATO "THE FRAME", 1938

KAHLO, Frida, *Self-Portrait – The Frame*, 1938 Oil on aluminium and glass, 28.5 cm × 20.7 cm. Musée National d'Art Moderne, Paris, France.

Extracted from: <listverse.com/2010/01/18/top-10-extraordinary-people-with-disabilities/>. Accessed on: Jun. 7, 2016.

striking: impressionantes
sorrow: tristeza
disguised: disfarçava

4. Read an excerpt of Paralympian Brody Roybal's interview with *Time for Kids Magazine* in 2014. Then circle the relative pronouns and underline the words they refer to.

TFK: What inspired you to be an athlete?

BRODY ROYBAL: When I was younger, I was looking for any disabled sport to play. I tried many different sports, like wheelchair softball and wheelchair basketball, but hockey was the only one that stuck with me.

[...]

TFK: Where did you have the opportunity to try and play sledge hockey?

BRODY ROYBAL: When I was looking for a sport to play, I found the RIC (Rehabilitation Institute of Chicago) Blackhawks, which is a [sledge hockey] team down in Chicago. They were an adult team at the time, but I started practicing with them. Then, they told me I should go play for the Chicago Hornets, which is the youth team here in Chicago. [...]

Extracted from: <www.timeforkids.com/news/dreams-ice/151306>. Accessed on: Jun. 7, 2016.

Should

5. Read the text in activity 4 again and answer the questions.

a. Did the RIC Blackhawks tell Brody he shouldn't practice sledge hockey with them?

____

b. What did the RIC Blackhawks tell Brody he should do? ______________________

6. Match the parts to form meaningful statements about the modal verb should.

a. We use **should** before the main verb

b. We use **shouldn't** (**should not**) before the main verb

☐ when we want to say that it is not advisable to do a certain thing.

☐ to give advice.

7. Complete the following quote from the English physicist Stephen Hawking with one of the verb forms from the box.

should have	shouldn't be

"We ____________ surprised that conditions in the universe are suitable for life, but this is not evidence that the universe was designed to allow for life."

Extracted from: <refspace.com/quotes/Stephen_Hawking/Q1729>. Accessed on: Jun. 7, 2016.

HANDS ON!

Finish the sentences with information you already have based on Paralympic Games and athletes. Compare your answers with a classmate. Then, decide which sentences reflect the most interesting ideas and report them to the class.

Claudiney Batista dos Santos is an athlete who ____________________.

The Paralympic Games, which ____________________.

Host cities are the cities where ____________________.

Relative pronouns

Relative pronouns are used when we want to add information about a person, thing, place, etc.

Examples:

She is the actress **who** played Juliet in the movie.

That's the restaurant **where** I eat every day.

Those are the moments **when** you realize how lucky you are.

My friend, **whose** name I prefer not to say, is a very famous celebrity.

The song, **which** was released in early December, is still a huge hit.

The relative pronoun...	refers to...
who	people
where	places
when	time
whose	possession
which	things

The relative pronoun **that** can be used for people or things, but mainly in informal situations.

Examples:

Glenn is someone **that** I really admire for being so brave.

The vases **that** cost $1,99 are the ones on the top shelf.

Should

Should is a modal verb that is used to give advice or suggestions. It is used before the main verb in the base form.

Affirmative

You don't look good.
You **should** rest.

THINKSTOCK/GETTY IMAGES

Negative

You **shouldn't** eat junk food, it's bad for you!

HOMER W SYKES/ALAMY/FOTOARENA

Interrogative

A: Should I have my hair cut?
B: Only if you want to. You look great with any hairstyle.

THINKSTOCK/GETTY IMAGES

1. Choose the correct relative pronoun to complete the sentences.

a. We sometimes spend our vacations in Igarapé Grande, Maranhão, __________ our grandparents live.

☐ which ☐ that ☐ where

b. That blond man over there, __________ brother is a senator, told me he knows your father.

☐ who ☐ whose ☐ where

c. Mr. Baxby, __________ is a bus driver, lives on the apartment next to mine.

☐ who ☐ whose ☐ where

d. 1974 was the year __________ my parents got married.

☐ which ☐ when ☐ where

e. This is the boy __________ comes from South Africa.

☐ that ☐ whose ☐ where

f. I just met the girl __________ bike was stolen last week.

☐ who ☐ whose ☐ which

g. Thank you so much for your gift, __________ was a hit with the kids at home.

☐ who ☐ when ☐ which

h. Where did you store that box __________ we brought from the old house?

☐ who ☐ where ☐ that

2. Write one affirmative (with **should**) and one negative (with **shouldn't**) piece of advice for each situation below.

a. "I never get enough rest. I always wake up very tired."

____

____

b. "I feel like I never have time for anything fun in my life."

____

____

c. "My doctor told me that I have to lose weight."

____

____

d. "My grades at school were not good last bimester."

____

____

e. "I want to be a better swimmer and, maybe one day, be a professional athlete."

____

____

LISTENING COMPREHENSION

BEFORE LISTENING

1. Based on the picture, answer the questions.

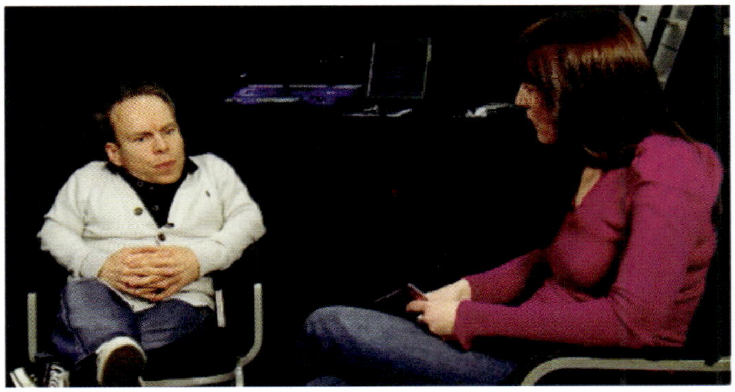

THE GUARDIAN

a. What is different about the man in the photo?

b. What are you going to hear in this audio?

2. Look at the pictures and check the ones you believe that represent difficulties a short person faces in everyday life.

KEITH MYERS/NEWSCOM/GLOW IMAGES

RODRIGO BUENDIA/AFP

PILAR OLIVARES/REUTERS/LATINSTOCK

CAREN FIROUZ/REUTERS/CORBIS/LATINSTOCK

EUAN CHERRY/ALAMY/LATINSTOCK

DAVID R/ALAMY/LATINSTOCK

3. The man in the picture in activity 1 is the actor Warwick Davis. The picture is of an interview with him and he's answering about difficulties he faces as a short person. What difficulties do you think he's going to mention?

LISTENING

4. Listen to the interview. Then go back to activity 3 and check if your prediction was correct.

21

5. Write **T** (true) or **F** (false) according to what you have just heard.

a. ☐ Being short makes Warwick feel pain when he walks.

b. ☐ He considers himself a disabled person all the time.

c. ☐ Being short has helped Warwick accomplish important things in his life.

d. ☐ He got the part in the movie because he was a friend of the director.

e. ☐ In the movie *Star Wars*, Warwick played an Ewok.

f. ☐ He got the part in *Star Wars* because he was short.

g. ☐ He doesn't like being an actor.

6. Listen to the interview again. Then work with a classmate to choose the correct answer to the questions.

22

a. Based on Warwick's accent, where do you think he is from?

☐ Spain.

☐ England.

b. Why did Warwick say that the interviewer's question *"Do you consider yourself to be disabled?"* is an interesting question?

☐ Because he could reflect about all the chances he has had as a disabled person.

☐ Because he considers himself to be a disabled person.

7. Complete part of Warwick's answer to one of the interviewer's questions with the words/expressions from the box. Then check your answers with the audio script.

actor	costume	height	in acting

"It's enabled me to have a career ______________. I wouldn't have been an ______________. I got the part in *Star Wars* because I was short, that was the only reason. It wasn't anything with acting at that point: 'Oh yeah, you're the right ______________ for the job. Come on in. Get fitted up for an Ewok ______________.'"

AFTER LISTENING

8. What can you learn from the stories of the people you saw in this unit and other stories you know of people who overcame their personal difficulties?

SPEAKING

1. Work in pairs. Choose one of the para-athletes below and tell your classmate what questions you would like to ask him/her and why.

A

DIBYANGSHU SARKAR/AFP

Xu Qing Jin, swimming

B

MOACYR LOPES JUNIOR/FOLHAPRESS

Fernando Fernandes, canoeing

C

ANASTASSELIS/REX FEATURES/GLOW IMAGES

Aimee Mullins, track and field

D

MATTHEW CHILDS/ZUMAPRESS/EASYPIX

Marcel Eric Hug, wheelchair racing

E

PETER WAYNE/ZUMA PRESS/EFEVISUAL

Alana Nichols, wheelchair basketball

F

ASP/AFP

Bethany Hamilton, surfing

Reflecting on the theme

- How important is it for athletes with disabilities to participate in the Paralympic Games?
- People who have a disability are victims of prejudice in many different situations. How important do you think events such as the Paralympic Games can be to change this?

WRITING

BEFORE WRITING

1. Read the fast facts about Stevie Wonder and write **T** (true) or **F** (false) for the statements below.

Stevie Wonder Fast Facts Personal	
Birth date	May 13, 1950
Birth place	Saginaw, Michigan
Birth name	Stevland Hardaway Judkins
Father	Calvin Judkins
Mother	Lula Mae Hardaway
Marriages	Karen "Kai" Millard Morris (2001-present, separated); Syreeta Wright (September 14, 1970-1972, divorced)
Children	With Tomeeka Robyn Bracy: Nia (female), December 2014, Zaiah (female), 2013; with Kai Millard Morris: Mandla Kadjaly (male), May 13, 2005; Kailand (male), 2001; with Melody McCulley: Mumtaz (male),1983; with Yolanda Simmons: Keita (male), 1977; Aisha (female), April 7, 1975; Mothers' names unavailable publicly: Kwame (male), August 6, 1988; Sophia
Education	Michigan School for the Blind
Other Facts	
Winner of 25 Grammy Awards, an honorary award, 74 nominations. Born prematurely; doctors believe he was blinded when he was accidentally given too much oxygen in his incubator. Learned to play piano, drums and harmonica by age nine. His first stage name was Little Stevie Wonder. Wonder is one of six children. His siblings use the last name Hardaway. According to his mother's authorized biography, Wonder's surname was legally changed to Morris, "an old family name," when he signed with Motown, and Berry Gordy gave him the stage name Wonder. [...]	

Extracted from: <edition.cnn.com/2013/06/07/us/stevie-wonder-fast-facts/>. Accessed on: Jun. 7, 2016.

a. ☐ Stevie Wonder was born blind.

b. ☐ He is a successful singer.

c. ☐ Wonder wasn't his original name.

2. Choose the correct alternatives.

a. Fast facts are basically

☐ lists of some of the most important information not only about people, but about products or services, too.

☐ lists of important information about people, products or services with the writer's opinion about them.

b. The objective of fast facts is

☐ to give advice – and that's why the writer's opinion is the most important part of fast facts.

☐ to inform – and that's why only real facts should be in fast facts.

WRITING

3. In pairs, follow the steps to write fast facts about a disabled person you admire.
   - In pairs, brainstorm names of disabled people you admire. It could be a famous person, someone you have heard about or a person you know in real life.
   - Choose one name to write about.
   - Search the internet, magazines and newspapers for information on that person.
   - Remember to include:
     - full name
     - birth date
     - birth place
   - Try to focus on what this person does.
   - Organize all the information about the person you chose and write fast facts about him/her.
   - You can choose a picture of this person to put in the fast facts.
   - Share your work with a classmate and revise it together.
   - Ask the teacher to revise your work. Then make all necessary changes.
   - Rewrite your fast facts on a piece of cardboard or A3 paper.

AFTER WRITING

- Present your person of interest to your classmates.
- Explain why you chose that person to talk about.
- Present your fast facts to the class and then pin them to the class bulletin board.

SELF-EVALUATION

Check the true sentences about your learning in Unit 7.
In this unit you have learned to:

- ☐ identify the main characteristics of fast facts and write a text with them;
- ☐ get to know Paralympic sports;
- ☐ use relative pronouns.

Reflecting...

- **What Paralympic sports, which I hadn't heard before, do I know now?**
- **What did I learn about fast facts?**
- **What questions do I still have about relative pronouns?**
- **What questions do I still have about the use of should?**

UNIT

8

Families

Icons are representations of objects or concepts presented in a simple way. They are all around us, in places such as shopping malls, airports, guides, manuals, maps, infographics, etc.

Icons allow people to quickly identify the object or idea that is being represented. Since they are images, we don't need any background knowledge on a certain language to understand them. The same icon can represent the same idea in different countries and languages.

Your learning objectives for this unit are…

- to report events that happened in the past, without mentioning when they happened;
- to identify different kinds of families and compare them;
- to read and write a testimonial.

EXCHANGING IDEAS

1. Look at the icons in the image. What kinds of families are they representing?
2. Besides the icons, what other elements are there in the image? What does this image represent to you?
3. Use your notebook and make a representation of your family using icons.

- ***Do jeito que a gente é***

  LEITE, Márcia. São Paulo: Ática, 2009.

  It tells the story of Beá and Chico. She is 14 years old and worried about her appearance. He is 17 years old and questioning his own sexuality.

- ***A história de Júlia e sua sombra de menino***

  BRUEL, Cristiane. São Paulo: Scipione, 2010.

  Júlia's parents have always criticized her appearance, saying that she looked like a boy. One day, Júlia notices that her shadow is shaped like a boy's and she starts to question her identity.

- ***Hoje eu quero voltar sozinho***

  Direction: Daniel Ribeiro. Brazil: Lacuna Filmes, 2014. 96 min.

  Internationally awarded coming-of-age movie about a teenager who has to deal with his parents, friends, feelings, and sexuality.

8 Families

READING COMPREHENSION

TEXT 1

BEFORE READING

1. You are going to read a news article about fathers who raise their children by themselves. What information do you think you will find in this news article?

READING

2. Read the text and answer the questions that follow.

www.theatlantic.com/national/archive/2014/02/the-rise-of-the-single-dad/284016/

The rise of single dad
More than 2.6 million households in America are headed by a single father.

When his son, Kyle, was four months old, Stefan Malliet woke up to his crying at three o'clock in the morning. Stefan tried to figure out what was wrong—Kyle wasn't hungry, his diaper wasn't dirty, but he still wouldn't settle down and go to sleep. He just kept screaming. With no one else in the house to take Kyle off his hands, Stefan called a friend, crying: "I had no idea what was going on."

When I asked Stefan how he decided to take on the responsibilities of a single dad, he said, "This is my child. I have to be here."

Today, more men than ever are making the same choice. A Pew Research study published this statistic this summer: 8 percent of households with minor children are now headed by a single father, up from just one percent in 1960. This represents a nine-fold increase, from fewer than 300,000 households in 1960 to more than 2.6 million in 2011. In contrast, the number of single-mother households increased four-fold during that time period, from 1.9 million in 1960 to 8.6 million in 2011.

[...]

Single dads are more easily discouraged than single moms, he [Malliet] says, because men suffer from a lack of parental training. While women often grow up tucking their dolls into bed at night, young men are rarely conditioned to take care of someone else. This lack of experience can make single dads begin to doubt whether they are really cut out for this, after all.

THINKSTOCK/GETTY IMAGES

Extracted from: <www.theatlantic.com/national/archive/2014/02/the-rise-of-the-single-dad/284016/>. Accessed on: Jun. 7, 2016.

a. The news article begins with the story of a father. What problem did he face? How did he feel in that situation?

____

____

b. Why is there a personal story in the beginning of the news article?

____

____

c. The news article compares the number of single dad families in 2011 and in 1960. What has changed?

____

____

d. Malliet talks about parental training. What is the example he gives for parental training?

____

e. Considering the example of parental training he gives, answer: What else can be part of parental training?

____

____

3. Write **T** (true) or **F** (false).

a. ☐ In 2011 the number of single dads was smaller than in 1960.

b. ☐ The number of single mothers had a three-fold increase from 1960 until the day the article was published.

c. ☐ According to Malliet, men are not educated to be fathers.

d. ☐ Women receive more parental training than men.

4. Check the answers that apply to the following question: What are the possible objectives of this text?

a. ☐ Criticize single fathers.

b. ☐ Present data about single fathers.

c. ☐ Report stories of single fathers.

d. ☐ Show how family formations change and the reasons for these changes.

AFTER READING

- Do girls and boys have the same kind of education to raise a child in the future? Give some examples to justify your answer.

TEXT 2

BEFORE READING

1. "The bond that links your true family is not one of blood, but of respect and joy in each other's life." (Richard Bach, writer)

Extracted from: <www.brainyquote.com/quotes/topics/topic_family.html>. Accessed on: Jun. 7, 2016.

Do you agree with his point of view about family? Explain.

____

2. Read the title of the testimonial below. What information do you expect to find?

____

READING

3. Scan the testimonial and answer the questions.

   a. Is the author still a child?

   ____

   b. Which part of the testimonial supports your answer?

   ____

www.musedmagonline.com/2012/04/life-with-my-two-dads/#sthash.yGqvY3Tc.dpuf

BY CAMRYN CRUMP/ Opinion April 17, 2012

Life With My Two Dads

regrets: arrependimentos
whether: se

[...]

MATTHEW JACQUES/SHUTTERSTOCK

I would never exchange my childhood experience with anyone else. I have no regrets for growing up in a home that, to society, is not perceived as normal. Having two fathers made me the strong intelligent individual I am today. Although it took some questioning, some learning, some fighting and some embarrassing moments, I am proud of my childhood and the person my fathers have helped me grow to be. My best friend and I are still friends today, and he recently told me he envied the amount of support I had in my household. Because of my life experience, I do believe that same sex couples should be allowed to adopt and care for a child as freely as any heterosexual couple. How they choose to love and live their lives doesn't mean they give less support and safety than a man and woman. In this world children need to be safe, secure and loved, whether it's a marriage between a man and a woman or a partnership between two men [...].

Extracted from: <www.musedmagonline.com/2012/04/life-with-my-two-dads/#sthash.yGqvY3Tc.dpuf>. Accessed on: Jun. 7, 2016.

4. Read the text again. Then write **T** (true) or **F** (false).

a. ☐ The text was written by Camryn's fathers.

b. ☐ The author feels happy about his childhood experience.

c. ☐ The author believes having two fathers made him famous.

5. Complete the questions with the words from the box. Then check the correct answers.

fathers	man	normal

a. According to the author, society doesn't perceive his family as ______________. Why does this happen?

☐ Because he wasn't raised by a mother and a father.

☐ Because he has no brothers.

b. What kind of ______________ is he today?

☐ He is a strong intelligent individual due to the way his fathers raised him.

☐ He is a good man with few regrets.

c. Was the situation of having two ______________ always easy to deal with?

☐ Yes. He didn't have any problems with friends because of that.

☐ No. There were embarrassing moments and some learning and fighting, too.

6. Which characteristic is not present in the testimonial?

a. ☐ The testimonial mentions true facts about the author's life.

b. ☐ The pronoun "I" and the possessive adjective "my" appear many times, making it clear that the text is centered on the narrator.

c. ☐ There are some pieces of information that do not support the theme.

d. ☐ The author expresses his opinions, feelings and point of view about some facts.

AFTER READING

- Read: "The child's optimal development seems to be influenced more by the nature of the relationships and interactions within the family unit than by the particular structural form that the family assumes".

Extracted from: <www.homophobie.org/default.aspx?scheme=4319> Accessed on: May 29, 2015.

- Comment this affirmation with your classmates and mention situations that justify your ideas about the relation between children development and their families.

FOCUS ON VOCABULARY

1. Go back to page 146, find the words and expressions below and read the sentences they are in again. Match each one to its corresponding synonym.

a. childhood

☐ infancy ☐ adulthood

b. growing up

☐ living ☐ aging

c. marriage

☐ divorce ☐ matrimony

d. partnership

☐ association ☐ union

e. safety

☐ security ☐ shelter

f. support

☐ assistance ☐ comfort

g. household

☐ size of the house ☐ people in a family

Extracted from: <www.merriam-webster.com/dictionary/childhood>; <www.merriam-webster.com/dictionary/growing%20up>; <www.merriam-webster.com/thesaurus/marriage>; <www.merriam-webster.com/thesaurus/partnership>; <www.merriam-webster.com/thesaurus/safety>; <www.merriam-webster.com/thesaurus/support>; <www.merriam-webster.com/dictionary/household>. Accessed on: Jun. 7, 2016.

2. What words does the author of text 2 use to describe himself as a grown up?

a. ☐ normal

b. ☐ strong

c. ☐ intelligent

3. In the sentence "Single dads are more easily discouraged than single moms...", from text 1, which word says how the tasks are done?

____

PRONUNCIATION PRACTICE

23 Listen and practice the pronunciation of these words.

equal – equally
particular – particularly
full – fully
emotional – emotionally
cognitive – cognitively
social – socially
sexual – sexually

4. Match each type of family with its corresponding description. Then label each picture accordingly.

a. Adoptive/Foster family

b. Extended family

c. Grandparent family

d. Nuclear family

e. Same-sex parent family

f. Single parent family

☐ This type of family has multiple generations and additional relatives.

☐ Grandparents raising their grandchildren.

☐ A man and a woman living together and raising their biological children.

☐ Two people of the same sex raising children from previous relationships or adopted children.

☐ One parent only – mother or father – raising his or her biological children.

☐ A couple or one person who raises children who are not their biological children.

PIXTAL/EASYPIX

____

THINKSTOCK/GETTY IMAGES

____

ADAM HESTER/CORBIS/LATINSTOCK

____

BLEND IMAGES/MASTERFILE/LATINSTOCK

____

CORBIS/LATINSTOCK

____

THINKSTOCK/GETTY IMAGES

____

IT'S YOUR TURN!

Choose two words from the ones you listened to in **Pronunciation Practice** and write sentences about the topic of the texts you have read. You can use a dictionary to help you. Share the sentences with the whole group.

____

____

LANGUAGE IN USE

Present perfect

1. The sentences below are an excerpt from text 2 on page 146 and part of a campaign against homophobia, respectively. Read them, and then check the correct answers to the questions that follow.

"[...] Although it took some questioning, some learning, some fighting and some embarrassing moments, I am proud of my childhood and the person my fathers **have helped** me grow to be. [...]"

a. **Has** it **been** easy for Camryn Crump to turn into the proud person he is today?

- [ ] Yes, it has.
- [ ] No, it hasn't.

b. **Have** Camryn's fathers **helped** him become the person he is?

- [ ] Yes, they **have helped** him and he is proud of the person he**'s become** with their support.
- [ ] Yes, they **have helped** him, but they **haven't succeeded** in making him a proud person.

"[...] Studies **have found** that lesbian and gay parents are just as likely as heterosexual parents to provide an environment favorable to the development of the child. [...]"

Extracted from: <homophobie.org/en/>. Accessed on: Jun. 7, 2016.

c. What **have** studies **discovered**?

- [ ] They**'ve found** that heterosexual parents are less likely to provide an environment of favorable development for a child.
- [ ] They**'ve found** that providing an environment of favorable development for a child doesn't depend on his or her parents' gender identity.

2. Refer to activity 1 again, pay attention to the words and expressions in bold and complete the rules for the present perfect tense.

a. The structures in bold describe actions that happened at unspecified times in the ____________ and have consequences in the present.

b. The main verbs ____________________, ____________________ and ____________________ are regular verbs in the past participle form while the main verbs ____________________, ____________________ and ____________________ are irregular verbs in the past participle form.

c. The auxiliary verb used in the present perfect is ______________. We use ______________, which is the verb form in the third person, with he, she, it.

d. Contractions in the affirmative form are formed using ____________ (for have) and ____________ (for has). In the negative form, ____________ and ____________ are the contracted forms.

3. Underline the present perfect verb forms in the text below. Then read the statements and write **T** (true), **F** (false), or **NM** (not mentioned).

Rise in racist, religious and homophobic hate crimes in London

Hate crimes motivated by racism, religion and homophobia have significantly increased in London over the past year, a new report has warned.

[...]

Police and LGBT community groups agree that the rise is due to people being more willing to come forward and report incidents, rather than a genuine increase in incidents of hate crime.

[...]

Hate crimes targeting the lesbian, gay, bi-sexual, and transgender (LGBT) community have risen to as many as 100 cases a month, with a monthly increase of 21.5 per cent since March 2014, according to the Metropolitan Police.

In June a record 175 cases of homophobic crime were reported to the Metropolitan police, while hate crime aimed at transgender people has risen from 58 to 108 cases, a rise of 86.2 per cent.

[...]

Extracted from: <www.independent.co.uk/news/uk/crime/rise-in-racist-religious-and-homophobic-hate-crimes-in-london-9899009.html>. Accessed on: Jun. 7, 2016.

a. ☐ People have become more willing to report incidents.

b. ☐ The fact that more people are reporting hate crimes means that the number of this kind of crime in London has increased.

c. ☐ People have considered London one of the safest cities in the world.

d. ☐ The report doesn't focus on hate crimes other than homophobia.

e. ☐ Among the cases of homophobic crimes reported to the Metropolitan police in June, 50% were online hate crimes.

4. Circle the correct verb forms to complete the following quotations.

a. "I know what I am. I know that **I've chosen/I have to choose** to identify as a transgender woman, and that I am – by and large – happy with where I am in this world. I'm far from perfect, and I could give you a list as long as my arms of the things I'd love to change. Nevertheless, I am still here, and I am still me, and no one can change that without my permission." (Gwendolyn Ann Smith, founder of the Transgender Day of Remembrance)

Extracted from: <dayagainsthomophobia.org/quotes/#sthash.ay1FO4A9.dpuf>. Accessed on: Mar. 11, 2015.

Transgender Day of Remembrance (TDOR) is an annual observance on November 20 that honors the memory of those whose lives were lost in acts of anti-transgender violence.

Extracted from: <www.glaad.org/tdor>. Accessed on: Jun. 7, 2016.

b. I learned compassion from being discriminated against. Everything bad **that's ever happened/that is ever happening** to me **have taught/has taught** me compassion. (Ellen DeGeneres, actress and TV host.)

Extracted from: <www.brainyquote.com/quotes/quotes/e/ellendegen451793.html>. Accessed on: Jun. 7, 2016.

5. Now complete these testimonials with the verbs from the box in the correct form of the present perfect.

be	face	have	react	report	speak

a. Maya

[...] Bullying in my current grade (7th) ______________________ that bad. I am on medication for my ADHD and it helps but it makes me angry, I ______________ never really ______________ any physical bullying, but sometimes I would come home with bruises from walking in the hall, getting back from lunch is HELL. The first classrooms are the 8th graders so they would push and shove and sometimes they would push other people into me. I ______________________ past bullying and the teachers ______________________ by punishing the kid who did it. I don't really have that problem anymore, well not yet anyway. [...]

Extracted from: <www.noplace4hate.org/real-bullying-stories/>. Accessed on: Jun. 7, 2016.

current: atual
ADHD: Transtorno do Déficit de Atenção/Hiperatividade
bruises: hematomas
shove: dar um empurrão
not yet: ainda não

b. Gemma

My name is Gemma. I have been bullied for most of my life. And I________________ never ________________ about it until now, 15 years after it first started.

I ______________ literally ________________ bullying for as long as I can remember; at least since pre-school. I had three very good friends, one of whom was a boy. I was never pretty, even as a kid, or athletic. Kids teased me mercilessly for it. I cried easily. I remember one day we had a substitute teacher who was telling us a story. The kids started teasing me in front of her until I cried. I asked her in front of everyone to make them stop, but she simply shook her head as if in disappointment. [...]

one of whom: um deles
teased: implicavam
mercilessly: impiedosamente
shook her head: fez que não com a cabeça

Extracted from: <www.noplace4hate.org/real-bullying-stories/>. Accessed on: Jun. 7, 2016.

HANDS ON!

Let's take a class survey! Write down 3 questions about things you want to know whether your friends have done or not. You can ask questions about different topics: *Have you suffered any kind of prejudice? Have you studied in another school? Have you eaten Mexican food?* Take notes on their answers. Finally, report your findings to the class.

Present perfect

We use the **present perfect** to talk about past events and actions that happened at an unspecified time and have consequences in the present.

THINKSTOCK/GETTY IMAGES

I **have washed** the dishes.

(Consequence in the present: There aren't any dirty dishes on the sink.)

CHRIS ROUT/ALAMY/ FOTOARENA

She **hasn't found** her car keys.

(Consequence in the present: She can't open the car.)

THINKSTOCK/GETTY IMAGES

A: Has Bruna **walked** the dog?

B: Yes, she has.

(Consequence in the present: The dog walked a lot and is resting now.)

To form the present perfect we need the auxiliary verb **have** and a main verb in the **past participle**.

Affirmative

Have/Has + verb in past participle

Regular verbs
I **have washed** the dishes.
Kevin **has helped** many people.

Irregular verbs
I **have seen** the new Avengers movie three times!
My sister **has been** to many countries.

Negative

Haven't/Hasn't + verb in the past participle

Regular verbs
Justin **hasn't started** his composition.
We **haven't cleaned** the room.

Irregular verbs
They **haven't found** their car keys.
Mariana **hasn't taken** photos with her new cell phone.

Interrogative

Have/Has + subject + verb in past participle

Regular verbs
Has Marta washed her hands?
Have they signed the petition?

Irregular verbs
Have you gone snorkeling?
Has the cat eaten?

1. Analyze the images and complete the sentences with a verb from the box in the present perfect (affirmative or negative).

arrive	ask	climb	get on	hurt	ride

THINKSTOCK/GETTY IMAGES

The teacher ______________ a question.

THINKSTOCK/GETTY IMAGES

They ______________ at their final destination.

THINKSTOCK/GETTY IMAGES

The students ______________ the bus.

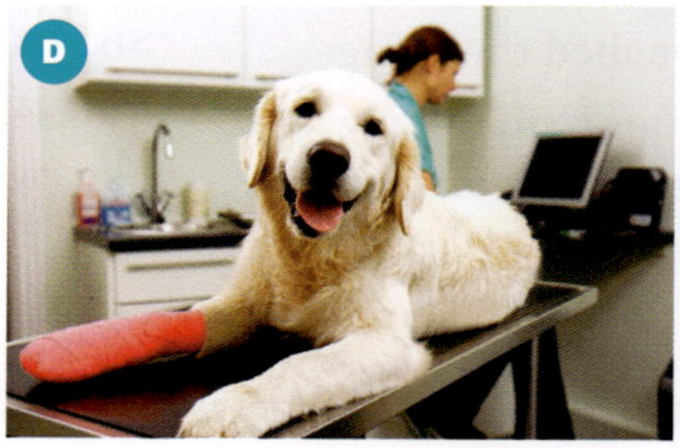

THINKSTOCK/GETTY IMAGES

My dog ______________ his leg.

THINKSTOCK/GETTY IMAGES

She ______________ a mountain.

THINKSTOCK/GETTY IMAGES

They ______________ their bikes all the way to the river.

2. Complete the questions with the present perfect of the verb in parentheses and then write personal answers.

a. ______________ you ______________ to Buenos Aires? (be) ______________

b. ______________ you ______________ to your best friend recently? (talk) ______________

c. ______________ your mother ______________ a rock concert? (see) ______________

d. ______________ your best friend ______________ a birthday cake for you? (make) ______________

e. ______________ you and your cousins ______________ a sport together? (play) ______________

LISTENING COMPREHENSION

BEFORE LISTENING

1. Read the first paragraph of Article 16 from the Universal Declaration of Human Rights.

Article 16.

- (1) Men and women of full age, without any limitation due to race, nationality or religion, have the right to marry and to found a family. They are entitled to equal rights as to marriage, during marriage and at its dissolution.

a. Look at the pictures and check who can get married, according to the first paragraph of Article 16.

SHUTTERSTOCK

IMAGESOURCE/AGB PHOTO

SHUTTERSTOCK

SHUTTERSTOCK

SHUTTERSTOCK

REUTERS/LATINSTOCK

b. Read the paragraph again and, based on it, answer: Who can the people on the pictures get married to?

☐ Women can get married only to men and men can get married only to women.

☐ Men and women who are of full age can get married to other men or women in the same condition, as long as both agree.

2. Do you think the right to marry is equal for everyone in every country? Say a few examples to justify your answer.

____

LISTENING

3. Listen to Riley Roberts, an American teenager from the state of Nevada. What is he going to talk about?

24

____

____

4. Listen to Riley as he continues his testimony and answer:

25

a. How old is Riley? __________

b. How long do his parents have been together? __________

c. Why does his mother Pam will not receive the survivor spouse benefit if his mother Gretchen dies?

____

____

5. Riley says: "They're denied the rights, the freedoms, and the ability to be a full and equal citizen of the United States of America in this great state of Nevada." Why does he say his parents are not full and equal American citizens and what is the cause for this difference?

____

____

____

____

____

6. Listen to the end of the testimony and answer.

26

a. How does Riley describe his parents?

- [ ] As regular people, who love, breathe, speak, and feel pain.
- [ ] As special people, who deserve special treatment.

b. Why does the idea of an opposition to equal rights bewilders Riley? Take your answer on the previous question into account.

____

____

____

____

AFTER LISTENING

7. Riley's testimony was made in 2013 in favor of a change in law that would recognize all marriages, regardless of gender. This amendment was approved in May 28, 2013. After listening to Riley's testimony, what is your position on the subject? Justify your answer.

SPEAKING

1. Read the statement and write **A** if you agree or **D** if you disagree.

☐ "Differences in social and emotional development result from a child's inborn temperament, cultural influences, disabilities, behaviors modeled by adults, the level of security felt in a child's relationships with adults, and the opportunities provided for social interaction."

Extracted from: <www.pbs.org/parents/childdevelopmenttracker/one/socialandemotionalgrowth.html>. Accessed on: Jun. 7, 2016.

2. List the reasons why you agree or disagree with the statement.

____

____

____

____

____

3. Work in pairs. Take turns and tell each other your opinion about the statement. Below you will find some useful expressions to give your opinion.

In my opinion,...
To my mind,...
From my point of view,...
In my eyes,...
Speaking personally,...
I have the feeling that...
My impression is that...
I have no doubt that...

4. Try to reach a conclusion about your discussion.

5. Report your discussion to the whole group. Mention if your opinions are similar or not.

Reflecting on the theme

- If you consider social interaction part of someone's social and emotional development, how can your attitudes help build an environment with less prejudice?

BEFORE WRITING

1. Read the text and answer the questions.

us.reachout.com/real-stories/story/count-your-blessings

Count your blessings

My name is Robyn, and I am perfectly imperfect. I laugh too loud, get distracted too easily, and dance like a fool. [...]

Life is a funny thing sometimes. I am exactly like my father: same stature, same obsession over correct grammar, same love for debate and argument (He's a lawyer), and same artistic eye (even if he does deny it, he is an artist.). My mother calls us the "human dictionaries," and we can't help but laugh. Now here's the funny thing: my father isn't really my father; I was adopted.

I don't ever remember my parents ever telling me that I was adopted. It's like I've always known and that was normal for me. [...] I have two parents that love me, and that's all that matters.

Extracted from: <us.reachout.com/real-stories/story/count-your-blessings>. Accessed on: May 29, 2015.

a. Who are the members of Robyn's family?

____

____

____

b. How does Robyn feel about her family?

____

____

____

2. Match the columns and find the most common characteristics of testimonials.

a. A testimonial is a letter or written statement

b. Testimonials are often intended to make the reader

c. True testimonials usually

d. There are testimonials about

e. A testimonial is commonly broadcast

☐ don't show the writer's complete name.

☐ on the appropriate media for its target audience.

☐ trust the person or product they refer to.

☐ about the qualities of a person, product or service.

☐ family relationships.

WRITING

3. You read different testimonials about family relationships in this unit. Now you're go ng to write a testimonial about your family or about friends who are very close to you.
   - Remember the characteristics of a testimonial:
     - A testimonial mentions true facts about the author's life.
     - A testimonial is written in first person.
     - The author expresses his/her opinions, feelings and points of view.
   - Choose a situation that you lived with this person. Why was this situation important?
   - How did you feel that day?
   - What was the reaction of the people who were with you?
   - Write a draft of the testimonial.
   - If necessary, use a dictionary to check vocabulary or spelling.
   - Exchange your text with a classmate and evaluate your testimonials.
   - Show your text to your teacher and make the necessary adjustments.

AFTER WRITING

- Schedule a day with your teacher to read your testimonial to your classmates.
- When you finish, allow your classmates to comment the parts of the testimonial they found most interesting.
- If you feel comfortable with it, pin your testimonial to the class bulletin board.

SELF-EVALUATION

Check the true sentences about your learning in Unit 8.

In this unit you have learned to:

- [ ] report events that happened in the past, without mentioning when they happened;
- [ ] identify different kinds of families and compare them;
- [ ] read and write a testimonial.

Reflecting...

- **What did I learn about different kinds of families?**
- **What questions do I still have about testimonials?**
- **What questions do I still have about the use of the present perfect?**
- **What did I like best about this unit?**

Connections

English • Physical Education

Traditional games

UNICEF

All around the world, children love sport. It gives them the chance to have fun and be active. Yet sport is also a way of learning important values and life skills, including self-confidence, team work, communication, inclusion, discipline, respect and fair play. For this reason, sport is an important part of childhood.

Although some sports are popular around the world, some are widespread in a specific culture or country, like the ball game called shomba.

Shomba

A dodging and tagging game played widely throughout Zambia.

Age: 5+

Players: Two teams, with a minimum of three players per team up to as many as you like.

Pitch: An open flat playing space with no specific boundaries.

Time: Unlimited.

Rules: One player from team A – the dodgers – begins by filling a bucket with sand from a pile, and transferring the sand to a sand pit.

Team B – the taggers – take it in turns to throw a soft ball at the dodger from an agreed distance.

When tagged (hit with the ball) this player goes to the back of team A and the next dodger steps forward to continue filling the sand pit.

The game continues until either the dodgers fill the sand pit and count to 10 or the taggers eliminate the dodgers before they complete the task.

Equipment

- An ichimpombwa (traditional Zambia ball), soft ball or similar.
- A bucket or similar vessel.
- A sand pit.
- Sand.

Safety

- Players can only be tagged below shoulder height.

Adapted from: <www.unicef.org.uk/Documents/Education-Documents/Resources-Documents/UNICEF_TraditionalGames_resource.pdf>. Accessed on: Jun. 8, 2016.

1. Do you know any other traditional games from other countries? Research online. How are they played? Which one is the most interesting in your opinion?

____

____

____

____

____

____

____

2. What traditional Brazilian games did you use to play when you were a kid? Do you still play them? Which one is your favorite traditional Brazilian game? How would you explain the rules of this game to a foreigner?

____

____

____

____

3. Ask for the help of your Physical Education teacher and organize a match of shomba. How do you like playing it? Would you adapt any rule? How so?

____

____

____

____

1. Read the poem below and check the correct answers to the questions.

English Is Everywhere

English language is known worldwide
From all languages that were collide
English is known everywhere
It is great to use it anywhere

Upholding English to everyone
Speaking in English is very fun
Don't be shy and show your greatness
Use it when showing competitiveness

Speaking in English is as good as gold
The language of English we need to uphold
It's very fun when you come to think of it
When you're with your friends who also love it

When you go to any country
This is the language of everybody
Being expressed in different place
Different accents on different place

The English language is my proficiency
Never be shy and express it freely
Just be confident and you'll be okay
Uphold English Proficiency and have a great day

** I wrote this for our English Month Activity-Poem Writing Contest for the 1st year High School students-1st Place!! =)) **

Geneen Meyers

Extracted from: <www.poemhunter.com/poem/english-is-everywhere/>. Accessed on: Jun. 8, 2016.

a. Why did Geneen Meyers write this poem?

☐ To participate in an English Month Activity-Poem Writing Contest.

☐ Because she was learning English.

b. In which stanzas did she say that people need to overcome shyness and speak English without being afraid?

☐ In the first and the last stanzas.

☐ In the second and in the last stanzas.

c. According to her, is English the same everywhere? Why?

☐ No, it isn't. Because English is spoken in different places and people have different accents.

☐ Yes, it is. Because people show their greatness when they speak English.

2. Complete the table with the past form of the verbs.

verb	regular	irregular
answer	*answered*	–
ask		
be		
come		
drive		
go		
want		

3. Complete the post below with the verbs from activity 2.

linguaholic.com/general-discussion/funny-language-situations

Jellyfish

Funny language situations

« on: September 04, 2013, 01:36:27 PM »

I was driving by the train when two girls ____________ to me and asked if I could help them. They ____________ from Mexico and ____________ me to help them buying tickets. We ____________ by the train to the station and ____________ to the ticket shop.

The women there ____________ me where they want to go and so on. Then she asked me what language they speak. I ____________: Mexican.

Well, not quite funny. More embarrassing.

How about you?

Extracted from: <linguaholic.com/general-discussion/funny-language-situations/>. Accessed on: Mar. 4, 2015.

4. Match the questions to the answers according to the post in activity 3.

a. What was Jellyfish doing when the two girls came to him?

b. Where were the girls from?

c. What did they want?

d. Why was the situation embarrassing?

☐ They wanted help to buy tickets.

☐ He was driving by the train.

☐ Because Jellyfish got confused and made a mistake. The girls spoke Spanish, not Mexican. Mexican is their nationality.

☐ They were from Mexico.

5. Write **T** (true), **F** (false) or **NM** (not mentioned) according to what you hear about the Dead Sea. (27)

a. ☐ The Dead Sea is the lowest point on Earth.

b. ☐ There aren't any living things in the Dead Sea.

c. ☐ There is no fish swimming there.

d. ☐ The only mineral in the water is salt.

6. Check the best alternative to complete the excerpt of the text you have just heard. Then listen and check. (28)

> [...]
>
> The Dead Sea is about ____________ saltier than the ocean, and that salt will sting. But with the yin comes the yang. Even the ____________ here is good for you, helping with everything from arthritis to wrinkles, which is why you'll see ____________ lathering it on and then baking a bit before heading in. If you like to ____________ your spa treatments outdoors, the Dead Sea is a good place to do it.

Transcripted from: <www.budgettravel.com/video/float-in-the-dead-sea,58/>. Acessed on: Mar. 26, 2015.

☐ 20 times – salt – tourists – enjoy

☐ 2 times – water – people – relax

☐ 10 times – mud – people – enjoy

7. The pictures below are from the Dead Sea. Label them using some expressions extracted from the audio you heard in activity 5.

A

JAN GREUNE/LATINSTOCK

B

ALAMY/MASTERFILE/LATINSTOCK

C

MENAHEM KAHANA/AFP

A: ____________ B: ____________ C: ____________

The Dead Sea is a salt lake bordered by Jordan, Israel and the West Bank. Its unique characteristic is that its water has 300 grams of salt per liter. The normal amount of salt in the ocean for the same amount of water is 30 grams.

8. Read about Wales, a country in the United Kingdom, and answer the questions.

Wales

WOLFGANG MEIER/CORBIS/LATINSTOCK

Wales, the land of Merlin (Myrddin Emrys in Welsh) and the red dragon. The mist rising from these dark green valleys is an invitation to explore further with kids – from great crumbling 13th century castles on rocky crags to underground caverns and mines, deep under the mountains.

[...]

Tip: Wales has steam trains, originally built to carry ore or timber. These trains pass through some absolutely glorious scenery, some places you can't get to by car. Steam trains have appeal for kids (is it all that puffy white smoke) and this is the perfect thing for a day trip.

Fun food
At tea time, try Welsh Rarebit, essentially cheese on toast, or Bara Brith (Speckled Bread) with lots of honey. The "speckles" are dried fruit or dates.

Shopping
Celtic jewellry is fun, earrings, bracelets, rings and brooches. For the more industrially minded, bring back a real miner's lamp or other souvenirs from the coal, slate and gold mines.

Extracted from: <www.travelforkids.com/Funtodo/Wales/wales.htm>. Accessed on: Jun. 8, 2016.

jewellry (UK): jewelry (USA)

crags: penhascos
steam trains: trens a vapor
dried fruit: frutas secas
slate: ardósia

a. What can you see if you travel by steam train?

b. What is Welsh Rarebit made of?

c. Which mines can you buy souvenirs from?

d. What is Celtic jewellry?

1. Match the pictures to the travel tips they represent.

IMAGENS: GREENING YOUR LIFE

Extracted from: <www.applevacationsblog.com/2013/04/greening-your-life/>. Accessed on: Jun. 8. 2016.

a. ☐ 

d. ☐ 

b. ☐ 

e. ☐ 

c. ☐ 

f. ☐ 

2. Read the travel tips again and answer the questions.

a. Which tips aren't represented in the image?

b. Which icons would you use to represent them? Make a drawing in your notebook.

3. Write **T** (true) or **F** (false) according to the text on page 166.

a. ☐ Unplug electric devices and save energy.

b. ☐ You can help save fuel by choosing non-stop flights to your destination.

c. ☐ Don't worry about saving energy when you are a guest in a hotel.

d. ☐ There are four tips about what you can do before leaving home.

e. ☐ You should not touch coral formations when snorkeling.

4. Write explanations to the true sentences in activity 3.

____

____

____

____

5. You are going to listen to John Kerry, the US Secretary of State, talking about what we can do to help protect our ocean. Before you listen, order the parts below in a logical sequence. Then listen and check.

29

☐ The good news is, it doesn't have to be that way. Governments, communities, and individuals can act now to reverse these trends.

☐ The ocean covers almost three quarters of our planet, but our ocean today is at grave risk and the damage is not happening by accident. Human activity is the cause.

☐ We can protect the ocean if we all start treating it like "our ocean". Wherever you live, you can help in some way.

☐ Harmful fishing practices, even illegal fishing; giant garbage patches, hundreds of dead zones, and rising carbon dioxide levels – all of it threatens life under the sea. That is the bad news.

Extracted from: <www.state.gov/secretary/remarks/2014/06/227042.htm#>. Accessed on: Jun. 6, 2016.

ANADOLU AGENCY/GETTY IMAGES

6. Listen to the second part of John Kerry's remarks and check the correct answers to the questions below. 30

a. How many things does he mention people can do to have a healthier ocean?

☐ Four. ☐ Two.

b. What will leaders around the world be asked to do?

☐ To act now to create a healthier ocean together.

☐ To make a public commitment for a healthier ocean.

7. John Kerry's message is from June 2, 2014. What are the ocean's condition now? Has anything changed?

---

8. Read about the singer and political activist Miriam Makeba and check YES or NO.

Miriam Makeba

Miriam Makeba (1932-2008) was an award-winning singer and political activist born in Johannesburg, South Africa. She was one of the most visible opponents of the apartheid regime, resulting in the revocation of her South African citizenship by the regime due to her activism. She toured internationally and collaborated with artists including Harry Belafonte with whom she won a Grammy award.

JORDI VIDAL/REDFERNS/GETTY IMAGES

Extracted from: <en.unesco.org/womeninafrica>. Accessed on: Jun. 8, 2016.

The apartheid was a system of racial segregation enforced in South Africa from 1948 to 1994. Besides Miriam Makeba, there were many other anti-apartheid activists, such as Nelson Mandela, the most famous of them all.

	YES	NO
a. Miriam Makeba was well-known just because she was an awarded singer.		
b. She fought against racial segregation.		
c. She didn't like to deal with political issues.		
d. Miriam and Belafonte were awarded a Grammy.		
e. Because she was an opponent of the apartheid regime, her South African citizenship was canceled.		

9. Read the comic strips and answer the questions.

a. Why is Jon upset?

____

b. What will Jon do about it?

____

c. Why does Jon use *'ll* in his sentence?

____

d. According to Garfield, is Jon's plan good or bad?

____

e. Why does Jon say he is afraid?

____

f. Is Garfield ironic? Explain.

____

g. Which word shows Garfield's irony? How do you know that?

____

h. Why does Jon want to be good enough for Liz?

____

1. Read about the Mexican artist Frida Kahlo and complete the chart with the symbolic elements mentioned in the text, according to the cues given.

www.theartstory.org/artist-kahlo-frida.htm

Self-Portrait with Thorn Necklace and Hummingbird (1940)

The frontal position and direct stare of Kahlo in this self-portrait directly confronts and engages the viewer. The artist wears Christ's unraveled crown of thorns as a necklace that digs into her neck, signifying her self-representation as a Christian martyr and the enduring pain from her failed marriage. A dead hummingbird, a symbol in Mexican folkloric tradition of luck charms for falling in love, hangs in the center of her necklace. A black cat – symbolic of bad luck and death – crouches behind her left shoulder, and a spider monkey gifted from Rivera, symbolic of evil, is included to her right. Kahlo frequently employed flora and fauna in the background of her bust length portraits to create a tight, claustrophobic space, using the symbolic element of nature to simultaneously compare and contrast the link between female fertility with the barren and deathly imagery of the foreground.

FRIDA KAHLO, AUTORRETRATO COM COLAR DE ESPINHOS, 1940

KAHLO, Frida. *Self-portrait with Thorn Necklace and Hummingbird.* 1940. Oil of canvas, 61.25 cm × 47 cm. Harry Ranson Center, University of Texas at Austin, USA.

Extracted from: <www.theartstory.org/artist-kahlo-frida.htm>. Accessed on: Jun. 8, 2016.

thorns: espinhos
necklace: colar
luck charms: amuletos da sorte
crouches: agacha-se

a. An element of bad luck and death.	
b. It's a luck charm for falling in love.	
c. It symbolizes evil.	
d. It symbolizes Frida's failed marriage.	

2. Complete this excerpt from the Frida Kahlo website using the words from the box.

calm	feelings	pain	symbolic

[...]

Her expression is ____________________ and solemn. It also seems she is patient y enduring the ____________________ .

Frida Kahlo put so many ____________________ creatures in this painting. She was not painting a realistic scene but using these symbolic elements to express her ____________________ .

[...]

Extracted from: <www.fridakahlo.org/self-portrait-with-thorn-necklace-and-hummingbird.jsp>. Accessed on: Jun. 8, 2016.

3. Listen to part of Frida Kahlo's story and check True or False.

31

	True	False
a. Frida Kahlo transformed her life by painting herself.		
b. She was born in 1907.		
c. She didn't have to deal with serious problems during her life.		
d. Due to an accident, she had to live with permanent injuries.		
e. During her convalescence, she stopped painting.		

4. Listen to another part of the story and complete the text.

32

She herself would become a legend, making her own life into a ____________________ and coming to feel at home with some of the most celebrated ____________________ and visionaries of her day. And yet, ironically, her ____________________ would remain virtually ____________________ during her lifetime – an obscurity that did not matter to her. She painted, she said, for herself and, in the process, created some of the most indelible images of the ____________________.

Transcripted from: <www.youtube.com/watch?v=jYWKoMFjnbs>. Accessed on Jun. 6, 2016.

5. Check the best alternatives to answer the questions about the comic strip.

a. Which part of sentence from the comic strip makes us believe that Jon is going to read a fairy tale aloud?

- ☐ "This sounds familiar"
- ☐ "Once upon a time there was..."

b. Which house do you think Jon refers to?

- ☐ His own house.
- ☐ The house from the story he is reading.

c. Who are the real fat cat and the happy dog?

- ☐ Garfield and Oddie.
- ☐ Characters from the story.

d. Why is Jon angry?

- ☐ Because he is tired of reading stories aloud.
- ☐ Because Garfield and Oddie have ruined his morning.

e. Look at Jon's facial expressions in the first and second panels and compare them to the one in the last panel. What can you notice?

- ☐ In the first and second panels, Jon is focused. In the third one, he is much more upset.
- ☐ In the first and second panels, Jon's face doesn't show any emotion at all. In the third one, it's crystal clear that he is very upset.

f. Look at Garfield's and Oddie's faces in the three panels. Do they react the same way?

- ☐ No, they don't. Garfield seems not to worry about Jon's anger, but Oddie does.
- ☐ Yes, they do. Both seem to be worried about Jon's irony.

6. Underline the correct words to form true sentences about the cartoon.

"Why was she roaming the forest looking for porridge?
A girl her age should know how to microwave a breakfast sandwich!"

a. The woman probably **buys/reads** to her daughter before the girl goes to sleep.

b. The girl has doubts about **her mother's/the character's** behavior.

c. From the girl's point of view, the character is too **dependent/independent** and not so smart.

d. The girl's mother is **surprised/excited** because she didn't expect that kind of question.

7. Complete these fragments of famous stories with the correct alternative.

a.

> [...]
> "Well, no," said Simba sadly. "My father has forbidden me to go there."
> "Quite right," said Scar. "Only ____________________ lions go there. An elephant graveyard is no place for a young prince." [...]

Extracted from: *The Lion King*. Ladybird Books Ltd: Leicestershire, United Kingdom, 1994. p. 7.

☐ the bravest ☐ braver than

b.

> [...]
> Jafar raised his head to strike Aladdin. "Did you think you could beat ____________________ being on Earth?" he snarled.
> Aladdin thought quickly of a way to trap Jafar. "The Genie has much more power than you!" he taunted.
> [...]

Extracted from: *Aladdin*. Ladybird Books Ltd: Leicestershire, United Kingdom, 2003. p. 7.

☐ more powerful than ☐ the most powerful

FURTHER PRACTICE 4

1. Look at the campaign poster and check the sentence that is NOT true.

DPA PUBLIC EDUCATION CAMPAIGN 2013

a. ☐ The people inside the elevator pretend not to see the man in the wheelchair.

b. ☐ The man in the wheelchair can move in a single direction.

c. ☐ The poster is directed only to people who use elevators.

2. Correct the sentence you checked in activity 1 and justify.

____

____

3. In pairs, answer the following question: Are pictures usually more relevant than sentences in posters? Why?

____

____

4. Listen to the testimonial of a seventeen-year-old boy named Sam Berns who suffers from a disease called Progeria. Check the correct option to complete the sentences you have heard.

33

What is progeria?

Progeria is a progressive and rare genetic disorder which has no known cure. The main symptons of progeria are a very old-looking appearance, hair loss and excessive thinness. Life expectancy for people who have this disorder is about 20 years.

Based on: <www.minhavida.com.br/saude/temas/progeria>. Accessed on: Mar. 22, 2015.

a. [...] It affects only about ____________ kids today, worldwide. [...]

☐ 350 ☐ 150

b. [...] So, it's pretty rare and effects of Progeria include tight skin, lack of weight gain, stunted growth, and ____________ disease. [...]

☐ bone ☐ heart

c. Last year ____________ and her team of ____________ published the first successful Progeria Treatment Study [...]

☐ parents / doctors ☐ my mom / scientists

5. Listen to Sam Berns again and correct the wrong sentences.

34

a. His answer to the question "What is the most important thing that people should know about you?" is "I have a fantastic mother."

____

____

b. Even though Sam faces many problems, he doesn't want people to feel bad about him.

____

____

c. Sam thinks about the obstacles all the time, but he knows that he is able to overcome most of them anyway.

____

____

6. Use the words from the box to complete the excerpt from Sam's testimonial. Then listen and check your answers. 35

challenges	hard	obstacles

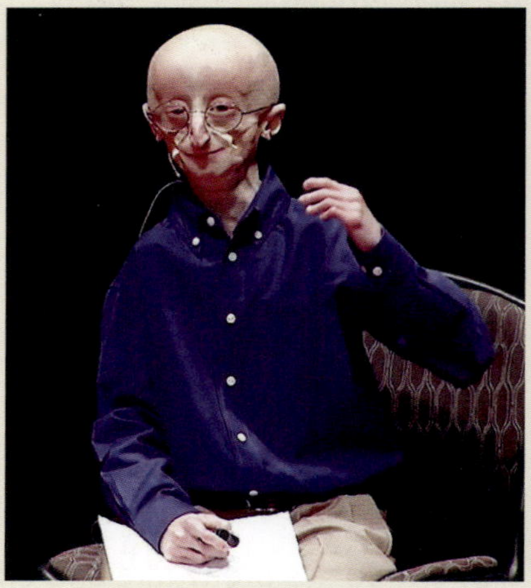
TEDX

Now people sometimes ask me questions like, "Isn't it ______________ living with Progeria?" or "What daily ______________ of Progeria do you face?" And I'd like to say that, even though I have Progeria, most of my time is spent thinking about things that have nothing to do with Progeria at all. Now this doesn't mean that I ignore the negative aspects of these ______________. When I can't do something like run a long distance or go on an intense roller coaster, you know, I know what I'm missing out on. But instead, I choose to focus on the activities that I can do through things that I'm passionate about like scouting, or music, or comic books, or any of my favorite Boston sports teams.

Extracted from: <www.youtube.com/watch?v=36m1o-tM05g>. Accessed on: Jun. 6, 2016.

7. Underline the correct options to complete this blog post about Brett and Justin.

fam2fam.org/adoptive-families/passionate-about-helping/

Brett and Justin are passionate about helping others.

Posted on July 3, 2014 by rgm

Brett and Justin are best friends **which/who** fell in love. They **married/have married** on January 3, 2014 after four very happy years together.

They are a loving couple who are devoted to their family, friends, and pets. Brett and Justin love trips and exploring new places. They **have traveled/traveled** from San Antonio, to South America, to the Caribbean and more!

Justin is in pre school education and Brett is a business owner. They are both passionate about their jobs **where/when** they are able to help children and the community. They love children and often spend time with their nephews **who/whose** state that they are fun and kind. Brett and Justin cannot wait to spoil their own children with love and adventures.

They are anxious to begin their own family through adoption and state that their child's birth mother "will always be the hero that gave us the chance to be parents".

[...]

Extracted from: <fam2fam.org/adoptive-families/passionate-about-helping/>. Accessed on: Mar. 23, 2015.

8. Read the text about Brett and Justin again and match questions and answers.

a. When did Brett and Justin get married?

b. How long did they stay together before getting married?

c. What do they love doing?

d. Why do they love their jobs?

e. What do they say about their future child's birth mother?

☐ Because they are able to help children and the community.

☐ Exploring new places.

☐ For four years.

☐ On January 3, 2014.

☐ They compare her to a hero because she will give them the chance to become parents.

9. Look at the picture, read the poster and check the true sentences.

a. ☐ The baby girl is the women's daughter.

b. ☐ The poster supports marriage equality.

c. ☐ Families like the one in the poster have their rights preserved.

d. ☐ The reader is invited to think about the issue the poster presents.

MARRIAGE QUALITY

PROJECT 1

Indian culture fair: a fascinating display of culture

In this project you will be:

- reflect on cultural differences that come from having different languages in the same country;
- get to know what Indian people are doing in order to minimize the social gap resulting from the language differences across the country;
- hold a Culture Fair about Indian languages and other aspects of Indian culture in order to share knowledge with the community.

1. Read the text *Languages in India* and write **T** (true), **F** (false) or **NM** (not mentioned).

www.kwintessential.co.uk/resources/global-etiquette/india-country-profile.html

Languages in India

The different states of India have different official languages, some of them not recognized by the central government. Some states have more than one official language. Bihar in east India has three official languages – Hindi, Urdu and Bengali – which are all recognized by the central government. But Sikkim, also in east India, has four official languages of which only Nepali is recognized by the central government. Besides the languages officially recognized by central or state governments, there are other languages which don't have this recognition and their speakers are running political struggles to get this recognition. Central government decided that Hindi was to be the official language of India and therefore it also has the status of official language in the states.

[...]

TPG/AGB PHOTO

PETER SCHICKERT/IMAGEBROKER/AGB PHOTO

Extracted from: <www.kwintessential.co.uk/resources/global-etiquette/india-country-profile.html>. Accessed on: Jun. 8, 2016.

struggles: batalhas

a. ☐ Hindi, Urdu, Bengali, and Nepali are some of the languages recognized by the central government.

b. ☐ Hindi is the only official language in India.

c. ☐ Each Indian state has its own official language.

d. ☐ Each state speaks one language only.

e. ☐ Speakers of non-recognized languages are fighting for recognition.

Group discussion

There are 22 major languages in India, written in 13 different scripts, with over 720 dialects. The official Indian languages are Hindi (with approximately 420 million speakers) and English, which is also widely spoken.

[...]

Extracted from: <www.justlanded.com/english/India/India-Guide/Language/Languages-in-India>. Accessed on: Jun. 8, 2016.

- In your opinion, what are the personal, social, and economic consequences of not understanding people from other states in your own country?

Project

- In groups, decide on which aspect of the Indian culture you are going to talk about during the Indian Culture Fair. You can talk about facts and statistics, languages, hierarchy, the role of the family, social behavior, table manners, dress etiquette or any similar topic.
- Talk to teachers of other subjects for specific information, depending on which aspect you choose. For example, if you choose languages, ask the Geography teacher for information about languages spoken in each part of the country; if you choose dress etiquette, talk to the History teacher about the social-economic meaning of clothes in India.
- Search the internet for information on the topic you chose, or look it up at the school library.
- Decide on how you are going to present the information you have collected. For example, you can prepare infographics, cook traditional Indian food or present pictures of traditional outfits.
- Create the written part of your exposition. If you are cooking a traditional dish, write the recipe and present it. If you are showing traditional outfits, prepare a picture gallery with captions. If you are presenting information about languages, produce fact files or some posters. Ask the teacher to correct your texts before writing them over.
- Set the date and place for the event and then prepare invitations of different kinds – traditional ones, posters and flyers – to inform and invite other students, teachers, coordinators, family and members of your community to the Indian Culture Fair. This way you can share your knowledge on Indian culture with as many people as possible.

Research suggestions

- <www.mapsofindia.com/culture>
- <www.bbc.com/news/world-south-asia-12557384#facts>
- <memory.loc.gov/frd/cs/profiles/India.pdf>
- <www.youtube.com/watch?v=HrrW3rO51ak>

Accessed on: Jun. 8, 2016.

PROJECT 2

Influence and intertextuality in everyday life

In this project you will:

- reflect on the new meanings that a text gains when it is influenced by others;
- learn to recognize intertextuality in different types of text;
- create different forms of intertextuality and share them with other students and school members.

1. Do you usually borrow phrases, quotes, images and so on from previous texts when you communicate? Why do you do that? Share some examples with the whole group.

2. Look at the pictures. Then check the correct alternative.

LEONARDO DA VINCI, MONA LISA, C.1503-6

Mona Lisa
(Leonardo da Vinci – 1452/1519)
c. 1503-1506 – Oil on poplar
77 cm × 53 cm
Musée du Louvre, Paris
France

MAURICIO DE SOUSA EDITORA LTDA.

Mônica Lisa
1989 – Acrylic on canvas
71 cm × 61 cm

a. ☐ *Mônica Lisa* is an example of intertextuality from the artwork *Mona Lisa*.

b. ☐ *Mona Lisa* and *Mônica Lisa* were probably painted by the same artist.

c. ☐ *Mônica Lisa* is as famous as *Mona Lisa*.

3. Read the definition of intertextuality again on page 109. Based on that definition, what other uses of intertextuality can you think of?

____

____

____

Group discussion

Intertextuality as a Literary Device

Do you borrow phrases and concepts from other works in your own? If yes, then you're using intertextuality, perhaps even without knowing it.

Though it sounds intimidating at first, it's quite a simple concept really:

Intertextuality denotes the way in which texts (any text, not just literature) gain meaning through their referencing or evocation of other texts.

[...]

Extracted from: <thewritepractice.com/intertextuality-as-a-literary-device>. Accessed on: Jun. 8, 2016.

Project

- In groups, choose any text you want to revisit. It can be a painting, a song, a poem, a book, a TV commercial, a cartoon, a fable, a fairy tale or any other.
- Think of the intertextual analysis you want to do and talk to your teacher.
- You can exchange some ideas with your Portuguese or Art teacher as well, depending on what kind of text you have decided to work with.
- Create your text.
- If it is a written text, let your teacher revise it. Then make all the necessary changes. If you are drawing, painting, sculpting, or molding, make some notes about how you intend to explain it to the group and show these notes to your teacher.
- Present your work to your classmates. You can invite other students, teachers and coordinators to this presentation.
- At the end, discuss the most creative and interesting works with the whole group.

Research suggestions

- <pt.slideshare.net/lauraraxten/intertextuality-im-music-videos>
- <study.com/academy/lesson/intertextuality-in-literature-definition-examples.html>
- <humanities.wisc.edu/assets/misc/What_Is_Intertextuality.pdf>
- <www.youtube.com/watch?v=U5DyOgvmizE>

Accessed on: Jun. 8, 2016.

Simple past

We use the **simple past** of regular and irregular verbs to talk about something that started and finished at a definite time in the past.

We add **-ed**, **-d** or **-ied** to make the simple past form of regular verbs. Irregular verbs don't follow the **-ed** ending rule and have their own forms.

In the negative form, we insert **not** after the auxiliary verb **did**, before the main verb.

To make the interrogative, we invert the position of the auxiliary verb **did** and the subject.

Look at the examples in the charts below. As you can see, when we use the auxiliary verb **did** (or the negatives **did not/didn't**), the main verb form remains in the base form.

Affirmative	Negative	Interrogative
I **bought** a new software for my PC.	I **did not/didn't buy** a new software for my PC.	**Did** I **buy** a new software for my PC?
You **found** the car keys.	You **did not/didn't find** the car keys.	**Did** you **find** the car keys?
He **drove** me to school.	He **did not/didn't drive** me to school.	**Did** he **drive** me to school?
She **slept** on the couch.	She **did not/didn't sleep** on the couch.	**Did** she **sleep** on the couch?
It **snowed** two days ago.	It **did not/didn't snow** two days ago.	**Did** it **snow** two days ago?
We **visited** granny last week.	We **did not/didn't visit** granny last week.	**Did** we **visit** granny last week?
You **traveled** abroad.	You **did not/didn't travel** abroad.	**Did** you **travel** abroad?
They **lived** in a house.	They **did not/didn't live** in a house.	**Did** they **live** in a house?

Short answers – affirmative and negative

Question	Affirmative	Negative
Did he go to Barcelona?	Yes, he did.	No, he didn't.
Did they work downtown?	Yes, they did.	No, they didn't.

In the simple past we often say when the action happened, so time expressions like **yesterday**, **last night**, **last week**, **last month**, **last year**, **two hours ago**, **four months ago**, **three years ago**, **in 2010**, etc., are common to reinforce the completion of the action.

Look at the following examples:

Gus played soccer with his friends **last Saturday**.
We didn't leave home **yesterday** morning.
Did you send your reports **two days ago**?

Past continuous

We use the **past continuous** to talk about an action that was in progress at a certain time in the past.

To make the affirmative form of the past continuous, we use **was** or **were** before the main verb in the **-ing** form.

In the negative form, we use **was not/wasn't** or **were not/weren't** followed by the main verb in the **-ing** form.

In the interrogative form, we invert the position of **was** or **were** and the subject and then add the main verb in the **-ing** form.

Look at the examples in the charts below.

Affirmative	Negative	Interrogative
I **was working** yesterday morning.	I **was not/wasn't working** yesterday morning.	**Was** I **working** yesterday morning?
You **were taking a shower** at 9:00.	You **were not/weren't taking a shower** at 9:00.	**Were** you **taking a shower** at 9:00?
He **was driving** downtown.	He **was not/wasn't driving** downtown.	**Was** he **driving** downtown?
She **was listening** to music.	She **was not/wasn't listening** to music.	**Was** she **listening** to music?
It **was raining** when I got up.	It **was not/wasn't raining** when I got up.	**Was** it **raining** when I got up?
We **were studying** in our bedrooms.	We **were not/weren't studying** in our bedrooms.	**Were** we **studying** in our bedrooms?
You **were watching** a movie last night.	You **were not/weren't watching** a movie last night.	**Were** you **watching** a movie last night?
They **were talking** to the teacher.	They **were not/weren't talking** to the teacher.	**Were** they **talking** to the teacher?

Short answers – affirmative and negative

Question	Affirmative	Negative
Was she eating a hot dog?	Yes, she was.	No, she wasn't.
Were you looking for Jane?	Yes, we were.	No, we weren't.

Past continuous x simple past

The **past continuous** is also used to talk about actions that were in progress simultaneously in the past or about an action that was in progress when another one happened. In these situations, the adverbs **while** and **when** are often used and the **simple past** is used for the completed action or the action that interrupted the one in progress.

Take a look at the following examples:

Kelly **was reading** a book **while** her husband **was playing** tennis with his friends.
My friends **weren't watching the movie when** the lights **went** off.
What **were** you **doing when** I **arrived**?

Future (going to)

In English, there are different ways of talking about the future. Using **going to** is one of them.

We use **going to** to talk about our plans or intentions for the near future.

In the affirmative form, we use the verb **to be** (**am**, **are** or **is**) followed by **going to** and the base form of the main verb.

In the negative form, we use **not** between the verb **to be** and the **going to** form.

In the interrogative form, we invert the position of the subject and the verb **to be**.

Check the examples in the chart below.

Affirmative	Negative	Interrogative
I **am**/I'**m going to swim** in that pool.	I **am not**/I'**m not going to swim** in that pool.	**Am** I **going to swim** in that pool?
You **are**/You'**re going to talk** on the phone.	You **are not**/**aren't going to talk** on the phone.	**Are** you **going to talk** on the phone?
He **is**/He'**s going to eat** in the cafeteria.	He **is not**/**isn't going to eat** in the cafeteria.	**Is** he **going to eat** in the cafeteria?
She **is**/She'**s going to travel** for a month.	She **is not**/**isn't going to travel** for a month.	**Is** she **going to travel** for a month?
It **is**/It'**s going to be** hot today.	It **is not**/**isn't going to be** hot today.	**Is** it **going to be** hot today?
We **are**/We'**re going to take** an exam.	We **are not**/**aren't going to take** an exam.	**Are** we **going to take** an exam?
You **are**/You'**re going to come** for the wedding.	You **are not**/**aren't going to come** for the wedding.	**Are** you **going to come** for the wedding?
They **are**/They'**re going to have** breakfast.	They **are not**/**aren't going to have** breakfast.	**Are** they **going to have** breakfast?

Short answers – affirmative and negative

Question	Affirmative	Negative
Am I going to need some help?	Yes, you are.	No, you aren't.
Are you going to visit Claire on Monday?	Yes, I am.	No, I'm not.

We often use time expressions such as **next** (**week**, **month**, **class**), **tomorrow**, **tonight**, **this** (**afternoon**, **evening**), **in** (**year**, **month**) with the **going to** future. They are usually placed at the end of the sentence. Although it's not so common, they can also be used at the beginning of sentences.

Look at these examples:

The teachers are going to talk to the director **tomorrow**.
Next year we are going to talk about sustainability.
Is the school going to be closed **in January**?

Present continuous (future plans)

Besides the future with **going to**, we can also use the **present continuous** to talk about future plans. We usually use it when we know the date, the time, and the place something is happening.

Take a look at these sentences:

What **are** you **doing** tonight?
I'm playing an online game with my friends tomorrow afternoon.
They **are doing** the laundry this weekend.

Future: will

We can also use **will** to talk about the future. We use it to express a prediction for the future, to indicate a promise to do something in the future and to talk about decisions for the future we make at the moment we speak.

Look at the examples below:

It **will rain** this afternoon.
I **will do** everything I can to help you.
It's cold in here. I **will close** the windows.
In the affirmative form, we use **will** followed by the main verb in the base form.
In the negative form, we add **not** between **will** and the main verb in the base form.
In the interrogative form we invert the position of **will** and the subject.

Read the examples in the charts.

Affirmative	Negative	Interrogative
I **will/I'll have** salad for dinner tonight.	I **will not/won't have** salad for dinner tonight.	**Will** I **have** salad for d nner tonight?
You **will/You'll be** home soon.	You **will not/won't be** home soon.	**Will** you **be** home socn?
He **will/He'll buy** me a new dress.	He **will not/won't buy** me a new dress.	**Will** he **buy** me a new dress?
She **will/She'll call** us for help.	She **will not/won't call** us for help.	**Will** she **call** us for he p?
It **will/It'll snow** in 3 days.	It **will not/won't snow** in 3 days.	**Will** it **snow** in 3 days?
We **will/We'll see** about the cake for the party.	We **will not/won't see** about the cake for the party.	**Will** we **see** about the cake for the party?
You **will/You'll enjoy** your trip.	You **will not/won't enjoy** your trip.	**Will** you **enjoy** your trip?
They **will/They'll arrive** late today.	They **will not/won't arrive** late today.	**Will** they **arrive** late today?

Short answers – affirmative and negative

Question	Affirmative	Negative
Will he answer the questions?	Yes, he will.	No, he won't.
Will they rent their apartment?	Yes, they will.	No, they won't.

Modals: must, have to

To express obligation or necessity, we use the modal verbs **must** and **have to** before the main verb in the base form.

Must has only one form for all persons, but **have to** changes to **has to** in the 3rd person singular (he, she, it).

Read the examples below:

Students **must/have to wear** a uniform in my school.
One **must/has to take** driving lessons to get a driver's license.

Mustn't and **don't have to** (or **doesn't have to**), on the other hand, are used to express prohibition or lack of necessity, respectively.

Read the following examples.

We **mustn't cross** the street when the traffic light isn't green.
You **don't have to carry** all your books to school every day. Just take the ones you really need.

Modals: may, might

Modal verbs come before the base form of main verbs. They often have only one form for all persons; that is, they do not frequently change in the 3rd person singular.

We use **may** and **might** to indicate a possibility, something that has the chance of happening in the present or in the future. **Might** suggests a smaller chance than **may**.

In the affirmative form, we use **may** or **might** before the base form of the main verb.

In the negative form, we use **not** between the modal verb and the base form of the main verb.

Look at the sentences below:

Andres **may/might come** for dinner tonight.
Shannon **may not be/might not be** at home by now.

May and **might** are used in questions mainly to ask for and give permission, especially in a more formal style.

May I help you?
Might I ask you a question?

Adjectives

Adjectives are used to describe or qualify nouns (things, people or places).

In English, adjectives don't have plural forms or gender distinctions. They are often positioned before the nouns they describe or after a linking verb such as the verb to be.

Take a look at these examples:

Those **young** girls are our **new** neighbors.
The author of the book isn't **famous**.

A compound adjective is an adjective that contains two or more words that are usually connected by hyphens.

Read these examples carefully:

Christian Bale is a **well-known** British actor.
That **3,000-piece** puzzle is amazing! Can you help me with it?

When we have more than one adjective to describe a noun, we order them from the most general to the most specific. Then, opinion adjectives come before fact adjectives.

Look at the examples below:

I met an **intelligent young** man at the theater yesterday evening.
Were you reading that **small yellow** magazine when I arrived?

Comparative adjectives

Adjectives can be used to compare two things, people, places or actions.

To make the comparative form of most short adjectives, we add **-er** to the end of the word. However, we use **more** before long adjectives. In both cases, we use **than** to mention the second item being compared.

Take a look at the following examples:

Allan's apartment isn't **smaller than** my house.
In your opinion, is surfing **more difficult than** skateboarding?

Superlative adjectives

Adjectives can also be used to compare people, things, places or actions in a group to which that person, thing, place or action belongs.

To form the **superlative** of most short adjectives, we add **-est** to the end of the word. Before long adjectives, we use **most**.

Note that the article **the** is used before short adjectives, as well as before long adjectives.

Read the following examples:

Kleyton is **the smartest** guy I know.
This isn't **the most interesting** movie, in my opinion.

Comparative and superlative spelling rules

1. For many short adjectives (one-syllable and most two-syllable adjectives), we add **-er** in the comparative form and **-est** in the superlative form.
Observe:
fast – fast**er** than – the fast**est**
great – great**er** than – the great**est**
young – young**er** than – the young**est**

2. For adjectives that end in **-e**, we add only **-r** in the comparative and **-st** in the superlative.
Observe:
large – large**r** than – the large**st**
safe – safe**r** than – the safe**st**
brave – brave**r** than – the brave**st**

3. For one-syllable adjectives that end in the consonant-vowel-consonant pattern, we double the consonant and add **-er** in the comparative form and **-est** in the superlative form.
Observe:
big – bigg**er** than – the bigg**est**
hot – hott**er** than – the hott**est**
sad – sadd**er** than – the sadd**est**

4. For adjectives ending in **-y**, we replace the **y** for **i** and add **-er** in the comparative form and **-est** in the superlative form.
Observe:
funny – funn**ier** than – the funn**iest**
pretty – prett**ier** than – the prett**iest**
easy – eas**ier** than – the eas**iest**

5. These are irregular comparatives and superlatives. They do not follow a spelling rule or a pattern.
good – better than – the best
bad – worse than – the worst

There to be (simple past)

We use **there was** and **there were** to talk about the existence of someone or something in the past.
The verb form **there was** refers to the singular and **there were** refers to the plural.
In the negative form, we use **there was not** (**there wasn't**) and **there were not** (**there weren't**).
In the interrogative form, we use **was there** and **were there**.
Look at the following examples:

Affirmative

There was a charity campaign at school in 2016.
There were two girls behind me in class today.

Negative

There was not/wasn't a good talk show on TV last night.
There were not/weren't any good ideas for the talent show.

LANGUAGE REFERENCE

Interrogative

Was there a restaurant on this street?
Were there a lot of games on sale?

Short answers

Affirmative	Negative
Yes, there was.	No, there wasn't
Yes, there were.	No, there weren't

Contracted forms

There was not = There wasn't

There were not = There weren't

When we have a list of things and the first item of that list is singular, we use **there to be** in the singular form.

Observe this sentence:

There was a mom, her daughter and her husband in the doctor's waiting room.

Relative pronouns (who, which, where, when, whose)

Relative pronouns are used when we want to introduce additional information about a person, a thing, a place, etc.

When we refer to people, we use **who**. To refer to things, animals or ideas we use **which**. **That** is also a relative pronoun and it can often replace **who** and **which**, but it is more informal.

Take a look at the following sentences:

The girl **who/that** lives next door is going to study in my class.
The tables **which/that** aren't old don't need to be replaced.

The relative pronoun **where** is used for places and **when** for time.

Observe these sentences:

Can you take me to a restaurant **where** they serve Japanese food?
December is the month **when** summer begins in Brazil.

The relative pronoun **whose** is used to indicate possession and it is always followed by a noun.

The woman **whose** dress is black is my mother.

Should

We use the modal verb **should** to give some advice or recommendation.

In affirmative sentences, we use **should** before the main verb in the base form.

In negative sentences, when we want to say that it is not advisable to do a certain thing, we use **shouldn't** (**should not**) before the main verb in the base form.

In interrogative sentences, **should** comes before the subject.

Look at the examples below:

The doctor told me I **shouldn't drink** so much soda.
You look sick. You **should stay** in bed today.
What **should** I **do** to be a good student?

Present perfect

We use the **present perfect** to describe actions that happened at an unspecified time in the past and have consequences in the present.

To form the affirmative form, we use **have** or **has** followed by the past participle of the main verb.

In the negative form, we insert **not** after **have** or **has**, before the main verb.

To make the interrogative, we invert the position of **have** or **has** and the subject.

Contractions in the affirmative form are formed using **'ve** (for **have**) and **'s** (for **has**). In the negative form, **haven't** and **hasn't** are the contracted forms.

The past participle of regular verbs has the same form of the simple past. The past participle of irregular verbs, on the contrary, does not follow that rule. See the list of irregular verbs at the end of the book.

Look at the examples in the following charts.

Affirmative	Negative	Interrogative
I **have**/I'**ve decided** to take up piano lessons.	I **have not**/**haven't decided** to take up piano lessons.	**Have** I **decided** to take up piano lessons?
You **have**/You'**ve traveled** to India.	You **have not**/**haven't traveled** to India	**Have** you **traveled** to India?
He **has**/He'**s drunk** milk.	He **has not**/**hasn't drunk** milk.	**Has** he **drunk** milk?
She **has**/She'**s had** lunch with her friends.	She **has not**/**hasn't had** lunch with her friends.	**Has** she **had** lunch with her friends?
It **has**/It'**s been** quite hot.	It **has not**/**hasn't been** quite hot.	**Has** it **been** quite hot?
We **have**/We'**ve seen** him around.	We **have not**/**haven't seen** him around.	**Have** we **seen** him around?
You **have**/You'**ve cooked** dinner.	You **have not**/**haven't cooked** dinner.	**Have** you **cooked** dinner?
They **have**/They'**ve left** the office.	They **have not**/**haven't left** the office.	**Have** they **left** the office?

Short answers – affirmative and negative

Question	Affirmative	Negative
Has she told you the good news?	Yes, she has.	No, she hasn't.
Have you cleaned your bedroom?	Yes, I have.	No, I haven't.

AUDIO SCRIPTS

UNIT 1

TRACK 2

Page 24, activity 2

Listen to a Brazilian exchange student who has studied in the UK. Order the reasons she gives about the importance of speaking English.

Hi everyone. My name's Juliana. I'm from Florianópolis, Brazil, but now I live in Birmingham, United Kingdom, to study for my Master's in future media, digital marketing. And today I'm gonna talk to you a little bit about the importance of speaking English. Obviously speaking English was important for me when deciding to move and study in another country. It also made a lot easier for me to adapt to a different culture. But apart from that, speaking English opened doors and gave me opportunities I wouldn't have otherwise. I work as a digital marketing consultant, and even back at home in Brazil clients would hire me because I could create content in English and communicate with their foreigner customers, which turned out to be really good for their businesses. As we all know our country is a growing economy, and speaking English helps us doing business abroad.

Not to mention we're gonna host two of the biggest world events over the next three years, and that will create loads of opportunities regarding tourism and services and part of being prepared to seize these opportunities is speaking English. And you all want to be ready, don't you? Hope that helped you! Bye!

Extracted from: <www.youtube.com/watch?v=uGGWMZ9nc9Q> (0:00-1:10). Accessed on: Jun. 6, 2016.

TRACK 3

Page 24, activity 3

Listen to Juliana again and write **T** (true) or **F** (false).

Hi everyone. My name's Juliana. I'm from Florianópolis, Brazil, but now I live in Birmingham, United Kingdom, to study for my Master's in future media, digital marketing. And today I'm gonna talk to you a little bit about the importance of speaking English. Obviously speaking English was important for me when deciding to move and study in another country. It also made a lot easier for me to adapt to a different culture. But apart from that, speaking English opened doors and gave me opportunities I wouldn't have otherwise. I work as a digital marketing consultant, and even back at home in Brazil clients would hire me because I could create content in English and communicate with their foreigner customers, which turned out to be really good for their businesses. As we all know our country is a growing economy, and speaking English helps us doing business abroad.

Not to mention we're gonna host two of the biggest world events over the next three years, and that will create loads of opportunities regarding tourism and services and part of being prepared to seize these opportunities is speaking English. And you all want to be ready, don't you? Hope that helped you! Bye!

Extracted from: <www.youtube.com/watch?v=uGGWMZ9nc9Q> (0:00-1:10). Accessed on: Jun. 6, 2016.

TRACK 4

Page 24, activity 4

Complete part of Juliana's speech with the words from the box, according to the audio. Then read the audio script and check your answers.

Not to mention we're gonna host two of the biggest world events over the next three years, and that will create loads of opportunities regarding tourism and services and part of being prepared to seize these opportunities is speaking English. And you all want to be ready, don't you? Hope that helped you! Bye!

Extracted from: <www.youtube.com/watch?v=uGGWMZ9nc9Q> (0:49-1:10). Accessed on: Jun. 6, 2016.

UNIT 2

TRACK 5

Page 34, activity 1

Listen to the descriptions of some sea animals. Label the pictures using the names from the box.

a. For over a hundred million years the stingray has roamed the oceans, an almost mithological animal, extraordinarily graceful and yet considered potentially lethal.

Extracted from: <video.nationalgeographic.com/video/stingray> (00:00-00:15). Accessed on: Jun. 6, 2016.

b. [...] Sharks are large carnivorous fish with sharp teeth, a dorsal fin on their back, and strong powerful tails so they can swim fast.

Extracted from: <www.youtube.com/watch?v=agqgBkpbCoY> (00:25-00:36). Accessed on: Jun. 6, 2016.

c. Dolphins on the hunt strategize one another. They coordinate their movements with whistles and clicks. But it is just as important what they don't say as what they do say.

Extracted from: <video.nationalgeographic.com/video/weirdest-dolphin-talk?source=searchvideo> (00:06-00:18). Accessed on: Jun. 6, 2016.

d. Sea lions are very similar to seals. It's hard to spot the difference. Sea lions have small external ears and large strong front flippers, which they use to propel themselves under water. [...]

Extracted from: <www.youtube.com/watch?v=4k00xSYABjs> (00:36-00:52). Accessed on: Jun. 6, 2016.

TRACK 6

Page 42, activity 2

Listen to a woman talking about Singapore and check the correct sentences.

One of the smallest and most densely populated countries in the world, Singapore is a breeze to explore – nothing is more than an hour away from the central business district.

Built at the crossroads of maritime trading routes, for well over a century, Singapore was the jewel in Britain's empire. When the city became a republic in 1965, few thought a country with so few resources and of vastly different ethnic groups could succeed. But succeed it has, on an unimaginable scale!

Singapore today is one of the four Asian economic tigers, a futuristic bridge between East and West. Yet despite blossoming into one of the great global cities, Singapore is a nation that still cherishes its Asian traditions.

[...]

Extracted from: <www.youtube.com/watch?v=XTjDU4TiPlg> (00:00-00:55). Accessed on: Jun. 6, 2016.

TRACK 7

Page 42, activity 3

Listen again and answer.

One of the smallest and most densely populated countries in the world, Singapore is a breeze to explore – nothing is more than an hour away from the central business district.

Built at the crossroads of maritime trading routes, for well over a century, Singapore was the jewel in Britain's empire. When the city became a republic in 1965, few thought a country with so few resources and of vastly different ethnic groups could succeed. But succeed it has, on an unimaginable scale!

Singapore today is one of the four Asian economic tigers, a futuristic bridge between East and West. Yet despite blossoming into one of the great global cities, Singapore is a nation that still cherishes its Asian traditions.

Extracted from: <www.youtube.com/watch?v=XTjDU4TiPlg> (00:00-00:55). Accessed on: Jun. 6, 2016.

TRACK 8

Page 42, activity 4

Listen further and answer: According to the audio, what are two Singaporean obsessions?

[...]

One thing unites all Singaporeans – food – it's the national obsession!

For an authentic Singaporean 'Makan' experience, follow the satay smoke to the nearest hawker center. For more upscale dinning, head to the bright lights of Boat and Clarke Quays.

[...]

Singapore enjoys a hot tropical climate. When the cooling afternoon rains come, indulge in that other Singaporean obsession, shopping! Orchard Road offers miles of retail indulgence. For a change of pace, head to the Bugis Markets to really rub shoulders with bargain-hunting locals.

[...]

Extracted from: <www.youtube.com/watch?v=XTjDU4TiPlg> (01:42-02:01; 02:53-03:15). Accessed on: Jun. 6, 2016.

UNIT 3

TRACK 9

Page 57, Pronunciation practice

Listen and practice the pronunciation of the standard form of **going to** and the contracted form **gonna**, which is normally used in informal speech.

I'm going to have dinner at 9:00 pm.

I'm gonna have dinner at 9:00 pm.

TRACK 10

Page 57, Pronunciation practice

Listen and write **going to** or **gonna**.

a. We're gonna have pizza and soda after the movies.

b. My grandma is going to live next door to us.

c. John is gonna have his tooth pulled today.

d. Mandy is going to study in Australia next year.

TRACK 11

Page 62, activity 2

Listen to the beginning of the program *Curiosity Quest Goes Green* and answer the questions.

Joel: Hey there, I'm Joel Greene. Welcome to Curiosity Quest Goes Green, the show that explores what you, the viewer, are curious about. Well, today our quest sort of came to us from Lassandra in Villa Park, California. Lassandra wrote: "Dear Joel, I have a question about your show Curiosity Quest. How can we help the planet? Can we help the planet by recycling or not polluting? Can we help the planet by walking more instead of driving?" Well, Lassandra, because of you, we have made our way out of here to Grand view Elementary in Manhattan Beach, California, we're gonna learn about planet pals and literally, get schooled on how we can help protect the environment. So let's get start on today's Curiosity Quest Goes Green. Bell rings! Let's go to school.

[...]

Extracted from: <www.youtube.com/watch?v=MiS46BxV6Sg> (00:00-00:47). Accessed on: Jun. 6, 2016.

TRACK 12

Page 62, activity 3

Listen to another part of the program and check the picture that matches the subject they are talking about.

[...]

Joel: Right, so now Allie, tell us... a trash-free lunch, what exactly does that mean?

Allie: A trash-free lunch means that you don't have any trash of it, not even a juice box or a bag. You just store everything in the compartments, like this, and you... it comes with a water bottle so you don't have to have a plastic one, and you just store everything in here and it stays safe and when you open it, it's all just fresh and you can eat it.

Joel: Now, Shelby, I noticed you have this bottle next to you. Is this yours?

Shelby: Yeah. I lost mine of this, so my mom bought me this.

Joel: OK. But this is still trash-free, right?

Shelby: Yeah.

[...]

Joel: What's the coolest thing about having these trash-free lunches?

Allie: The coolest thing about having these is that you can just bring'em from home; you don't have to waste time because you go straight from lunch to recess, so you don't have to waste time crowding around the trash can throwing everything away, and so it's just easier. You just put this in your lunch bin that your class has and then you just walk away and go to recess.

Joel: Again, you are not throwing any plastic, any paper, any trash away and what you do end up putting in a composter is your... like you said, your fruits and vegetables, right?

Collin: Yeah.

Extracted from: <www.youtube.com/watch?v=MiS46BxV6Sg>. (02:57-03:29; 03:47-04:17). Accessed on: Jun. 6, 2016.

UNIT 4

TRACK 13

Page 79, activity 3

Listen to the introduction of a speech and identify which woman made it.

Today on this 100th anniversary of International Women's Day, we celebrate a century of progress, a century of women using their collective voice to organize for change. It is very appropriate that at the same time we're celebrating the creation of UN Women – an ambitious international commitment to accelerate the realization of women's right and gender equality, and I am honoured to be the first leader of this new United Nations Organization.

[...]

Extracted from: <www.youtube.com/watch?v=4SZUUUS46qk> (00:00-00:37). Accessed on: Jun. 6, 2016.

TRACK 14

Page 80, activity 5

Listen to the continuation of the speech and check the themes she addresses.

[...]

Much has been achieved over 100 years. When the first International Women's Day took place, women could vote only in two countries. Today that right is virtually universal, and women have now been elected to lead governments in every continent. Women are participating in the workforce in greater and greater numbers, and 67 countries have laws mandating equal pay for men and women. And 126 countries have guaranteed maternity leave. As we see on our television screens every day, women and girls are mobilizing alongside men and boys to advance political freedoms worldwide. While the achievement of gender equality is closer than ever before, we still have far to go. Our vision in UN Women is a world where men and women have equal opportunities and capacities, and the principles of gender equalities are embedded in the development, peace and security agendas. Realizing this vision involves opening up spaces for women's political leadership as trade and peace negotiators, as head of corporations. It involves free women from gender based violence and convincing key policymakers that where women fully contribute to our economies and societies, the gains for everyone are greatly increased.

Evidence shows that where women have access to good education, good jobs, land, and other assets, national growth and stability are enhanced and we see lower maternal mortality, improved child nutrition, greater food security and less risk of HIV and AIDS.

[...]

Extracted from: <www.youtube.com/watch?v=4SZUUUS46qk> (00:38-02:31). Accessed on: Jun. 6, 2016.

TRACK 15

Page 80, activity 6

Listen again and write down at least one sentence that justifies each of the items you checked in activity 5.

[...]

Much has been achieved over 100 years. When the first International Women's Day took place, women could vote only in two countries. Today that right is virtually universal, and women have now been elected to lead governments in every continent. Women are participating in the workforce in greater and greater numbers, and 67 countries have laws mandating equal pay for men and women. And 126 countries have guaranteed maternity leave. As we see on our television screens every day, women and girls are mobilizing alongside men and boys to advance political freedoms worldwide. While the achievement of gender equality is closer than ever before, we still have far to go. Our vision in UN Women is a world where men and women have equal opportunities and capacities, and the principles of gender equalities are embedded in the development, peace, and security agendas. Realizing this vision involves opening up spaces for women's political leadership as trade and peace negotiators, as head of corporations. It involves free women from gender based violence and convincing key policymakers that where women fully contribute to our economies and societies, the gains for everyone are greatly increased.

Evidence shows that where women have access to good education, good jobs, land, and other assets, national growth and stability are enhanced and we see lower maternal mortality, improved child nutrition, greater food security, and less risk of HIV and AIDS.

[...]

Extracted from: <www.youtube.com/watch?v=4SZUUUS46qk> (00:38-02:31). Accessed on: Jun. 6, 2016.

UNIT 5

TRACK 16

Page 100, activity 2

Listen to an artist talking about one of his paintings and answer.

Hello, my name is Dereck O'Connor. I'm the artist of this painting which is called *Melt*.

It is a painting about landscape but in a very general way. Landscape painting comes in many different pictorial forms; my interest has been from abstract to expressionism. The actual format of the canvas is a landscape format.

I was inspired by a series of photographs and film that I saw, which was talking about global warming and the impact on the Antarctic ice. What caught my attention was the refraction of Artic light through the ice and then the inflaction into the water.

I decided to use expressive marks and paint expressively as I felt that was more of a general way of encompassing the idea of a landscape.

[...]

Extracted from: <www.youtube.com/watch?v=YdHMCe0k15A> (00:00-01:09). Accessed on: Jun. 6, 2016.

TRACK 17

Page 100, activity 3

Listen to a description of the colors he used in this painting. What were they? Circle the correct ones. Then write their names.

Dereck: I decided to use these fan marks that go like this, and I used a spatula, not a brush, and as you can see there are various transparencies that appear which make the red come through uh, the blue and the white.

White was primarily used because, well, obviously the Antarctic ice is white and the ocean is blue, predominantly, and then it gave a good source of reflection. I placed these colors on a red background to advance the red and make the blue and the white recede.

[...]

Extracted from: <www.youtube.com/watch?v=YdHMCeOk15A> (01:11-01:43). Accessed on: Jun. 6, 2016.

TRACK 18

Page 100, activity 4

Listen to the last part of the audio. Where is it possible to see the painting *Melt*?

Dereck: In 2011 the National Gallery of Australia purchased this painting; I think it's within every artist's career that they hope for such a purchase.

I'm very, very pleased that the Australian public will be able to come and view this painting and make up their own mind and hopefully enjoy the painting.

Extracted from: <www.youtube.com/watch?v=YdHMCeOk15A> (02:38-02:55). Accessed on: Jun. 6, 2016.

UNIT 6

TRACK 19

Page 117, activity 2

Listen to John Green's interview and choose the best title for it.

Reading was really important in our house growing up. It was a big part of my life and it really has been ever since. When I was a little kid ah, the reading time I had with my parents was in many ways, like, the best quality time I had with them 'cause I didn't have to share it with my brother – which was awesome – and also because we got to talk about stuff that really interested both of them and me, so I was able to kind of feel like I was an active participant in the conversation, and not just a kid, and that was really important for me.

We especially read a lot of fairy tales. And I remember when I was pretty little, I read this book *Kon-Tiki* with my dad: the story of a guy's journey across the ocean on this little raft, and it was just so exciting and real and alive. And it was also a great time with my parents, kind of alone time, one-on-one time, and it was really special for me.

Extracted from: <www.youtube.com/watch?v=xopdxlgTH64> (00:10-01:10). Accessed on: Jun. 6, 2016.

TRACK 20

Page 118, activity 3

Listen to John Green's interview again. Check all the reasons why he enjoyed his reading moments as a kid.

Reading was really important in our house growing up. It was a big part of my life and it really has been ever since. When I was a little kid ah, the reading time I had with my parents was in many ways, like, the best quality time I had with them 'cause I didn't have to share it with my brother – which was awesome – and also because we got to talk about stuff that really interested both of them and me, so I was able to kind of feel like I was an active participant in the conversation, and not just a kid, and that was really important for me.

We especially read a lot of fairy tales. And I remember when I was pretty little, I read this book, *Kon-Tiki* with my dad: the story of a guy's journey across the ocean on this little raft, and it was just so exciting and real and alive. And it was also a great time with my parents, kind of alone time, one-on-one time, and it was really special for me.

Extracted from: <www.youtube.com/watch?v=xopdxlgTH64> (00:10-01:10). Accessed on: Jun. 6, 2016.

UNIT 7

TRACK 21

Page 138, activity 4

Listen to the interview. Then go back to activity 3 and check if your prediction was correct.

Nicky Clark: Do you consider yourself to be disabled?

Warwick Davis: You know, there's a lot of other, for me, complications and sort of other issues related to me being short than just being short, and sometimes those things are debilitating in the fact that, you know, walking any distance is painful and things like that. So in that side of things I do, but I see being short also as being... it's enabled me to do everything I've ever done. It's enabled me to have a career in acting. I wouldn't have been an actor. I got the part in *Star Wars* because I was short; that was the only reason. It wasn't anything to do with acting at that point: "Oh yeah, you're the right height for the job. Come on in. Get fitted up for an Ewok costume." That was it. So, whether that cancels out my thought of being disabled or not, I don't know. It's interesting. It's an interesting question.

Extracted from: <www.theguardian.com/society/video/2012/feb/22/warwick-davis-lifes-too-short-video> (06:47-07:49). Accessed on: Jun. 6, 2016.

TRACK 22

Page 138, activity 6

Listen to the interview again. Then work with a classmate to choose the correct answer to the questions.

Nicky Clark: Do you consider yourself to be disabled?

Warwick Davis: You know, there's a lot of other, for me, complications and sort of other issues related to me being short than just being short, and sometimes those things are debilitating in the fact that, you know, walking any distance is painful and things like that. So in that side of things I do, but I see being short also as being... it's enabled me to do everything I've ever done. It's enabled me to have a career in acting. I wouldn't have been an actor. I got the part in *Star Wars* because I was short; that was the only reason. It wasn't anything to do with acting at that point: "Oh yeah, you're the right height for the job. Come on in. Get fitted up for an Ewok costume." That was it. So whether that cancels out my thought of being disabled or not, I don't know. It's interesting. It's an interesting question.

Extracted from: <www.theguardian.com/society/video/2012/feb/22/warwick-davis-lifes-too-short-video> (06:47-07:49). Accessed on: Jun. 6, 2016.

UNIT 8

TRACK 23

Page 148, Pronunciation practice

Listen and practice the pronunciation of these words.

equal – equally
particular – particularly
full – fully
emotional – emotionally
cognitive – cognitively
social – socially
sexual – sexually

TRACK 24

Page 156, activity 3

Listen to Riley Roberts, an American teenager from the state of Nevada. What is he going to talk about?

Riley: Good evening Chairman Ohrenschall and members of the committee. My name is Riley Roberts, and my life is amazing. Thank you for the opportunity to talk to you about the issue of gay marriage and how it affects my life.

[...]

Extracted from: <www.advocate.com/politics/marriage-equality/2013/05/14/nevada-3-great-testimonies-marriage-young-people> (00:10-00:27). Accessed on: Jun. 6, 2016.

TRACK 25

Page 156, activity 4

Listen to Riley as he continues his testimony and answer:

[...]

Riley: What issue? I see no issue. I was born in Reno, Nevada, 18 years ago and guess who was there? My mom Pamela Roberts and Gretchen Miller, my loving parents.

[...]

My two loving parents. And who will be there to see me walk across the stage next month and receive my honor's diploma? My two gay loving parents who have been together for 22 years. They have been with me on my journey through life, and they have supported me through everything.

[...]

My mother Gretchen has been paying taxes for... paying into social security for at least 40 years, but if she dies my mom Pam will not receive the survivors' spouse benefit. Why? Because the government doesn't recognize their relationship and... as a marriage. They're denied the rights, the freedoms and the ability to be a full and equal citizen of the United States of America in this great state of Nevada. I love them very much and I want them to have the same rights that I and my friends have.

[...]

Extracted from: <www.advocate.com/politics/marriage-equality/2013/05/14/nevada-3-great-testimonies-marriage-young-people> (0:28-0:44; 01:04-01:23; 01:29-02:01). Accessed on: Jun. 6, 2016.

TRACK 26

Page 156, activity 6

Listen to the end of the testimony and answer.

[...]

My parents love, breathe, speak, feel pain, and most of all know that their love is more than any paper can do or say and that they will be together forever. The idea of an opposition to equal rights just bewilders me. I can't even fathom it.

[...]

Thank you for listening to what I have to say and I hope everyone knows how much equality means to me and my family and I hope that you'll vote, do pass on SJR13.

Extracted from: <www.advocate.com/politics/marriage-equality/2013/05/14/nevada-3-great-testimonies-marriage-young-people> (02:26-02:42; 02:55-03:03). Accessed on: Jun. 6, 2016.

FURTHER PRACTICE 1
(UNITS 1 & 2)

TRACK 27

Page 164, activity 5

Write **T** (true), **F** (false) or **NM** (not mentioned) according to what you hear about the Dead Sea.

[...]

Welcome to the lowest point on Earth: The Dead Sea. Though the name sounds fatal and it's true, there are no fish swimming here, this water is rich in minerals which are thought to have curative properties which is why people have been coming here to float for thousands of years.
You don't have to worry about a life preserver here. And don't try to swim either, just relax and float away. Now, if you have any small cuts, you're gonna feel some pain.

[...]

The Dead Sea is about 10 times saltier than the ocean and that salt will sting. But with the yin comes the yang. Even the mud here is good for you helping with everything from arthritis to wrinkles, which is why you'll see people lathering it on and then baking a bit before heading in. If you like to enjoy your spa treatments outdoors the Dead Sea is a good place to do it.

Extracted from: <www.budgettravel.com/video/float-in-the-dead-sea,58/> (00:21-00:52; 00:57-01:22). Accessed on: Mar. 26, 2015.

TRACK 28

Page 164, activity 6

Check the best alternative to complete the excerpt of the text you have just heard. Then listen and check.

[...]

The Dead Sea is about 10 times saltier than the ocean and that salt will sting. But with the yin comes the yang. Even the mud here is good for you helping with everything from arthritis to wrinkles, which is why you'll see people lathering it on and then baking a bit before heading in. If you like to enjoy your spa treatments outdoors the Dead Sea is a good place to do it.

Extracted from: <www.budgettravel.com/video/float-in-the-dead-sea,58/> (00:57-1:22). Accessed on: Mar. 26, 2015.

FURTHER PRACTICE 2
(UNITS 3 & 4)

TRACK 29

Page 167, activity 5

You are going to listen to John Kerry, the US Secretary of State, talking about what we can do to help protect our ocean. Before you listen, order the parts below in a logical sequence. Then listen and check.

The ocean covers almost three quarters of our planet, but our ocean today is at grave risk – and the damage is not happening by accident. Human activity is the cause. Harmful fishing practices, even illegal fishing; giant garbage patches; hundreds of dead zones; and rising carbon dioxide levels – all of it threatens life under the sea. That is the bad news. The good news is, it doesn't have to be that way. Governments, communities, and individuals can act now to reverse these trends. We can protect the ocean if we all start treating it like "our ocean". Wherever you live, you can help in some way. [...]

Extracted from: <www.state.gov/secretary/remarks/2014/06/227042.htm#> (00:00-00:47). Accessed on: Jun. 6, 2016.

TRACK 30

Page 168, activity 6

Listen to the second part of John Kerry's remarks and check the correct answers to the questions below.

There are things you can do to make a difference. Let's work toward a healthier ocean, for this generation and those to come. Show your support and tell others how you'll make this commitment. Don't throw trash into our ocean or waterways. Ask for sustainable seafood. Volunteer at least one day a year to clean our waterways or beaches. I intend to ask our leaders around the world to act now to create a healthier ocean together, and we'll help lead the way. What will you do to help protect our ocean?

Extracted from: <www.state.gov/secretary/remarks/2014/06/227042.htm#> (00:48-1:35). Accessed on: Jun. 6, 2016.

FURTHER PRACTICE 3
(UNITS 5 & 6)

TRACK 31

Page 171, activity 3

Listen to part of Frida Kahlo's story and check True or False.

Frida Kahlo was a Mexican woman who transformed her life by painting herself. Born in Mexico City in 1907 on the threshold of the great revolutions of the 20th century, she would improvise her own kind of freedom in order to gracefully transcend a life filled with pain. Crippled at 19 in a terrible accident that left her with permanent injuries, she would begin to paint during her long convalescence and spend the rest of her life articulating her experience into some of the most luminous and haunting images of the age.

[...]

Extracted from: <www.youtube.com/watch?v=jYWKoMFjnbs> (00:00-00:52). Accessed on: Jun. 6, 2016.

TRACK 32

Page 171, activity 4

Listen to another part of the story and complete the text.

She herself would become a legend, making her own life into a work of art and coming to feel at home with some of the most celebrated artists and visionaries of her day. And yet, ironically, her paintings would remain virtually ignored during her lifetime – an obscurity that did not matter to her. She painted, she said, for herself and, in the process, created some of the most indelible images of the 20th century.

Extracted from: <www.youtube.com/watch?v=jYWKoMFjnbs> (1:15-1:50). Accessed on: Jun. 6, 2016.

FURTHER PRACTICE 4
(UNITS 7 & 8)

TRACK 33

Page 175, activity 4

Listen to the testimonial of a seventeen-year-old boy named Sam Berns who suffers from a disease called Progeria. Check the correct option to complete the sentences you have heard.

I just wanna give you some more information about Progeria. It affects only about 350 kids today, worldwide. So, it's pretty rare and effects of Progeria include tight skin, lack of weight gain, stunted growth, and heart disease.

Last year my mom and her team of scientists published the first successful Progeria Treatment Study, and because of this, I was interviewed on NPR and John Hamilton asked me the question "What is the most important thing that people should know about you?" and my answer was simply that I have a very happy life. Thank you.

So, even though there are many obstacles in my life, with a lot of them being created by Progeria, I don't want people to feel bad for me. I don't think about these obstacles all the time, and I'm able to overcome most of them anyway.

[...]

Extracted from: <www.youtube.com/watch?v=36m1o-tM05g> (01:47-02:50). Accessed on: Jun. 6, 2016.

TRACK 34

Page 175, activity 5

Listen to Sam Berns again and correct the wrong sentences.

I just wanna give you some more information about Progeria. It affects only about 350 kids today, worldwide. So, it's pretty rare and effects of Progeria include tight skin, lack of weight gain, stunted growth, and heart disease.

Last year my mom and her team of scientists published the first successful Progeria Treatment Study, and because of this, I was interviewed on NPR and John Hamilton asked me the question "What is the most important thing that people should know about you?" and my answer was simply that I have a very happy life. Thank you.

So, even though there are many obstacles in my life, with a lot of them being created by Progeria, I don't want people to feel bad for me. I don't think about these obstacles all the time, and I'm able to overcome most of them anyway.

[...]

Extracted from: <www.youtube.com/watch?v=36m1o-tM05g> (01:47-02:50). Accessed on: Jun. 6, 2016.

TRACK 35

Page 176, activity 6

Use the words from the box to complete the excerpt from Sam's testimonial. Then listen and check your answers.

[...]

Now people sometimes ask me questions like, "Isn't it hard living with Progeria?" or "What daily challenges of Progeria do you face?" and I'd like to say that, even though I have Progeria, most of my time is spent thinking about things that have nothing to do with Progeria at all. Now this doesn't mean that I ignore the negative aspects of these obstacles. When I can't do something like run a long distance or go on an intense roller-coaster, you know, I know what I'm missing out on. But instead, I choose to focus on the activities that I can do through things that I'm passionate about like scouting, or music, or comic books, or any of my favorite Boston sports teams.

Extracted from: <www.youtube.com/watch?v=36m1o-tM05g> (03:14-03:58). Accessed on: Jun. 6, 2016.

GLOSSARY

A

- **able** capaz
- **about** sobre
- **abroad** em outro país
- **absolutely** completamente
- **abstract** abstrato
- **accelerate** acelerar
- **accent** sotaque
- **acceptable** aceitável
- **accident** acidente
- **accidentally** acidentalmente
- **accomplish** realizar
- **according to** de acordo com
- **achievement** conquista, realização
- **act** agir, ato
- **acting** teatro, interpretação
- **active participant** participante ativo
- **activist** ativista
- **activity** atividade
- **actor** ator
- **actual** real
- **adapt** adaptar
- **add** adicionar
- **addiction** vício
- **adequate** adequado
- **adjustment** ajuste
- **admire** admirar
- **adopt** adotar
- **adult** adulto
- **advise** aconselhar
- **aerodynamic** aerodinâmico
- **aesthetic** estética
- **affect** afetar
- **afraid of** ter medo
- **after** depois
- **afternoon** tarde
- **agree** concordar
- **agreement** concordância
- **aid worker** trabalhador humanitário
- **aim** visar
- **alive** vivo
- **allegorical** alegórico
- **allow** permitir
- **along** ao longo de
- **aloud** em voz alta
- **already** já
- **also** também
- **alternatively** em vez disso
- **although** apesar de
- **aluminium can** lata de alumínio
- **always** sempre
- **amazing** incrível
- **ambassador** embaixador
- **ambition** ambição
- **among** entre
- **amount** quantia, quantidade
- **amputated** amputado
- **angry** bravo
- **anniversary** aniversário
- **announcement** declaração
- **answer** resposta
- **anxiety** ansiedade
- **anxious** ansioso
- **anyway** de qualquer forma
- **anywhere** em qualquer lugar
- **apparently** aparentemente
- **appeal** apelo
- **apple** maçã
- **appreciate** apreciar
- **approve** aprovar
- **aquarium** aquário
- **archery** tiro com arco
- **arm** braço
- **array** coleção
- **arrival** chegada
- **art gallery** galeria de arte
- **arthritis** artrite
- **art installation** instalação artística
- **as well** também
- **ask** perguntar
- **assume** assumir
- **athlete** atleta
- **athletic** atlético
- **athletics** atletismo
- **at-risk** em risco
- **attached** ligado
- **attend** comparecer
- **attendant** acompanhante, assistente
- **attention** atenção
- **attitude** atitude
- **attraction** atração
- **autobiography** autobiografia
- **average** média
- **avoid** evitar
- **award** prêmio
- **aware** conscientizar
- **away** fora da cidade
- **awesome** incrível

B

- **B class** de classe B
- **baby** bebê
- **back cover** contracapa
- **background** fundo
- **balance** equilíbrio
- **bandaged** com atadura
- **bar code** código de barras
- **bargain-hunting** caçadores de pechinchas
- **barren** infrutífero
- **basketball** basquete
- **battery** bateria, pilha
- **be** ser, estar
- **beach** praia
- **bear** urso
- **because** porque
- **become** tornar-se
- **bed** cama
- **bedroom** quarto
- **bedtime** hora de dormir
- **before** antes
- **begin** começar
- **beginning** começo
- **behavior, behaviour** comportamento
- **behind the scenes** nos bastidores
- **believe** acreditar
- **bell** sino
- **belong** pertencer
- **below** abaixo
- **benefit** benefício
- **besides** além de
- **best** melhor
- **best friend** melhor amigo
- **best-known** mais conhecido
- **best-loved** mais adorado
- **between** entre
- **bias** preconceito
- **bill** proposta de lei
- **bio** biografia
- **biological children** filhos biológicos
- **birth name** nome de nascença
- **birth place** local de nascimento
- **blind** cego
- **block** quarteirão
- **blonde** loiro
- **blood** sangue
- **blossom** florescer
- **body** corpo

bold negrito
bond laço, ligação
book reservar
border fronteira
bored aborrecido
born nascido
borrow pegar emprestado
Botanic Garden Jardim Botânico
both ambos
bottle garrafa
boundary limite, fronteira
bowl tigela
box quadro, caixa
boy garoto
bracelet pulseira
brainstorm listar ideias de
break pausa, tempo
breakage estrago
breathe respirar
breeze fácil, moleza
brew preparar
bridge ponte
brief breve
bright claro
bring trazer
broken quebrado
bronze bronze
brooche broche
broom handle cabo de vassoura
brown marrom
brush escovar
building construção, prédio
bullet train trem-bala
bulletin board quadro
bully intimidar
bunch grupo, bando
bus ônibus
business negócios
bustle alvoroço
buy comprar
buyer comprador
by and large em geral

C

cable cabo
cacophony cacofonia
cafeteria cantina
can poder
candy doce
canoeing canoagem
canvas tela (de pintura)
capital capital
caption legenda
capture capturar
cardboard papelão
cardboard box caixa de papelão
care cuidar
career carreira
carpool compartilhar carro
carry carregar, trazer consigo
cartoon cartum
case caso
Castilian castelhano
castle castelo
Catalan catalão
cathedral catedral
caveat advertência, aviso
cavern caverna
celebrate comemorar
celtic celta
century século
chair cadeira
challenge desafio
challenging desafiador
change mudança
change your mind mudar de opinião
character personagem
chart tabela
chatter conversa
check checar, conferir
cheese queijo
cherish valorizar
chest peito
chicken-wire tela de arame
chief chefe
child criança
childhood infância
child-rearing task tarefa de criação de crianças
children crianças
Chinese chinês
choose escolher
circle circular
citizen cidadão
citizenship cidadania
class classe
classmate colega de classe
classroom sala de aula
clear claro
clearly claramente
cleverly brilhantemente
client cliente
climate clima
climate change mudança climática
close perto
closet armário
closing sentence frase de encerramento
cloth bag saco de pano
cloth roupa
coal carvão
cognitively cognitivamente
cold frio
collect recolher, juntar
collectible objeto colecionável
collector colecionador
college faculdade
color, colour cor
color-coded codificado por cores
combination combinação
come vir
comfort confortar
comfortable confortável
comic book gibi
comic strip tirinha
commemorate comemorar
committee comitê
common comum
communicate comunicar-se
communication comunicação
community comunidade
comparison comparação
compassion compaixão
competitiveness competitividade
complicated complicado
composed composto
concept conceito
concerning referente a
condition condição
conditioning programme programa de condicionamento
congenital congênito
connect conectar
consider considerar
consist consistir
contact contato
content conteúdo
contribute contribuir
control controlar
convince convencer
cook cozinhar; cozinheiro
copper cobre
copy copiar

coral coral
corresponding correspondente
costume figurino
counter fazer frente a
country país
couple casal
courageously corajosamente
course curso
cover capa (de livro), cobrir
cram ser cheio de
crazy louco
create criar
creature criatura
critical crítico
cross cruz
crossroad cruzamento
crouch agachar-se
crowd multidão
crown of thorns coroa de espinhos
crumbling desmoronando
crusader defensor
cry chorar
crystal clear evidente, óbvio
culture cultura
cup xícara
curtain cortina
customer cliente
cut cortar, corte

D

dad pai
daily basis diariamente
dance dança
Danish dinamarquês
dark escuro
date tâmara
daughter filha
day trip viagem de um dia
dead morto
Dead Sea Mar Morto
dead zone zona morta
deal lidar
deathly mortal
decide decidir
deep profundo
defeat derrota
definition definição
deforestation desflorestamento
delicious delicioso
democracy democracia
dependent dependente
describe descrever
design desenhar, projetar, planejar
desire desejo
despite apesar de
destination destino
detail detalhe
detailed detalhado
deteriorate deteriorar-se
development desenvolvimento
devise conceber
devotee devoto
diagnose diagnosticar
diagram diagrama
dialect dialeto
dictionary entry verbete de dicionário
die morrer
difficulty dificuldade
dig espetar
dinner jantar
direct direto
dirty sujo
disability deficiência
disabled deficiente
disagree discordar
disagreement discordância
discard descartar
disciplinary disciplinar
discover descobrir
discus arremesso de disco
disguise disfarçar
display exibição
district distrito, bairro
do fazer
doctor médico
document documento
dolphin golfinho
donate doar
door porta
doubt dúvida
draft rascunho
dragon dragão
dramatic dramático
drawing desenho
dream sonho
dress vestido
dress etiquette etiqueta para se vestir
drink beber
drive dirigir
drums bateria
due to devido a
dwarf anão

E

ear orelha
earlier antigo
earn ganhar (dinheiro)
earring brinco
Earth Terra
earthquake terremoto
easier mais fácil
easily facilmente
east leste, oriente
easy fácil
eco-friendlier mais ecologicamente correto
economic econômico
economy economia
education formação
effective efetivo
effort esforço
elderly idoso
elective optativo
electric elétrico
element elemento
embarrassing embaraçoso
emotionally emocionalmente
emperor imperador
empire império
employee empregado, funcionário
empty vazio
encompass abranger
encourage encorajar
encourager pessoa que incentiva
end up acabar
endangered ameaçado de extinção
endeavor, endeavour empenho
ending final
enduring duradouro
energy energia
engage comprometer-se
engaging encantador
enough suficiente
entertaining divertido
environment meio ambiente
envy invejar
equal igual
equally igualmente
erosion erosão
ESL (English as a Second Language) inglês como segunda língua

essential essencial
establish estabelecer
estimated estimado
ethnic étnico
Euskadi basco
event evento
everything tudo
everywhere por toda a parte
evidence evidência, prova
evil mal, mau
exactly exatamente
exchange trocar
exchange student estudante de intercâmbio
exciting animador
exhibition exposição
existence existência
expect esperar
expected esperado
expensive caro
experience experiência; viver experiência
expert especialista
explain explicar
explore explorar
explorer explorador
export exportação
express expressar
expression expressão
extended family família estendida
extract trecho
eye olho

F

fable fábula
face rosto
facet faceta
fact fato
failed fracassado
fairy fada
fairy tale conto de fadas
fall cair
fall, autumn outono
family família
family unit unidade familiar
famous famoso
fantastic fantástico
fantasy fantasia
far longe
father pai
faucet torneira
favorite, favourite favorito
feature característica
feel sentir
feeling sentimento
female feminino
feminist feminista
fencer esgrimista
fertile fértil
fever febre
fiberglass fibra de vidro
field campo
fight brigar, lutar
figure out descobrir, compreender
find encontrar
first primeiro
first glance primeira vista
first-grade primeiro ano escolar
fish stock criação de peixes
fitness center academia de ginástica
flight voo
float flutuar
floor chão
fly voar, viajar de avião
focus foco
folkloric folclórico
follow seguir, fazer o mesmo
foot pé
football futebol
football 5-a-side futebol de cinco jogadores em cada time
foreground primeiro plano
foreign estrangeiro
forest floresta
forget esquecer
forgive perdoar
formation formação
formed formado
fortunately felizmente
forward em frente
foster family família de criação
found fundar
founder fundador
fragile frágil
fragmentation fragmentação
free grátis; libertar
freezing gelado
friend amigo
frighten assustar
frightened assustado
frog sapo
front cover capa
fully completamente
fun divertido
funky maneiro
further information mais informações
future futuro
futuristic futurista

G

Galician galego
garbage patch mancha de lixo
gender equality igualdade de gêneros
general geral
genetic genético
genius gênio
genre gênero
genuine genuíno
German alemão
get out sair
gift shop loja de presentes
girlfriend namorada, amiga
give dar
glad contente
glass vidro
global warming aquecimento global
glue cola
go ir
go back voltar
goal objetivo
god deus
gold ouro
golden dourado
good bom
gorgeous lindo
governance governo, administração
government governo
graduation graduação
granite granito
graveyard cemitério
green ecológico
greeting cumprimento
ground solo, chão
group grupo
grow passar a
grow up crescer
guest hóspede
guys pessoal
gym academia de ginástica

GLOSSARY

H

habit hábito
hand mão
handicraft artesanato
hang pendurador
hang around andar
happen acontecer
hard difícil, duro
harm prejudicar
harmonica gaita
hate crime crime de ódio
have ter
hawker vendedor ambulante
hazy nebuloso
head ir, dirigir-se
health saúde
hear ouvir
heat calor
height altura
hell inferno
help ajudar
here aqui
heterosexist heterossexista
heterosexual heterossexual
hide esconder-se
high alto
high school ensino médio
higher education ensino superior
highlighted destacado
highlight destaque
hire contratar
holiday feriado
home casa, lar
home country país de origem
home grown cultivado em casa
homophobia homofobia
homophobic homofóbico
honest honesto
honey mel
honored, honoured honrado
hope esperança; esperar
horn buzina
host receber, hospedar
host city cidade-sede
hot quente
household casa, família
how como
how long quanto tempo
how many quantos
hug abraço
huge enorme
humanitarian humanitário
human being ser humano
humanitarian relief auxílio humanitário
hummingbird colibri
huntsman caçador
husband marido
hyperrealistic hiperrealista
hyphen hífen

I

ice gelo
identify identificar
ignore ignorar
illness doença
illustrate ilustrar
image imagem
imagery imagens
imagine imaginar
immerse mergulhar
impact impacto, efeito
impacting impactante
impairment deficiência
impressed impressionado
impression impressão
improve melhorar
inadvertent inadvertido
inborn inato
inch polegada
include incluir
increase aumentar
incubator incubadora
Indian indiano
indicate indicar
indigenous indígena
individual indivíduo
indulge entregar-se
indulgence luxo
infant mortality mortalidade infantil
inflection flexão
influence influenciar
influencer pessoa que influencia
infographic infográfico
inform informar
information informação
infrastructure infraestrutura
inherently inerentemente
initiate iniciar
injury ferimento
inside dentro
instruction instrução
intention intenção
interaction interação
interest interesse
interested interessado
interesting interessante
intertextuality intertextualidade
interview entrevista; entrevistar
intimidate intimidar
intuitive intuitivo
invitation convite
invite convidar
involved envolvido
ironically ironicamente
irony ironia
island ilha
isolated isolado
issue questão, tema
italics itálico

J

jealous com ciúmes, ciumento
jewel joia
jewelry, jewellery joias
join juntar-se a, juntar
journey viagem
joy alegria
jungle selva

K

keep manter
kill matar
kind tipo
king rei
kiss beijo
know saber
knowledge conhecimento
known conhecido
Kurdish curdo

L

lacquer resin resina de laca
lady dama, moça
lamp lamparina
land terra
landowner proprietário de terra
landscape paisagem
language língua
larger maior

last último
later mais tarde
Latin latim
laureate laureado
lavish luxuoso
law lei
leader líder
leadership liderança
leaflet panfleto
learn aprender
leave deixar, sair
leave behind deixar
leaves folhas (de plantas)
legacy legado
legislate legislar
leisure time tempo de lazer
lesbian lésbica
less menos
letter letra
letter-or-number-named nomeado por letras ou números
level nível
liberty liberdade
library biblioteca
lie in encontrar-se
life vida
life-size em tamanho real
light luz
limit limite
link ligar, unir
lion leão
listen ouvir
little pequeno
live up to estar à altura de
live morar, viver; ao vivo
lives vidas
loads of muitos
long jump salto em distância
long longo
look olhar
look up consultar
lot of muito(s), muita(s)
love amar, adorar; amor
lovely ótimo, delicioso
lower mais baixo
lucky sortudo
lucky charm amuleto da sorte
lunch almoço
lunch tray bandeja de comida
luxurious luxuoso
lying deitado

M

magazine revista
maid of honor dama de honra
main principal
mainly sobretudo
major formar-se, graduar-se
make fazer
makeover remodelação
make your bed arrumar a cama
man homem
manager gerente
market stall banca de mercado
marriage casamento
martial arts artes marciais
mass transit transporte coletivo
mastepiece obra-prima
match relacionar
matter importar
meaning significado
meaningful significativo
means of subsistence meios de subsistência
means of transportation meio de transporte
medal medalha
medication medicação
melt derreter
memorable memorável
mention menção; mencionar
middle meio
Middle East Oriente Médio
military dictatorship ditadura militar
milk crate engradado de leite
mind mente
mine mina
minimize, minimise minimizar
minority minoritário
mirror espelho
mist névoa
mistake erro
model modelar
mom mãe
money dinheiro
month mês
monthly mensal
moon Lua
mortar argamassa
mother mãe
motivate motivar
mountain montanha
move mudar-se
mud barro, lama
multiple choice question questão de múltipla escolha
museum museu
mystery mistério
myth mito

N

named nomeado
narrator narrador
nationality nacionalidade
native nativo
nature natureza
natural resource recurso natural
navigate andar, navegar
nearby próximo
nearer mais perto
neatly organizadamente
necessary necessário
need precisar
nephew sobrinho
nevertheless no entanto
new novo
newspaper jornal
next próximo
next weekend no próximo fim de semana
nicknamed apelidado
non-fiction não ficção
non-native não nativo
non-stop flight voo direto
nose nariz
notebook caderno
not-for-profit sem fins lucrativos
novelist romancista
nuclear family família nuclear
number número

O

obstacle obstáculo
occasionally ocasionalmente
occupation profissão
odd-looking aparência estranha
offer oferecer
officer funcionário de alto escalão
official oficial
often com frequência

oil on canvas óleo sobre tela
oil painting pintura a óleo
old velho
olive oil azeite de oliva
once uma vez
once upon a time era uma vez
only só, somente, único
open abrir
opportunity oportunidade
opposite oposto
optimal ótimo
option opção
orchard pomar
ore minérios
organic orgânico
organize organizar
origin origem
other outro(s), outra(s)
outfit roupa
outnumber ser mais numeroso que
overall geral
overcome superar
overnight da noite para o dia
own próprio

P

pace ritmo
page página
pain dor
painter pintor
painting pintura
pair par
palace palácio
pale claro
para-athlete para-atleta
paragraph parágrafo
paralympic paralímpico
paralyzed paralisado
parenting skills conhecimentos de como ser pai/mãe
parents pais
park parque
part parte
participate participar
particularly particularmente
partnership parceria
passenger passageiro
past passado
past year ano passado
pastoral care assistência pastoral
path caminho, percurso
pay pagar
peace paz
pediatrician pediatra
peek espiada
people pessoas
perceive considerar, perceber
percentage porcentagem
perfect perfeito
perhaps talvez
perk up animar-se
personal pessoal
personality test teste de personalidade
personnel pessoal (funcionários)
pesticide pesticida
philosophy filosofia
phone telefone
photo fotografia
phrase frase, expressão
pick up pegar, escolher
pictorial pictórico
picture fotografia, imagem
pie chart gráfico de *pizza*
piece of paper folha de papel
piece together montar (quebra-cabeças)
place lugar
plane avião
planet planeta
planet pal amigo do planeta
plant plantar
planting plantação
plastic bag saco plástico
platform plataforma
platinum platina
play tocar, jogar
please por favor
pleased satisfeito
poetry poesia
point of view ponto de vista
poisoned envenenado
police polícia
Polish polonês
polite educado
politics política
pollution poluição
poor pobre
population população
portrait retrato
possess possuir
potion poção
pound libra
poverty pobreza
powdered em pó
powerful poderoso
practice praticar
precisely precisamente
prediction previsão
prefer preferir
prematurely prematuramente
pre-school pré-escola
present apresentar; presente
preserve preservar
pretend fingir
pretty bonito
price preço
prince príncipe
princess princesa
print impressão
private privado
privilege privilégio
prize prêmio
produce produzir
profession profissão
proficiency proficiência
progress progresso
project projeto
promise prometer
promote promover
proud imponente, orgulhoso
prove provar
provide prover, oferecer
publish publicar
publishing house editora
puffy white smoke fumaça branca fofa
puppet marionete
puppeteer marionetista
purchase comprar
purpose objetivo, propósito
push empurrar
puzzle quebra-cabeça

Q

qualify qualificar
quality qualidade
quarried extraído
quay cais
queen rainha
question pergunta
quickly rapidamente
quotation citação
quote citação; citar

R

rabbit coelho
racing corrida
rain chuva
raise criar
rancher fazendeiro
range gama
rangeland pasto
rank classificação
rate taxa
rather than em vez de
reach chegar a, alcançar
read ler
reader leitor
ready pronto
realistic realista
reality realidade
really realmente
reason razão
receive receber
recently recentemente
receptionist recepcionista
rechargeable recarregável
recipient destinatário; ganhador
recognize, recognise reconhecer
record gravar
recycle reciclar
recycled reciclado
recycled paper papel reciclado
recycling bin lixeira de reciclável
red vermelho
reduce reduzir
refer referir-se
reference referência
reflect refletir
reflection reflexão, reflexo
refraction refração
regard considerar
regarding com respeito a
region região
rehearse ensaiar
related to relacionado a
relationship relação, relacionamento
relax relaxar
religion religião
remaining restante
remember lembrar
remind relembrar
remove remover
renowned de renome
repair consertar
report denunciar
represent representar
reproduce reproduzir
republic república
require requerer
research pesquisa
residence residência
resident morador
resin resina
resource recurso
respect respeito
responsibility responsabilidade
restored consertado
result resultado
retail comércio
reusable reutilizável
reusable lunch box lancheira reutilizável
reuse reutilizar
revise revisar
revocation revogação
rewrite reescrever
rice arroz
rich rico
right certo, direita, direito
ring anel
rise aumento
risk risco
road estrada
rocky rochoso
role papel, função
romance novel romance (história)
room quarto, sala
root raiz
rouse provocar
royal real
rule governar, chefiar
run administrar, correr

S

sad triste
sadness tristeza
safe seguro
safeguard proteger
safety segurança
salt sal
saltier mais salgado
same sex couple casal homossexual
sandbank banco de areia
save economizar
say dizer
scenery cenário
scent perfume
schedule agenda
school escola
science ciência
Science fair feira de ciências
science fiction ficção científica
scientist cientista
score marcar ponto
sculptor escultor
sculpture escultura
sea lion leão-marinho
seafood frutos do mar
search procurar, buscar
secure protegido
seem parecer
seize aproveitar, agarrar
selection seleção
self-evaluation autoavaliação
self-confident autoconfiante
self-portrait autorretrato
sense senso, sentido
sense of humor senso de humor
sent enviado
sentence sentença, oração
servant criado
service serviço
sexism sexismo
sexually sexualmente
shadow sombra
shadowy sombreado
shampoo bottle frasco de xampu
shape forma
share compartilhar
shark tubarão
sheer grande
sheet folha (de papel)
shock choque
shoemaker fabricante de sapatos
shoe sapato
shopping bag sacola de compras
shopping mall *shopping center*
short baixo
shot put arremesso de peso
shoulder ombro
show mostrar
showcased exposta
shower chuveiro
shy tímido

shyness timidez
siblings irmãos
sight vista
sign assinar
significance relevância
silence silêncio
silver prata
simple simples
simplified simplificado
since desde
singer cantor
site local
situation situação
size tamanho
skim ler por alto
skin pele
sky céu
slash reduzir drasticamente
slave escravo
sledge hockey hóquei sobre trenó
sleeping adormecido
sleepover noite passada na casa de amigo
small pequeno
smaller menor
smell cheiro
smoke fumaça
snow neve
soap sabão
so-called tão chamado
social social
social gap lacuna social
social worker assistente social
socially socialmente
society sociedade
soil solo
some algum, alguns
song canção
soon logo, em breve
sound som
source fonte
space espaço
Spanish espanhol
speak falar
speaker palestrante, falante (de uma língua)
species espécie
specific específico
speech discurso
spell feitiço
spicy apimentado
spider monkey macaco-aranha
spoil mimar
spoken falado
sport esporte
spouse cônjuge
spray pulverizar
spread espalhar
spring primavera
stage estágio, palco
stage name nome artístico
stand estar, ficar
stanza estrofe
start começar
state declarar
statement afirmação
statistics estatística
stature estatura
status situação, posição social
stay ficar
step passo
step out sair
stepmother madrasta
stick enfiar, grudar
stigma estigma
still mesmo assim, ainda
stilt-walker artista de perna de pau
stingray arraia
stone pedra
stop parar
strategy estratégia
street rua
street performer artista de rua
strength força
string barbante
strong forte
struggle luta, esforço
study estudar
styrofoam lunch tray bandeja de isopor de comida
subject assunto
substitute substituto
subway metrô
succeed ter êxito
successful bem-sucedido
suffer sofrer
suggestion sugestão
suit terno
suitable adequado
summarize, summarise resumir
summer verão
support apoio
supposed suposto
sure certeza
surfing surfe
surprised surpreso
survey questionário
survivor sobrevivente
sustainability sustentabilidade
sustainable sustentável
sustainable development desenvolvimento sustentável
swim nadar
swimmer nadador
swimming natação
swimming pool piscina
system sistema

T

table manner modos à mesa
take pegar
talk conversar
target visar; alvo
taunt provocar
tea time hora do chá
team time, equipe
teenager adolescente
teeth dentes
tell dizer
tempera on panel têmpera sobre painel
temperament temperamento
temperature temperatura
temple templo
tender age tenra idade
tense tempo verbal
terrible terrível
testimonial depoimento
text texto
than do que
then naquela época, então
there lá
therefore consequentemente
these estes, estas
think achar, pensar
threaten ameaçar
throw jogar
ticketing options opções de passagem
tight exíguo
tile work azulejaria
timber madeira tratada
tint tinta (de cabelo)

tiny minúsculo
tip dica
tired cansado
tireless incansável
tiring cansativo
title título
toast torrada
today hoje
together juntos
toilet banheiro
tomorrow morning amanhã de manhã
ton tonelada
tonight hoje à noite
top speed velocidade máxima
topic tópico
topper pote
totally totalmente
touch toque
tourism turismo
tourist turista
trading house empresa comercial
trading route rota comercial
traditional tradicional
train treinar; trem
transcend transcender
transparency transparência
trap pegar, prender
trash lixo
trash free que não gera lixo
travel viajar
traveller viajante
tray bandeja
treasure tesouro
tree árvore
trip viagem
truly verdadeiramente
try tentar
Turkish turco
turn on ligar, acender
twin gêmeo
type tipo
typical típico

U

UK (United Kingdom) Reino Unido
UN (United Nations) Nações Unidas
uncle tio
underline sublinhar
understand entender
understood compreendido
unique único
unit unidade
unite unir
universe universo
unplug desligar (da tomada)
unusual incomum
upgrade atualização
uphold defender
upload fazer *upload*, carregar
upper body parte de cima do corpo
upscale sofisticado
upset chateado
upstairs no andar de cima
urban urbano
urban density densidade urbana
use usar
useful útil
user usuário

V

vain vaidoso
Valencian valenciano
valley vale
vegetables legumes
vegetarian vegetariano
vegetation vegetação
veiled velado, coberto
version versão
vibrant animado
victim vítima
viewed visto
viewer espectador
violence violência
visible visível
visit visita; visitar
vocabulary vocabulário
voice voz
volleyball vôlei
volunteer fazer trabalho voluntário
vote votar

W

wake up acordar
Wales País de Gales
walk andar
want querer
warn advertir
wash lavar
waste desperdício
watch assistir, observar
water água
way caminho
weak fraco
wear vestir
wedding casamento (cerimônia)
week semana
weekend fim de semana
weigh pesar
weight peso
well bem
Welsh galês
west oeste, ocidente
what o que
wheelchair cadeira de rodas
whenever todas as vezes
which qual, quais
while enquanto
who quem
whole inteiro
whose cujo(s), cuja(s)
why por que
wide variety grande variedade
widely amplamente
wilder mais selvagem
willing disposto
win ganhar
winter inverno
witch bruxa
within dentro
without sem
woman mulher
wonderful maravilhoso
wood madeira
woods floresta
word palavra
work obra, trabalho; trabalhar
workforce mão de obra
world mundo
worldwide em todo o mundo
worry preocupar-se
wrinkle ruga
write down anotar
written escrito

Y

younger mais novo
youth juventude

Z

zoo zoológico

LIST OF IRREGULAR VERBS

Base form	Simple past	Past participle	Translation
awake	awoke	awoken	acordar
be	was, were	been	ser, estar
become	became	become	tornar-se
begin	began	begun	começar
break	broke	broken	quebrar
bring	brought	brought	trazer
build	built	built	construir
buy	bought	bought	comprar
choose	chose	chosen	escolher
come	came	come	vir
deal	dealt	dealt	lidar
do	did	done	fazer
draw	drew	drawn	desenhar
drink	drank	drunk	beber
drive	drove	driven	dirigir
eat	ate	eaten	comer
feel	felt	felt	sentir
fight	fought	fought	brigar, combater, lutar
find	found	found	encontrar, procurar
fly	flew	flown	voar
get	got	got, gotten	conseguir, receber
give	gave	given	dar
go	went	gone	ir
grow up	grew up	grown up	crescer, virar adulto
have	had	had	ter
hear	heard	heard	ouvir
hold	held	held	manter, segurar

Base form	Simple past	Past participle	Translation
know	knew	known	conhecer, saber
leave	left	left	partir, sair
let	let	let	deixar, permitir
lose	lost	lost	perder
make	made	made	fazer
mean	meant	meant	significar
meet	met	met	conhecer, encontrar
overcome	overcame	overcome	superar
pay	paid	paid	pagar
put	put	put	colocar
read	read	read	ler
rewrite	rewrote	rewritten	reescrever
run	ran	run	correr
say	said	said	dizer
see	saw	seen	ver
send	sent	sent	enviar
sleep	slept	slept	dormir
speak	spoke	spoken	falar
stand up for	stood up for	stood up for	defender
swim	swam	swum	nadar
take	took	taken	levar, pegar, tomar
teach	taught	taught	ensinar
tell	told	told	contar, falar
think	thought	thought	achar, pensar
understand	understood	understood	entender
wear	wore	worn	vestir, usar
win	won	won	vencer
write	wrote	written	escrever

BIBLIOGRAPHY

ABREU-TARDELLI, L. S.; CRISTOVÃO, V. L. L. (Orgs.) *Linguagem e educação*: o ensino e aprendizagem de gêneros textuais. Campinas: Mercado de Letras, 2009.

BRASIL. *Lei de Diretrizes e Bases da Educação Nacional*. Brasília: Ministério da Educação, 1996.

_____. *Parâmetros Curriculares Nacionais* – Língua estrangeira. Brasília: Ministério da Educação, 1998.

_____. *Ensino Fundamental de nove anos* – Orientações gerais. Brasília: Ministério da Educação, Secretaria de Educação Básica, Departamento de Políticas de Educação Infantil e Ensino Fundamental, Coordenação Geral do Ensino Fundamental, 2004. Disponível em: <portal.mec.gov.br./seb/arquivos/pdf/Ensfund/noveanorienger.pdf>. Acessado em: 8 jun. 2016.

COPE, B.; KALANTZIS, M. Multiliteracies: The beginning of an idea. In: COPE, B.; KALANTZIS, M. (Ed.) *Multiliteracies*: literacy learning and the design of social futures. London: Routledge, 2000. p. 3-8.

CROSS, D. *Large classes in action*. Hertfordshire: Prentice Hall International, 1995.

DIONÍSIO, A. P.; MACHADO, A. R.; BEZERRA, M. A. (Orgs.) *Gêneros textuais & ensino*. São Paulo: Parábola, 2010.

FREIRE, P. *Pedagogia da autonomia*: saberes necessários à prática educativa. São Paulo: Paz e Terra, 1996.

GRELLET, F. *Developing reading skills*. Cambridge: Cambridge University Press, 1981.

HEIDE, A.; STILBORNE, L. *Guia do professor para a internet*: completo e fácil. Trad. Edson Furmankiewz. 2. ed. Porto Alegre: Artmed, 2000.

HOFFMANN. *Avaliar para promover*: as setas do caminho. Porto Alegre: Mediação, 2001.

LAPKOSKI, G. A. O. *Do texto ao sentido*: teoria e prática de leitura em língua inglesa. Curitiba: Ibpex, 2011.

MARCUSCHI, L. A. Gêneros textuais: definição e funcionalidade. In: MARTINEZ, P. *Didática de línguas estrangeiras*. São Paulo: Parábola, 2009.

MOITA-LOPES, L. P. Ensino de inglês como espaço de embates culturais e de políticas da diferença. In: GIMENEZ, T. et al. (Org.) *Perspectivas educacionais e o ensino de inglês na escola pública*. Pelotas: Educat, 2005.

_____. *Oficina de linguística aplicada*. Campinas: Mercado de Letras, 2000.

RAIMES, A. *Techniques in teaching writing*. New York, Oxford: Oxford University Press, 1983.

RICHARDS, J. C.; RENANDYA, W. A. (Ed.) *Methodology in language teaching*: an anthology of current practice. New York: Cambridge University Press, 2002.

RODRIGUES, D. (Org.) *Inclusão e educação*: doze olhares sobre a educação inclusiva. São Paulo: Summus, 2006.

SOUZA, A. G. F. et al. *Leitura em língua inglesa*: uma abordagem instrumental. São Paulo: Disal, 2005.

TOMLINSON, B. *Developing materials for language teaching*. Londres: Continuum, 2003.

VYGOTSKY, L. S. *Pensamento e linguagem*. São Paulo: Martins Fontes, 1993.

WALESKO, A. M. H. *Compreensão oral em língua inglesa*. Curitiba: Ibpex, 2010.